GENDER
CLASS &
EDUCATION

GENDER CLASS & EDUCATION

Edited &
Introduced by
Stephen Walker
& Len Barton

The Falmer Press

(A Member of the Taylor & Francis Group)

London · New York · Philadelphia

UK The Falmer Press, Falmer House, Barcombe, Lewes, East Sussex, BN8 5DL

USA The Falmer Press, Taylor & Francis Inc., 1900 Frost Road, Suite 101, Bristol, PA 19007

First published 1983   Reprinted 1989

Library of Congress Cataloging-in-Publication Data

Main entry under title:

Gender, class & education.
  "Presentations made at the fifth Westhill Sociology of Education Conference in January 1982"—introd.
  Includes bibliographies and indexes.
  1. Educational sociology—United States—Congresses.
I. Walker, Stephen F. II. Barton, Len. III. Westhill Sociology of Education Conference (5th : 1982 : Westhill College). IV. Title: Gender, class and education.
LC191.4.G46   1983   370.19   83-8478
ISBN 0-8002-3300-X

Jacket design by Leonard Williams

Printed in Great Britain by Taylor & Francis (Printers) Ltd, Basingstoke

Contents

Preface

This is the fifth collection of papers to emerge from the annual Westhill Sociology of Education Conference. In preparing this particular volume we have departed from the established practice of selecting for publication only those papers which were presented at the conference and we have included three teaching bibliographies on gender and education which have been compiled specially for this book. Preparing bibliographies, though it provides such an important service to teachers and researchers, is not always particularly rewarding work, and we would like to express our thanks to Maggie Coats, Terry Evans and Emily Moskowitz for undertaking this task.

We are also grateful for the assistance given by Sally Collis, by Denise Woodhams, by Malcolm Clarkson and by Lyn Gorman in the preparation of material for publication.

Finally, we would like to thank Joan Barton and Sandra Walker for their seemingly inexhaustible support.

Introduction

The papers which appear in this collection, with the exception of the editorial introduction and the bibliographies at the end of the volume, are all versions of presentations made at the fifth Westhill Sociology of Education Conference in January 1982. The theme of the conference was 'Race, Class and Gender' — a theme selected because of its obvious topicality. But this was not the only reason behind such choice. Another was a concern to provide a framework for debate between educational researchers and teachers who share certain common practical goals — the clarification of the relationship between schooling and social reproduction and the formulation of policies aimed at the eradication of inequitable practices in education — but who also pursue such goals by using very different theoretical schemes and by concentrating on quite distinctive aspects of social life. Given this second concern, it might seem a little peculiar that the emphasis in all the contributions collected here is most decidedly towards the analysis of gender relations in education, even though a wide range of different analytical approaches to this area is represented. Indeed, the reader might ask if such emphasis reflects a failure at the conference in any attempts to forge crucial links among the distinctive but interrelated areas of class, gender and race relations in schools. We do not believe this was the case. In fact, the particular emphasis in this collection is a result of a purely practical decision to publish the papers which concentrate on class, gender and education separately from those which concentrate on class, race and education. This being so, we would encourage the reader to treat this collection as a companion work to *Race, Class and Education*, to be published by Croom Helm. A great deal of the discussion developed in each of the books has relevance for debate about gender *and* race relations in schools.

A variety of perspectives on gender relations in education and a wide range of problems associated with developing our understanding of these relations were introduced at the conference. It would be impossible to provide an adequate summary of all these concerns in this introduction. However, three particular issues achieved a certain prominence in conference debate and we have used these as a basis for developing an order, a sequentiality in the arrangement of the papers in this volume.

The first of these concerns was a fairly powerful call for an increase in emphasis in the analysis of gender relations and education upon the 'active response'[1] individuals make to the social conditions in which they live. It was argued that this response needs to be conceptualized not merely in terms of the typical reactions girls (and boys) make to the messages about gender relations they receive inside and outside of schools, but also, and more particularly, in terms of the contradictions embedded within the origins, the form and the content of these messages and in terms of these messages being resisted. In Chapter One we have tried to identify the relevance this particular concern has for certain key problems in the analysis of women's educational experience and for the formulation of policy. Recognition of the contradictory principles at work in social life, we argue, exerts a pressure to incorporate in analysis a notion of *contestation* within descriptions of how individuals in schools and colleges react to ideological and structural conditions. Of course, there is a real danger here — the possibility that in our attempts to avoid over-deterministic theory of the reproduction of gender relations we substitute a corrected version which over-emphasizes peoples' freedom to react or to struggle. A consideration of the tension implied here, between forms of domination and forms of struggle or resistance, is the main theme of Jean Anyon's paper. Using data collected in a study of five schools in the US, Anyon argues that we can find elements of both *accommodation and resistance* in the responses girls make to the ideologies to which they are exposed and, importantly, that these responses vary according to whether they are made privately or publicly and according to class location.

One of the benefits of making use of the concept of resistance in feminist analysis of educational processes is that it sharpens the focus upon how attempts at the exercise of power both succeed and fail and, thus, by providing for the identification of instances of resistance in everyday life, it can be used to extend understanding of exactly where and how political action is likely to be most effective. This possibility is reviewed by both Jean Anyon and Lynn Davies. However, Davies argues that to accomplish such insight requires some refinement in our definition of power and in our concept of how it is exercised and, using ethnographic material from which she has built up representations of the 'type-scripts' girls are offered and create in schools, she examines some of the experimental strategies teachers and pupils employ as they act out experiences structured by power relations. Clearly, these strategies involve both pupils *and teachers*, and in his contribution to this volume, Michael Apple offers an analysis of how social developments have resulted in a progressive restructuring of teaching and teacher's work. The notion of 'resistance' has relevance here too. Teachers have not been passive in their response to this restructuring. However, Apple argues that as teachers are educational workers, it is necessary to analyze their responses in terms which take into account how class and gender divisions condition how teaching is done and who does it, as would be the case in the analysis of any form of work.

The second issue given prominence at the conference was concern that the descriptions of ways in which schools reproduce class and gender relations are made more precise by the continued exploration of specific historical, situational and institutional processes through which such reproduction takes place. This is variously developed by Madeleine Arnot, Sara Delamont, Rosemary Deem and Sandra Acker. Arnot examines ways in which distinctive forms of class and gender ideologies have shaped both debate and practice with regard to the development of single-sex and co-educational schooling. One purpose, Arnot explains, for making this consideration of the sometimes 'hidden history' of co-education is to delineate the various forms the 'modalities of transmission' of gender relations taken at specific moments in history and also how this variety reflects properties of specific class formations and relationships. However, historical analysis can have other uses. It can be used to inspect how practices have persisted, and Delamont, by combining historical and modern ethnographic data, inspects ways in which schools, by failing to respond to changes in interpretations of gender relations which have developed outside educational settings, have become increasingly conservative in approach and practice.

An important strength provided by the use of historical data in sociological investigation is that it permits comparative analysis. However, there are other ways in which a comparative approach can be used to achieve greater precision in description, to test theory and to validate explanation. Comparisons can also be made of, say, different institutional arrangements and practices or of the different kinds of experience individuals have inside particular forms of institutional life. This kind of approach is used by Deem in her investigation of aspects of womens' adult education — of the knowledge base, the pedagogy and the response women make to this form of education. This study, however, should in no way be seen as an isolated investigation of a particular phenomenon. Rather, it is a documentation of further ways in which patriarchal and class hegemonic orders persist and are resisted.

Another way of increasing the precision of the descriptions of gender relations in schools with which sociologists of education work is through continued critical re-examination of the concepts and theories employed. Acker, in her discussion of the sexual division of labour in teaching, provides such a re-examination of certain aspects of these descriptive mechanisms. As in other contributions to this book, an important consideration in Acker's writing is the 'fit' between *theories* of gender relation and the reality — in this case between descriptions of women teachers' motives, interpretations and career patterns and a reality which does not always confirm the accuracy of this description.

All four of these writers suggest ways in which their particular concerns have implications for the formulation of policy aimed at removing forms of women's oppression — and this endeavour was the third major issue given prominence at the conference and is the main focus of two papers in this collection. In her contribution, Miriam David examines the impact on moral education and on the values embedded within educational practice of what she sees as successful attempts by conservative pressure groups to win control of areas where public and private values are structured and to redefine these values. What is crucial here is that by making this examination and, thus, by being able to show contradictions in the basis from which these pressure groups operate, David is able to indicate points toward which radical strategy might be directed.

Not unexpectedly, one of the key questions with respect to policy formulation at the conference was how to link class and gender analysis in policy, or, more specifically, how to interrelate socialist and feminist struggle. In their contribution, Culley and Demain critically review certain analyses of educational processes which, by working with notions of 'pre-given interests' at work on social relations, provide, in their view, limitations on the kind and range of political responses available for socialists and feminists. As a corrective to this they suggest a concentration upon the specific forms of domination, accommodation and resistance found in schools — and, in so doing, they state what became the overriding concern of the 1982 conference.

Note

1 We have borrowed this phrase from Jean Anyon's discussions.

1   Gender, Class and Education: A Personal View

Stephen Walker, Newman College and Len Barton, Westhill College

> You don't have to be any one thing to be a feminist, there's no signing on
> the dotted line ... if the issue is choice then we also have to be free to
> choose our own ideas.   (McRobbie and McCabe, 1981)

In writing this introductory chapter to a volume concerned with the educational
experience of women, we find ourselves in a somewhat peculiar position: we feel
a need to explain, or even to justify, our own interest. To some extent such
explanation would not be unusual. Inclusion of biographical information or of
personal histories is now fairly common in prefaces to sociological discussion. But
the relevance of this practice to the particular topics discussed in this book is more
pressing, and arises from our awareness that some analysts may have doubts about
the status of discussion of women's experience by men. In part, this caution would
seem to be based upon the following view. A major concern in the study of
women's educational experience is the ways in which schools operate so as to
reproduce and sustain gender differentiated identities, perceptions and cultural
visions which are legitimated through ideologies of male domination. It follows
that analysis offered by men, whose own consciousness has been shaped through
participation in this system, is, at best, distorted or, at worst, patronizing. The
question arises, therefore, whether men can ever achieve non-sexist understanding
of women's experiences.

The significance of this question becomes acute in the light of the fact that
although the extensive work in women's studies which has been developed over the
last ten years has produced considerable theoretical refinement and a growing body
of empirical data for the sociology of education, it is still tempting to coin the
phrase 'invisible men' to describe male involvement in this area. Why — we might
ask — have so few men been interested in joining the debates and the research
programmes in this crucial area? Is it a result of bias, of shortsightedness, of a
failure to appreciate the work's relevance of even, perhaps, of a forlorn attempt to
preserve some supposed form of academic neutrality? Whatever the explanation,
our own recent experiences as teachers have convinced us that a slavish and
unreflective adherrance to a narrow perspective or to a fixed set of assumptions is
always counter-productive. Our motive, then, for entering this field — and we do
so with some trepidation — is not with a view to attempting chauvinistic correction
or to assimilating feminist insights into our own male world-views, rather, we see
such an effort as part of a process in which reciprocal challenge is a key and exciting
feature.

However, it is not through reference to these 'academic' considerations that
we would want to make the main reason for our interest in women's studies,
feminist analysis and gender differentiation in schools. Our motivation comes from
our interpretation of the basic purpose for doing sociological work. In this respect

we follow the direction and justification so clearly articulated by Wright Mills (1970) in his discussion of the politics of doing social science. He argues:

> The interest of the social scientist in social structure is not due to any view that the future is structurally determined. We study the structural limits of human decision in an attempt to find points of effective intervention, in order to know what can and what must be structurally changed if the role of explicit decision making in history-making is to be enlarged.... We study history to discern the alternatives within which human reason and human freedom can now make history. We study historical social structures, in brief, in order to find within them the ways in which they are and can be controlled. For only in this way can we come to know the limits and the meaning of human freedom.

It follows that interest in both the public and private troubles of women (or men) is inextricably related to the broader aim of discovering particular forms of structural and interactional limitations on the possibilities of human freedom. In short, for us as men to ignore or to accept exclusion from a concern for the position women occupy and the experiences they encounter in our society would be tacitly to accept a status quo, to treat it as unproblematic and, by so doing, to limit the possibilities in the common struggle which inspires our intellectual and political endeavours.

Gender and Schooling

> The development of mass education in England and Wales since the beginning of the nineteenth century has been marked by three crucial divisions: social class, ability and sex. (Deem, 1978)

Although the tendency to treat educational practices and assumptions as unproblematic has met increasing resistance from sociologists of education during the last decade, a new trend has replaced it. This is the practice of identifying an educational issue *as* problematic and then treating the area within which the problematic pertains as being relatively unified, homogeneous or well-bounded. However, this criticism cannot be applied to sociological analyses of women and education. Indeed, one of the problems which has resulted from the rapid increase in research interest in women's educational experience in the last few years is the development of a series of analytical forms and explanations which are diverse, heterogeneous and, sometimes, underrelated to a main theoretical platform. It is useful to examine these forms, not with a view to offering a detailed description or a synthesis, nor with the intention of suggesting orders of priority, but rather with a view to identifying what would appear to be some unifying concerns of this research — albeit concerns which themselves pose diverse problems in any programme aimed at change.

Issue 1: Ideology and Patriarchy

The education system is a key means of production and reproduction of the ideological structure — for this system not only in its very organisation and mode of functioning, embodies the dominant ideology of the society, but also functions to reproduce this ideology in its specific form.

(Wolpe, 1977)

A major focus in the study of women's education and gender differentiation has been the impact of ideological formations which work outside and above education and, crucially, their influence upon the processes of schooling and upon the reactions girls and boys make to these processes. These ideological formations have been depicted as encompassing a variety of features. The crude depiction of educational practice and experience as strongly influenced by a set of ideologies and relations which permeate the whole social order and which are characteristically patriarchal in form has been refined by writers like Kuhn and Wolpe (1978), Deem (1978, 1980), Arnot (formerly MacDonald) (1980, 1981) and David (1981) who chart critical dimensions of this influence. These dimensions generally include the following observations of the impact of patriarchy upon schooling:

(a) At the level of the individual, the dominant ideology works to regulate cultural norms of appropriate gender behaviour with respect to personal identity, social roles, work and marriage roles; these are norms which are *carried into the schools* by the pupils and involve quite specific gender differentiation. Specific illustration of sex stereotyping and gender differentiation through exposure to the socializing influences of the family, the media and other cultural agencies abound in Delamont's *Sex-Roles and the School* (1980). The important concern, however, is that not only do different cultures define sex roles and identities differently but also that the power to define the differences is itself in the hands of men. Patriarchy, then, operates a form of differentiation at both deep and surface levels of the structuring of reality.

(b) At the level of the social structure, the dominant ideology works so as to regulate appropriate forms of gender differentiation in terms of the practices made possible in the economic and political spheres. The way resources are distributed, the rights and obligations determined by law, the form of state intervention in personal life and welfare, can all be seen as preserving gender distinction, as reinforcing gender discrimination and, often, as sustaining the marginal position of women. Thus, girls and boys not only experience a process of acculturation at the individual level which is strongly patriarchal in form, but also the social structure works to legitimate this ideology at the collective level. Legislation which purports to concentrate on welfare provision, employment patterns or social services is never framed in a climate separate from a more pervasive social ideology and, hence, it is possible to identify reflections of patriarchy in most of the activities of state agencies. Commenting upon recent state economic policy, for example, Deem (1981) suggests that

> Reductions in public expenditure during Labour's period in office (in the 1970s) hit women's education particularly hard, as if to further underline the inconsistencies between the existence of legislation against sex discrimination and specific policies of different state apparatuses upholding that discrimination. Teacher training received one of the largest cuts at a time when it was still one of the major avenues for women's higher education ...

3

(c) An important element in the kinds of analysis we are examining is the conceptualization of the dominant ideology, that is, patriarchy, as being realized inside a series of complex relations within and among different social settings or sites. Gender differentiation is produced and reproduced through the operation of patriarchal ideologies in places of work or production, in family life and in cultural forms and practices — all of which are themselves necessarily class specific and differentiated. Thus, the ways in which the reactions of girls and boys to schooling are ideologically shaped will take a variety of forms. These will depend upon the dialectic between the class norms of a child's family and that family's experience of work, community and sub-cultural practices. Clarricoates (1980), in her study of the construction and reinforcement of gender stereotypical behaviour in schools which drew pupils from class differentiated catchment areas, remarks that she was led to believe that the

> models [of gender appropriate behaviour] presented to the children, with their demarcation between masculine and feminine, are based on ecological factors which pertain to that school, i.e., the value structure of the school in relation to community values.

But the question arises as to how the different influences of patriarchy should be seen as interrelated whilst being realized in different settings. Clarricoates (1980) herself expresses the fairly general view that 'it is patriarchy — the male hierarchical ordering of society, preserved through marriage and family *via the sexual division of labour* — that is the core of women's oppression' (our emphasis). This view exposes some of the difficulties which emerge in analyses which propose an interrelation between patriarchy and class, a linkage between gender differentiation and the sexual division of labour. The following difficulties can be noted.

1   Firstly, the location of the crucial defining element in the sexual division of labour is problematic. Essentially, one can question the relative influence of the sexual division of labour in the family upon the sexual division of labour in production, or, vice versa, the relative influence of the sexual division of labour in production upon family life. At one level, it can be argued that these two manifestations are inseparable. A sexual division *of labour* in family life, irrespective of how it originated, provides several advantages for the operations of economic production organized under a capitalist mode. It serves to legitimate the division and segmentation of productive authorities; it provides for the cheap and efficient reproduction of labour power by hiving off domestic work from paid employment and by giving the former an identifiable group — female non-waged workers; and it results in effective maintenance of an industrial reserve army whose contribution to production can be exploited on a part-time and insecure basis. Nevertheless, the key question is whether or not the sexual division of labour in the family is an essential condition of the mode of production. This is an important question because the ways in which individuals such as teachers can find a point of intervention in these processes are dependent on the answer. Thus, if one maintains a relative autonomy between forms of gender differentiation in the family and the wage-labour process, intervention will be required on two fronts. Or, if one reduces the sexual division of labour in the family to a particular manifestation of the social relations which arise from the organization of the forces of production,

then interventions which are aimed solely at changing attitudes to familial roles can only achieve limited reforms. But, in the final analysis, the answer has to be that the sexual division of labour in the family is *not* an *essential* condition of capitalism. Whilst its present form may *contribute* to the need of capital to establish effective control of labour processes, it is vital to recognize the full impact of MacDonald's (1981) insight when she argues:

> New forms of control may develop under capitalism which do not rely so heavily on patriarchal relations.... It is perhaps the changing nature of the capitalist economy and its demands for certain types and quantities of labour that allows for the possibility of 'progressive' attempts to reduce the inequalities between men and women. The success of these attempts, however, are likely to be determined to a large extent by the resilience of patriarchy as a power structure that also maintains a relative independence from economic forces of production since it is also based ideologically and materially in the family and other social institutes such as religion, newspapers, broadcasting etc.

2   A second difficulty is that the form of patriarchical relations, as many feminists have insisted, assumes different characteristics at specific moments in history. The 'male hierarchical ordering of society' works through a variety of forms and modes. Any crude depiction of this ordering in terms of a simple sexual division of labour would result in analysis which seriously misrepresents a subtle and shifting reality and which would be blind to quite crucial ways in which male cultural and economic power is exerted. The implication is that descriptions of the specificities of patriarchal relations require not only precise and detailed ethnographic charting but also constant revision and re-assessment.

3   A third difficulty with class-patriarchy linked models is that gender differentiation works both within and across class formations. Theoretical generalizations about the form of patriarchal domination in specific settings must be received cautiously and inspected to determine at which level of class formation they apply. More importantly, interventionists will have to struggle with the problem of determining if they are directing their programmes at *all* women, at specific class groups and, crucially, if the possible unintended consequence of programmes of action aimed at one class groups is an exacerbation of the problems of gender differentiation being experienced by another, different class group.

Issue 2: Gender Stereotyping in Schools

Girls are taken to cricket matches and given toy trains if they ask for them, while boys are allowed to knit, play with dolls' houses and cry. Yet, in school, institutional pressures, teachers and peers enforced stereo-typed sex roles, and are intolerant of idiosyncrasies.

(Delamont, 1980)

A second major focus of research into gender differentiation and sexism in education has been the stereotypical images of men and women prevalent in school and classroom activities and on the impact these images have upon pupils. Research into this area has been prolific. Its main direction has been towards demonstrating how culturally created differentiations among gender-appropriate traits, conduct and roles which find expression in the world outside school are either reproduced and reinforced in classrooms or, even, subtly transformed by educators to construct new bases for gender stereotyping. Generally, this kind of research draws upon literature in which the images of women and men, of femininity and masculinity commonly sustained in current social life have been described, and is then involved with a search for the presence of these images in educational processes. It is difficult to summarize this literature but the main concerns seem to be definitions of female and male typing in terms of sexuality (de Beauvoir, 1972; Millet, 1977), personality traits (Hutt, 1972), occupational roles and destinies (Burman, 1979) and relations and rights (Oakley, 1972; Mitchell and Oakley, 1976; Chetwynd and Hartnett, 1978).

Although the forms these cultural inventions take are complicated, three main aspects of gender stereotyping can be isolated as representing all forms. Firstly, the processes of assigning typical traits and roles to individuals on the basis of their sex almost invariably involves the association of males and the masculine with characteristics which are positively evaluated in crucial aspects of social life — work, politics and sexual relations. Secondly, following this, images of females and the feminine are seen usually through negative reference to men. As De Beauvoir (1972) observes,

> The terms *masculine* and *feminine* are used symmetrically only as a matter of form, as on legal papers. In actuality the relation of the two sexes is not quite like that of two electrical poles, for man represents both the positive and the neutral, as is indicated by the common use of *man* to designate human beings in general, whereas women represents only the negative, defined by limiting criteria, without reciprocity.

Thirdly, commonsense accounts of the rationale for this kind of stereotyping make implicit and frequent reference to the 'naturalness' of this phenomenon. The 'logic' of this last point is nicely pointed by Brunsdan (1978) in her comment, 'naturally different to men through their procreative ability, women are understood as closer to nature than men, more natural; and femininity as culturally constituted is seen as the natural expression of these differences, finding its natural fulfilment in the family.'

The perpetration (and transformation) of gender stereotypes in school has been described in terms of three points of entry — through the communication of teacher expectations, through classroom practices and through school rituals. Teacher expectations address many different educational concerns — norms of behaviour, notions of academic achievement and anticipated occupational careers. There is evidence that many of these expectations are organized around gender stereotypes. Thus, Arnot (1981) summarizes Clarricoates' findings that the teachers she researched assumed boys to be 'livelier, adventurous . . . independent, energetic' whilst they assumed girls to be 'obedient, tidy, conscientious . . . and gossipy.' Delamont (1980) reports Ingleby's and Cooper's findings where 'girls were seen [by teachers] as superior in character, brightness, schoolwork, home background and language skills.' Similarly, ethnographic accounts of aspects of classroom practice often illustrate various dimensions of behaviour based on notions of gender differences. Seating arrangements, the provision of appropriate play or work activities, the operation of communication structures, the devices used in classroom management have all been cited as evidencing an appeal to expected different pupil responses according to gender. Perhaps 'appeal' is the wrong word here. It seems likely that the idea of a 'naturalness' about these practices is taken for granted by many teachers. As King (1978) comments, in his study of infants' classrooms,

> In every classroom boys hung their coats separately from the girls. They were lined up in separate rows at the door. They were divided for activities.... These practices were completely taken for granted by the teachers, who when I talked to them, generally said they had 'never thought about it' and that to divide the class by sex was 'convenient' and 'natural'.

It is tempting to speculate that the same taken-for-grantedness permeates ritualized and ceremonial practices in schools such as assemblies, the wearing of uniforms and speech days, where gender roles and identities are symbolically represented as different.

As with the debate identified as issue one above, there are some difficulties with this kind of ethnographic work which traces the perpetuation of gender stereotypical images through schooling. Whilst we are not suggesting that many researchers are unaware of these problems, it is important that we take notice of their implications if the credibility of critique is to be maintained and if effective intervention is to be made possible.

One allegation about this kind of analysis is that it involves the adoption of a somewhat mechanistic conceptualization of socialization. For the claim to be sustained that expectations and practices in schools based upon gender stereotypes both *draw upon* and *reproduce* images of masculinity and femininity used to sustain asymetrical gender relations in wider society, research needs to be sensitive to the responses pupils make to the images with which they are presented. The extent to which both girls and boys may *resist* the sexist messages they receive as part of their school experience has become an important question for many. Not unrelatedly, the possibility that these messages may be differently defined in particular school settings needs attention; research already suggests that expectations and practices in primary schools refer to generalized images of femininity and masculinity and those in secondary schools are organized around attitudes to future work roles. For educational researchers and social scientists there is an even more fundamental question: in what sense can this sort of work lead to practical political action? Ethnography is quite deliberately descriptive and yet, in the work of many writers who follow the tradition developed by researchers like Sara Delamont, we sense a combination of description and reaction, characterized by a strong sense of indignation. The question is, then, can (or should) description ever be neutral, impartial or undertaken solely for the purpose of data collection? What we are asking for is an extension of the practice whereby ethnographic researchers make their interpretative work more explicit and more open to constructive assessment. This concern would address three elements: the processes involved in the selection of material which constitutes 'evidence'; the processes involved in the use of this evidence to support (or challenge) a priori assumptions; and the processes involved in the movement in which 'evidence' is used to construct and extend grounded theory. Unless these moments in the research process are rigorously explored, the prospect of translating indignation into an effective programme for social and political intervention will be lost.

Issue 3: Curriculum Differentiation and Gender Differentiation

Today
It is maths and science
Which are considered very important
For those who want to get on in a technological world.
Maths and Science are the entry qualifications
Which sort those who are capable
From those who are not.

Girls, it seems
Are not.
(Spender, 1980)

Since about 1971 — especially following the publication of Young's *Knowledge and Control* (1971) and of the Open University *School and Society* Course E202 (1972) — the emphasis given to the development of a sociology of knowledge as part of educational analysis has been considerable. This has meant that the *curriculum* has come to be seen increasingly as one of the major 'regulators of the structure of experiences' (Bernstein, 1971). It is not surprising that feminist critique aimed at identifying crucial aspects of school life should reflect this emphasis and should come to attach some importance to charting ways in which various curricular practices might be identified as sexist.

Before we consider this kind of critique, it is worthwhile reminding ourselves of the main challenge articulated in the 1970s by those writers who called for the redirecting of concern in the sociology of education towards detailed consideration of forms of knowledge and the curriculum. This is worthwhile for two reasons: it provides some measure against which research into the relationship between curriculum differentiation and gender differentiation can be assessed; and it is related to more general criticism levelled recently at work undertaken within this field — criticism concerning the weakness of the empirical base of the approach. As Arnot and Whitty (1982) observe, following the initial flush of enthusiasm at the theoretical level with the *idea* of making the school curriculum a problematic, there is a real danger that unless a more developed collection of *substantive* explorations of curricular *practices* is produced this approach will be 'written off in Britain as an eccentric interlude in the history of the discipline'. The contributions to the *Knowledge and Control* reader and those influenced by the ideas of the 'new direction' it established share an important perspective: a desire to avoid persistent reification in descriptions and analyses of the ways schools work by developing a programme based on the promise that,

to explore situationally defined meanings in taken-for-granted institutional contexts such as schools, very detailed case studies are necessary which treat as problematic the *curricular*, *pedagogical* and *assessment* categories held by school personnel. (Young 1971, our emphasis)

Summarized crudely, the direction was pointed towards the study of curriculum definitions, processes and outcomes. However, these three analytically distinct categories were never depicted as separate activity fields of curricular practice. Indeed, in the only detailed case study to appear in the *Knowledge and Control* collection, Nell Keddie is at pains to map the interrelations of these conceptualizations. Nevertheless, each individual emphasis was seen as critical. Both educational success and failure and less evaluative responses to schooling were quite explicitly related to pedagogical processes and curriculum arrangements, which were themselves crucially shaped by particular definitions and interpretations of knowledge. As Esland (1971), quoting Holzer, observed,

> ... curriculum, pedagogy and evaluation should be considered in relationship: together, they constitute an epistemology, and vocabularies of motive which will 'dictate broad preferences for the kinds of experiential bases on which knowledge is to be constructed'.

Much analysis of the impact of curriculum organization upon the formation of gender identities and relations has concentrated on the forms those 'experiential bases' take. It is possible to use the insights into the study of curricular practices developed in the 1970s to scrutinize some the main directions this kind of analyses has taken.

The analysis appears to have three strands — a review of the access boys and girls have to curricular provision, a consideration of sexist expectations which surround notions of subject suitability and an exploration of how ideologies of gender differentiation permeate and invade texts and the forms of discourse employed in classrooms.

Research which falls into the category identified as the first strand above is sometimes believed to be the most accessible and convincing evidence of gender discrimination through curricular practices. Such work typically involves consideration of statistical data showing the subjects selected and studied by girls and boys in schools, the different patterns of examination entry and success rates and the numbers following particular further education or vocational courses. This consideration is aimed at seeking to establish how patterns of curriculum differentiation limit post-school career prospects and life chances for girls. Thus, for example, Deem (1978), using this kind of evidence, notes a tendency for girls' curriculum choices and CSE examination successes to cluster around arts subjects against a consistent trend for boys, in terms of these variables, to be considerably overrepresented in the scientific, mathematical and technical areas.

> Arts subjects are of limited value for direct entry into jobs and usually lead to different routes in higher and further education, so that after leaving school girls are likely to follow very different paths to those taken by boys of comparable ability levels and social class background.

Similarly, Byrne (1978), using the same statistical evidence, argues,

> Secondary schools may well be guilty of pre-empting the future career choices of girls by 'persuading' them by direct or indirect means to 'choose' subjects that are a less useful or relevant foundation for future adult 'working' roles than those followed by boys.

Byrne's use of inverted commas around key words in this extract provides us with a clue to possible reservations she might have about some dimensions of this kind of practice. Certainly, the practice is not without problems. Firstly, there is the danger of cause and effect being too easily or too readily attributed. Whilst we share a concern about gender differentiation in curriculum choices and examination performances, the nature of the linkage between data and explanation, between statistical enumerations of selected aspects of pupils' behaviour in schools and what are taken to be contributory or consequential properties of this behaviour, is to be demonstrated, not assumed. Secondly, and not unrelatedly, there is the possibility that important assumptions in the research process receive insufficient inspection. Is there not a possibility that unexplored assumptions have crept into the practices of data collectors? Thus, whilst not invalidating a particular collection of numbers these may well operate so as to blind the user of these figures to the influence of other more critical variables. Also, however, is there not a danger that the categories and connections used by the analysts themselves in these procedures involve, to borrow Seeley's phrase (1966), 'taking' educators' problems and interpretations rather than 'making' them? Thirdly, and most importantly, this approach inevitably makes the researcher vulnerable to the charge of losing sight of the subjectivity of social action. When Byrne suggests, in this equivocal manner, that teachers may 'persuade' girls on curriculum matters or that pupils 'choose' particular curriculum packages, she reminds us, consciously or unconsciously, of the need to preserve a strong sense of the interpretative work involved in the categorizations sociologists use to describe the social world. The researcher's interpretation of action as involving 'persuasion' and 'choice' may fail entirely to catch the significances the individuals involved attach to these affairs.

The essence of this last issue is the possibility of researchers substituting their own interpretations and understandings of reality for those of the subjects of their inquiry, and then being faced with the difficulty of explicating the resources on which they have drawn to produce these descriptions and of defending their validity. In short, it is the problem of the infinite extendability of second-order descriptions and interpretations. This problem is also present in what we have called the second two strands of investigation of gender differentiation through curriculum practices — sexist expectation and sexist modes of discourse.

In terms of the first of these areas, the study of expectations associated with the gender-appropriateness of certain subjects in the curriculum, the problem has influence at several different points, as can be seen in the following illustration. It is well established that only a small percentage of women in Britain are involved in scientific work. To explain this some writers have sought to indicate ways in which girls and boys are encouraged to identify with different subject areas, and thereby open or close specific career options, by making reference to the expectations teachers have of subject appropriateness and the processes by which these expectations are communicated to the pupils. This is illustrated in the comment by Kelly (1975):

> Primary school teachers, having themselves accepted a traditional female role, and having in general very little scientific or mathematical background, often label boys and activities as 'for boys' or 'for girls' and direct their pupils accordingly. So it is not surprising if most girls get the message, and develop little interest in science.

We strongly support the attempt to trace emergent properties of social life back to the interactional setting from which they developed. However, we still question the *grounds* on which certain motives, practices and outcomes are given particular characterizations and are imbued with particular significances and, moreover, the extent to which both preserve the participants' perceptions and relevances.

In terms of the second of these areas, sexism in school texts, the problem is even more acute. We have in mind the work of Lobban (1977) and her analysis of sex-role presentations in reading schemes, of Spender (1980) and her discussion of gender differentiation in patterns of classroom talk and of Scott (1980) and her examination of textbooks used in a comprehensive school. This work is mainly concerned with showing the ways in which the predominant forms of discourse used in schools serve, as Spender (1982) summarizes it, not only to 'enhance the image of men at the expense of women, they frequently present a distorted representation of the world which is even more sexist than the real world.' This image and this distortion are described as characteristically involving an emphasis on the depiction of women which, at best, portrays them as passive and domestic or, at worst, as invisible. To some extent, it is tempting to focus debate on the validity of the claim made by Spender in the quotation above. Are the images which invade written and spoken school texts *'more sexist than the real world'*? Are the representations created by the producers of these school texts direct copies, replications of those which work to sustain female subordination outside school, or are important transformations made at the point of their production? But this speculation detracts from a more crucial issue — what pupils in school *do* with these images, messages and representations. As Arnot and Whitty (1982) observe,

> Even when we have established some understanding of the historical origins of school curricula and examined the ideological features of school texts, it remains important to recognize that the effectivity of curricula is also crucially dependent upon the pedagogical context in which they are used and the different knowledges, prejudices and resistances that pupils bring into the classroom.

This call to keep separate and evenly balanced those interpretations of the definitions of experience represented in school texts which are developed by researchers from those which are developed by participants does not emanate from a concern with theoretical and methodological niceties (although such a practice would seem to be a prerequisite in any project seeking to avoid an overdeterministic weighting in descriptions of social reproduction). More precisely, it stems from anxiety about the implication of a failure of this kind for the movement from analysis to intervention. Is it not more than likely that policy proposals which fail to relate to the feelings and interpretations of the individuals in the social world under examination, through a thorough analysis of these understandings, will be viewed by those individuals as either suspicious or unbelievable? A significant strength of the movement considered at the beginning of this section, the 'new directions' approach to the development of curriculum analysis inspired by ideas drawn from phenomenological sociology, was that because it was able to show how curricular definitions, practices and outcomes were most strongly shaped and structured through the commensense understandings of teachers and pupils, then it could also show that reforms which fail to act on these understandings are likely to be superficial. In short, our concern is with the danger that the very people such reforms are designed to help have both description *and* prescription imposed upon them.

This is not to undervalue existing investigation of the relationship between curriculum differentiation and gender differentiation. Rather, it to request that the outcomes of curricular practices are given the same attention as the forms of their definition and transmission, that the daily struggle undertaken by girls and boys, men and women, by which they construct, confirm *and contradict* gender identities inside a curriculum framework, is quite deliberately established as an essential component of any adequate analaysis.

Issue 4: Women and Educational Work

> Women teachers are most specifically mentioned in discussions of commitment, careers and claims of the occupation to professional status. What seems to run through such discussions is a conception of women teachers as damaging, deficient, distracted and sometimes even dim.
>
> (Acker, 1982)

The final issue in this introductory discussion is the nature of the involvement of women as academic workers at various levels of the educational system and with analysis of this involvement. Such a topic is difficult, not least because the form and scope of women's educational work varies from one level to another. However, in her discussion of the 'subtle problems . . . embedded in everyday life' which face women teachers and academics, Acker (1980) has suggested three analytical targets which have a general applicability.

The first concerns the demands made on women from what Acker (borrowing some phraseology from Coser) calls 'greedy institutions' — in this case familial and educational. Both these institutional forms require from core members high degrees of loyalty, commitment and productivity. For many women teachers and academics the problem is not merely that success in one institutional setting necessarily carries penalties in the other (although for many this is a real dilemma). More, this dual involvement in two 'greedy institutions' means that these women are under pressure to demonstrate quite unequivocally that they have indeed come to terms with this dilemma and that their successful performance in one of these institutional life forms is not being achieved at the expense of underperformance in the other. Whilst it might be argued that men also experience a tension created by involvement in, say, familial and waged work, the difference between women's and men's involvement is that the female experience is both surrounded and defined through an ideology and domesticity. This ideology, supported by state and cultural practices, preserves a sexual division of labour in the home by which the male commitment is to relatively fixed operations and the female commitment is to constantly extendable domains.

The second analytical target identified by Acker concerns the access women in educational work have to positions of seniority or influence within organizational hierarchies — that is, the visible-invisible dilemma for women. Clearly, the presence of women in academic work finds different expression or manifestation in schools from those in higher and further education. In the former the marginality of women teachers relates not to the number involved in the work but to the difficulties they have in gaining promotion or posts which carry opportunities for influence. In the latter marginality is a consequence *both* of numerical underrepresentation and a lack of opportunity to gain supervisory status. This token presence decreases women's bargaining power in the sense that they become identified as members of a largely invisible minority and, at the very same time, increases the likelihood of them being held accountable for their activities as individuals visibly different from most other members of the community. We might question why access and opportunities for women in academic work are progressively more restricted as one moves from primary to higher education. Here again, many commentators have suggested that we need to think in terms of the operation of an ideology in which femininity is associated with domesticity and domesticity with maternalism. Thus, the massive presence of women in primary education is explained, in part, if it is recognized that this *kind* and *level* of work is often seen by educators, employers and, sadly, by some women themselves, as an extension of women's maternal role. Similarly, women teachers leaving their work (and thereby, in many cases, forfeiting promotion rights) are also seen as achieving a personal fulfilment of this maternal role, which compensates for loss of career opportunities and of parity in the competition for promotion. In this way, inequitable practices are disguised as moral imperatives; the successful female educational worker who is also a mother is always vulnerable to the change of unethical behaviour, of unavoidably neglecting her child in the pursuit of selfish and unnatural ends. The possibility always exists for women to be subjected to moral blackmail in both social worlds.

Finally, these two problems are compounded in higher education in general and in sociology of education in particular by the difficulty women have, as educational workers, in gaining access to the networks by which knowledge is developed and distributed. Many feminists have pointed out that, although there has been a steady increase in women's studies in education during the last five years, both 'mainstream' analysis, and any other investigation which is not primarily defined as feminist analysis has tended to be designed in such a way as to reproduce an interpretation of reality in which women's marginality is either taken for granted or seen as unproblematic (see Acker, 1982). Furthermore, the reduced opportunities women have to direct research projects, to find proper funding for educational work, to edit journals, might also be seen as reflections of this marginality. Whether this situation results from conscious or unconscious manipulation by the 'gatekeepers' of knowledge is difficult to determine. Certainly, however, explanation and justification for these exclusions is now a public issue, and failure to confront this *as* an issue will be to compromise the credibility of the academic community.

Credibility, however, is also dependent upon the strength of the explanatory work being presented and some caution is, perhaps, necessary when approaching the ways in which women's educational work has been depicted. Wajeman (1981) in her criticism of wider analyses of women's work experience has raised a number of concerns which are equally applicable to the more specific conceptualizations and interpretations of the work experiences of women in education. As we have hinted above, *explanations* of this experience make frequent reference to the operation of an ideology in which domestic and familial commitments for women are presented as having priority over involvement in waged work. Wajeman argues, however, that such reference can be over simplistic and misleading. Firstly, this arises when women's experience both in the family and in the workplace is treated as uniform; in this way important differences related to type of work, amount of work, class position, the number and age of children in a family, the particular developmental stage of the family of which a person is a member, are all glossed over. Secondly, it arises when accounts stop at this single reference point and, thereby, not only neglect consideration of how roles in domestic and productive work are designed and built, but also fails even to imagine the influencing elements of the context which conditions such construction. This last point is crucial to a consideration of women's educational work. Some women teachers and some academics *use* their educational involvement to redefine domestic roles, to challenge oppressive ideologies and practices and to win space inside the schools and colleges in which they work. Thus, is it not essential to look beyond a rather closed family-work articulation of cultural settings and identify the properties conditioning *some* domestic settings and *some* workplaces in such a way as to provide an opportunity for resistance?

The Analysis of Gender Relations in Education

Far from patriarchy and its associated world being an unexplained relic of previous societies, it is one of the very pivots of capitalism in its complex and unintended preparation of labour power and reproduction of the social order. It helps provide the real human and cultural conditions which in their ... unintended and contradictory ways actually allow subordinate roles to be taken or 'freely' within liberal democracy.

(Willis, 1977)

In the last section, we raised some issues relating to particular approaches to the study of women's educational experience. A more fundamental concern, however, was to work towards an identification of some general dilemmas confronting all those involved in this kind of investigation — dilemmas which exist at the level of conceptualization, analysis and policy formulation. Clearly, these dilemmas are many and various. However, it seems that there is great merit in employing the concept of 'contradiction' as introduced in the quotation above, as an important notion around which discussion of the main issues can be organized.

The concept of 'contradiction' is fairly frequently (and sometimes cavalierly) used in sociological literature and it is necessary to clarify how we are using the term here. In one sense the concept has decidely materialist references. Giddens (1979), restricting application of the term to an analysis of the structural properties of social systems, defines contradictions as '... principles [which] operate in *terms of each other* but at the same time *contravene one another*'. It has to be remembered, however, that Giddens interprets 'structural properties' in a specific way, that is, as elements which both condition and arise from social action. 'Contradictions' have a dual location. Firstly, they exist in the principles of institutional life which make social action possible. Secondly, they exist in the principles of the practices and experience constituted by social action. It is in terms of this dual reference that we wish to use the concept in this discussion.

The questions that arise, then, are what are those principles in institutional life which both confirm and negate one another, and how are these principles related to an analysis of gender relations and gender differentiation? Clearly, all social life involves a central contradictory principle in the sense that a person's individuality is both realized and restricted through participation in group life.

However, contradictory principles are more usually associated with the workings of a mode of production. In terms of the capitalist mode of production, contradictions operate in various parts of the social structure. Production itself operates through a contradiction in that workers are locked into sets of technical and social relations which at one and the same time *sustain* and *exploit* their social being. The organization of institutionalized life under capitalism operates through a contradiction in that this organization is always under pressure to remain *stable* and thereby manage the continuity of social relations whilst, at the same time, there is a constant demand for *evolution* in such organization to accommodate changes in productive forms and processes. The social system under capitalism operates through a contradiction in that social settings like schools, family life or work places are predicated upon and articulated through norms and values which both *promote* and *inhibit* individual development, such contrary outcomes arising because these norms and values establish both necessary social constraints and possible individual rights. The cultural practices which arise under capitalism operate on a contradiction in that forms of cultural life whilst *reproducing* attitudes, activities and artefacts which support the particular arrangements of the social order in which they occur also *produce* recognitions, reactions and responses which provide for the development of a critical and challenging stance towards that order. Perhaps this last contradictory principle is the most important in that this cultural contradiction is a manifestation of a most fundamental social tension between demands for conformity at a collective level and the struggle for self-fulfilment at an individual one. It should not be imagined that the balance between principles which work towards conformity and those which contravene this pressure is equal. The very notion of 'contradiction' emphasizes tension and conflict between opposing elements and, in the sense that at different moments in time or order one element will gain ascendency, then the balance between contradictory principles is always precarious.

We wish to maintain that the insights provided in the recognition of contradictory principles listed above are very useful in any consideration of the four issues concerning the analysis of women's educational experience we have presented. This is not to suggest the list is complete or that feminist analysis should be exclusively materialist. However, an awareness of the impact of contradictions seems to provide several ways of clarifying some of the problems which attend these important issues.

The notion of contradiction is highly relevant in the debate about the conceptualization of patriarchal ideologies and about the way in which these invade educational settings. It is immediately apparent that, working with this notion, there is a need to extend our view of what patriarchy is and of how patriarchal domination is effected. This is so because recognition of the contradictions at work across a variety of crucial aspects of social life suggests that we might expect both patriarchal representation and hegemony to vary according to structural, institutional or cultural location — that patriarchal domination in, say, the family, will be different in form and method from, say, that which operates in the work place. But to which particular ideological formation are we referring when we speak of schools embodying and sustaining a patriarchal ideology? This question is further complicated by the fact that awareness of contradictions means that we cannot expect a uniform response to these forms. If we accept that teachers and pupils can and will use their experience to develop cultural practices which stand in contradiction to dominant definitions and authority systems, then it is not acceptable to assume a common response by such individuals to the patriarchal or sexist ideologies and orders which invade educational settings. For this reason, the particular nature of patriarchy, of ideological domination and of the responses developed by individuals and groups needs to be demonstrated. The subtle differences from setting to setting and the unique cultural responses specific teachers, pupils or groups struggle to create require careful and detailed empirical investigation if we are to produce theory which is firmly related to the reality it purports to explain.

But this complication can be turned to real advantage. To recognize that patriarchal ideologies and the practices through which such ideologies are realized embody contradictions is to achieve a most important insight into social life: that the principles which shape social behaviour and the real actions which give substance to these principles involve conflictual elements. The importance of this awareness is not just that it means that analysis of sexism in schools needs to account for both conformist and resistant reactions by teachers and pupils to the diverse ideological forms which support different aspects of male domination. More fundamentally, this recognition provides the basis for the kind of political response we introduced at the beginning of this chapter as the motivating force behind such analysis. If employment of the notion of *contradiction* gives centrality to a recognition of *conflict*, then this concept in turn serves to preserve primacy for the notion of *contestation*. It is our contention that investigations of gender relations in education which use a notion of contestation as a central conceptual premise, and which endeavour to identify the ways in which contestations are enacted, will go a long way towards realizing two crucial goals. One is the achievement of considerable analytical purchase on the four key issues we have identified as vital in the debate. The other is the provision of a practical foundation upon which the struggle for alternative perspectives, practices and policies can be based. This contention draws upon the following beliefs about the relevance of the concept 'contestation'.

Firstly, usage of this concept brings *people* back to the centre of inquiry. Descriptions of gender relations in education which fail to recognize that patriarchal ideologies may be contested by teachers, that curricular definitions and pedagogical practices may be challenged by pupils, that educational work roles may be redefined by academics, can only provide partial understanding. The notion of contestation not only reminds us of the dynamic character of social interaction; it also asserts its primacy.

Secondly, usage of the concept means that adequate analysis of women's educational experience will necessarily incorporate a concern with power relations. If, using this concept, we refuse to depict women's experience solely in terms of the observable conformities to dominant ideologies and interpretations but, rather, add the possibility of a subjective, creative response which in some ways transforms or contests these constraints, then we cannot avoid being sensitive to the quite specific ways in which domination is achieved or opposed.

Essentially, we are arguing that the use of the related concepts of contradiction and contestation in the analysis of women's educational experience, by alerting us to the ways in which real people expose real weaknesses in the operation of a social system as *they* experience it, will not only provide us with illustrations that certain practices are not inevitable, that procedures are changeable, but also identify points of opposition and intervention.

References

ACKER, S. (1980) 'Women, the other academics', *British Journal of Sociology of Education*, 1, 1.

ACKER, S. (1982) 'Women and teaching: A semi-detached sociology of a semi-profession', this volume.

ARNOT, M. (formerly MACDONALD, M.) (1980) 'Schooling and the reproduction of class and gender relations' in BARTON, L. *et al.* (Eds), *Schooling, Ideology and the Curriculum*, Barcombe, Falmer Press.

ARNOT, M. and WHITTY, G. (1982) 'From reproduction to transformation: Recent radical perspectives on the curriculum from the USA', *British Journal of Sociology of Education*, 3, 1.

BEAUVOIR, S. de (1972) *The Second Sex*, Harmondsworth, Penguin.

BERNSTEIN, B. (1971) 'On the classification and framing of educational knowledge', in YOUNG, M.F.D. (Ed.), *op. cit.*

BRUNSDEN, C. (1978) 'It is well known that by nature women are inclined to be rather personal', in WOMEN'S STUDIES GROUP, *Women Take Issue*, London, Hutchinson/CCCS.

BURMAN, S. (Ed.) (1979) *Fit Work for Women*, London, Croom Helm.

BYRNE, E. (1978) *Women and Education*, London, Tavistock.

CHETWYND, J. and HARTNETT, O. (1978) *The Sex-Role System*, London, RKP.

CLARRICOATES, K. (1980) 'The importance of being Ernest ... Emma ... Tom ... Jane', in DEEM, R. (Ed.) *Schooling for Women's Work*, London, RKP.

DAVID, M.E. (1981) *The State, Family and Education*, London, RKP.

DEEM, R. (1978) *Women and Schooling*, London, RKP.

DEEM, R. (Ed.) (1980) *Schooling for Women's Work*, London, RKP.

DELAMONT, S. (1980) *Sex Roles and the School*, London, Methuen.

ESLAND, G. (1971) 'Teaching and learning as the organization of knowledge' in YOUNG, M.F.D. *op. cit.*

GIDDENS, A. (1979) *Central Problems in Social Theory*, London, Macmillan.

HUTT, C. (1972) *Males and Females*, Harmondsworth, Penguin.

KEDDIE, N. (1971) 'Classroom knowledge' in YOUNG, M.F.D., *op. cit.*

KELLY, A. (1975) 'The fate of women scientists', *Women Speaking*, 4 (July)

KING, R. (1978) *All Things Bright and Beautiful? A Sociological Study of Infants' Classrooms*, Chichester, Wiley.

KUHN, A. and WOLPE, A.M. (Eds) (1978) *Feminism and Materialism*, London, RKP.

LOBBAN, G. (1977) 'Sex-roles in reading schemes', *Educational Review*, 27, 3.

MACDONALD, M. (1981) *Class, Gender and Education*, Course E353, Units 10–11, Open University.

McROBBIE, A. and McCABE, T. (Eds) (1981) *Feminism for Girls: An Adventure Story*, London, RKP.

MILLETT, K. (1977) *Sexual Politics*, London, Virago Press.

MITCHELL, J. and OAKLEY, A. (Eds) (1976) *The Rights and Wrongs of Women*, Harmondsworth, Penguin.

OAKLEY, A. (1972) *Sex, Gender and Society*, London, Temple Smith.

OPEN UNIVERSITY (1972) *School and Society*, E202, Open University Press.

SCOTT, M. (1980) 'Teach her a lesson: Sexist curriculum in patriarchal education', in SPENDER, D. and SARAH, E., *op. cit.*

SEELEY, J. (1966) 'The "making" and "taking" of problems', *Social Problems*, 14.

SPENDER, D. (1982) *Invisible Women*, London, Writers and Readers.

SPENDER, D. and SARAH, E. (Eds) (1980) *Learning to Lose*, London, The Women's Press.

WAJEMAN, J. (1981) 'Work and the family: Who gets "the best of both worlds?"', in THE CAMBRIDGE WOMEN'S STUDIES GROUP, *Women in Society*, London, Virago Press.

WILLIS, P. (1977) *Learning to Labour*, Farnborough, Saxon House.

WRIGHT MILLS, C. (1970) *The Sociological Imagination*, Harmondsworth, Penguin.

WOLPE, A.M. (1977) *Some Processes in Sexist Education*, London, Women's Research and Resources Centre.

YOUNG, M.F.D. (Ed.) (1971) *Knowledge and Control*, London, Collier-Macmillan.

Acknowledgement

We would wish to thank Maveleine Arnot for her very helpful comments on a previous version of this chapter.

2. Intersections of Gender and Class: Accommodation and Resistance by Working-Class and Affluent Females to Contradictory Sex-Role Ideologies*

Jean Anyon, Rutgers University

Many researchers have documented the stereotypical sex-role expectations common among parents, teachers, and others who are influential in the lives of young girls.[1] In addition, writers have described in detail the stereotyped images of women that pervade television programs and ads, school textbooks and tradebooks, and other commercial materials such as toys.[2] Feminist researchers often assume, and sometimes state explicitly, that stereotyped sex-role messages (as part of the overall sex-role socialization experience) are 'successful'. They may argue, for example, that girls believe the messages, and ultimately exhibit the attitudes and behaviors transmitted (for example, submissiveness to males; sexual passivity; the desire to nurture children and husbands; and reluctance to compete with men in non-domestic situations).[3]

I acknowledge the pervasiveness of sex-role stereotypes in the present environment, and deplore any limits they would place on the development by females of a full range of behaviors, roles, and personality traits. However, I will take issue here with the current focus on sex-role socialization as 'successful'. While it is true that most women learn what is socially approved, and often behave in ways that are expected, I will argue that complete acceptance (as well as complete rejection) of sex-role appropriate attitudes and behaviors is actually rather rare. Indeed, neither 'acceptance' nor 'rejection' accurately describes what occurs. A more accurate description is what Eugene Genovese has called, in regard to the reactions of black American slaves to their enslavement, a simultaneous process of accommodation and resistance.[4]

In addition to taking issue with the assumption of success implied by most research on female socialization, I will differ as well with the prevalent view that gender development is primarily a one-way process of imposition by society of values and attitudes that girls internalize. I will argue instead that gender development involves not so much passive imprinting as *active response to social contradictions*. Thus, for girls, gender development will involve a series of attempts to cope with — and resolve — contradictory social messages regarding what they should do and be. Girls are presented not only with ideologies regarding what is appropriate behavior for themselves as females (for example, nurturance of men and children in a domestic situation, submissiveness and non-competitiveness with men outside the domestic situation, and sexual submissiveness),[5] but also with ideologies of what are appropriate means in US society of achieving self-esteem (for example, through success in the *non*-domestic, competitive world of work). These two sets of ideologies, as others have noted,[6] are in direct contradiction.

This chapter explores female responses to this contradiction between femininity and self-esteem as follows: a brief discussion of the differing social class characteristics of the contradictory ideologies; an analytical discussion of accommodation and resistance as active responses by adult women to social (for example, gender) contradiction; and a presentation of empirical examples of accommodation and resistance in fifth-grade girls in working-class and affluent elementary schools. In conclusion, the implications of accommodation and resistance for how we work towards social change for women are discussed.

Class Difference in Contradictory Ideologies

There are subtle class differences in the ideology of what is appropriate female behavior, and in the contradictions between femininity and self-esteem for women of the working and professional classes.

For most white working-class girls in the US, there exists the expectation that they adhere closely to 'feminine' behavior, with clear-cut distinctions between male and female.[7] The expectations regarding girls' futures do not usually include college and a 'career' but rather marriage and a family — with perhaps part-time work,[8] although many working-class women report that they *want* to work outside the family, at least part-time.[9] When asked to give their reasons for wanting to work, working-class women do not usually cite the desire for self-development or careers, but the desire to be considered a useful and valued member of society — (and housework does not provide this).[10] Also, many say that they want a measure of independence from their husbands, and that work provides this; finally, many women also cite the need for an additional paycheck in the family.[11]

A major contradiction faced by many of these working-class and lower-middle-class women is that the charge of femininity — to be submissive, subordinate to their men, dependent and domestic, is in sharp dysjunction with the imperatives of their daily lives — the need, for example, to aggressively struggle for actual survival. In addition, for many working-class women the contradiction is manifest in the dysjunction between the demands of their (working-class) husbands that they be in the home and submissive, and the women's own need for recognized competence and self-esteem.

For middle-class professional and affluent families, the definition of femininity and the female sex-role is less rigid than for working-class females,[12] but it still impinges on the free development of personality traits and roles. For girls who grow up in professional and affluent families, for example, the expectation of achievement through success in the world of public work is often a *part* of the set of expectations that the family has for the girl.[13] Professional families usually expect their daughters to go to college, often to graduate school, and indeed, in many cases, to have a career and to 'fulfil their potential' as human beings.[14] However, I would argue that this is usually expected to occur before, not instead of, having children. Thus, although these girls may be expected to achieve in the world of work, they are also expected to be feminine, and to fulfil domestic roles. Herein lies not only a contradiction, but a difficult task. The contradiction for professional women is manifest in several ways. For example, after she has, say, received an advanced degree and expended efforts to excel in a profession, all of a sudden the social expectation that she be a mother and a housewife may be felt. Not only may the personality traits differ for successful domesticity and professionalism, but there are severe biological and occupational time constraints on child bearing as well.

Somewhat differently, if a professional woman does attain success in her profession, she may paradoxically be (and be seen as) an outsider to the profession itself. This may occur because the concerns of most professions have been defined by males, most academic research is male oriented, and most professional societies and universities are administered largely by males.[15] (Education is no exception, despite the relatively large number of females in this field.)

In conflictful situations such as these neither working-class nor more affluent females are passive; contrary to the myth, women — and girls — actively struggle to come to terms with, or to transcend, the conflicts involved in being female.

Accommodation and Resistance to Gender Contradictions

In order to describe (and characterize) the responses of females to their contradictory situation I make use of Eugene Genovese's description of the ways black slaves responded to their contradictory situation of being human beings who were — nevertheless — owned outright, as non-human physical property.[16]

Antebellum slave law defined black slaves as property. They were not considered human beings, by the law, but as animals or as other physical property. Because of this, there was no need to pay the slaves for their work. However, this legal definition was daily and blatantly contradicted by the fact that slaves were human beings, responded to daily conditions as human beings, and needed to be treated by slave owners as *if* they were human beings, if the owners were to derive sufficient labor from the slaves to make their ownership profitable. A social ideology of paternalism developed in the south which resolved this contradiction for slaveholders by absolving them; the ideology of paternalism, however, also gave the slaves a tool with which to coerce better and more humane treatment from the slaveholders.

The ideology of paternalism was that the slaveholders were responsible for the welfare of the slaves, and the slaves were to yield their labor to their owners without pay. Paternalism thus included a web of personal duties and obligations on both sides, and bound slave and owner to each other. It implicitly recognized slaves as human beings who got sick, needed food and shelter and who had feelings; thus the ideology of paternalism softened somewhat the dehumanization of the antebellum code of law. However, while the ideology of paternalism may have encouraged more humane treatment by slaveowners, the fact that it obligated the owners to take care of the slaves effectively disguised the fact that the slaves' labor was free and unpaid. That is, the ideology of paternalism disguised the slaves' social exploitation.

The slaves understood paternalism as a way to make the owners more sensitive to their needs. They appropriated this ideology to their own ends. They interpreted the ideology very differently from the owners, and used it daily against the owners for small favors, big favors, and as a way of resisting the psychological degradation inherent in their situation. The contradiction, of course, between their biological humanity and their ownership as physical property, still remained.

Genovese argues that although there was a number of slave rebellions, the vast majority of slaves neither totally acquiesced in slavery by agreeing to it or wholly supporting it, nor overtly attempted to destroy the system by outright rebellion. Rather, he says, most slaves engaged in a process of daily accommodation and resistance:

> Accommodation and resistance developed as two forms of a single process by which slaves accepted what could not be avoided and simultaneously fought individually and as a people for moral as well as physical survival.[17]

As examples of accommodation and resistance — or, (as he explains it) accommodation *in* acts of resistance, and resistance *within* accommodation — Genovese cites the slaves' appropriation of this ideology of paternalism, as well as their appropriation of the whites' religion. The slaves were obligated by their owners to go to church services at which they were preached to by white ministers on their holy obligation to obey their white masters. The blacks, however, developed on their own a partially autonomous religion that taught them that everybody was equal in the hereafter, and that whites would have to pay for their sins; their religion taught them to love and value each other; to take a highly critical view of slavery; and to reject the ideological rationales for their own enslavement (that blacks were not human beings). Secret religious meetings after work hours were necessary to develop this religion, and during these meetings the slaves were preached to by their own black preachers who exhorted self love and equality in life after death. The congregations sang songs that deftly ridiculed the white masters and mistresses. While black religion (and most black preachers) stopped short of suggesting overt rebellion, their religion did become the organizing center of the slaves' resistance to slavery — a resistance that clearly embodied a great deal of accommodation. Slave religion may have reflected the hegemony of the master class, but it also set firm limits to that hegemony. It narrowed down what was due to the white master (daily labor) and what was not due: the free spirit or soul, and the perpetuity of equality in the afterlife. Black religion, understood as a critical world view, emerged as the slaves' most formidable weapon for resisting slavery's moral and psychological aggression. Their religion was an example of resistance in accommodation, just as it was also an accommodation to slavery that had a critical or resistant edge to it.

Another example of resistance in accommodation was the slaves' appropriation of the word 'nigger'. According to Genovese,

> [The word nigger] was a brutal, violent word that stung the soul of the slave more than the whip did his back. But the slaves took this ugly word and like the white man's religion, made it their own. [Although they also sometimes used the word to deprecate themselves], in their mouths it could become an affectionate, endearing word. As much as was possible, they robbed it of its ability to spiritually maim them.[18]

This process of accommodation in resistance — and resistance in daily accommodation — was also apparent in 'slow downs' by slaves at work, in their wounding themselves so they could not work (and paternalism bound the owner to take care of them while they were sick); in breaking machinery; in appearing to misunderstand or not understand directions, and in their own use of intentionally vague language (to avoid suspicion or punishment by owners, etc.). There were of course slaves who overtly resisted slavery and who took part in the occasional slave rebellions. And there must have been some who were so indoctrinated that they fully acquiesced in the belief that they were sufficiently cared for by the master class and did not need distinct civil rights such as their freedom.

It should be obvious from the discussion of accommodation/resistance by slaves in the antebellum south that the dialectic of accommodation and resistance is a part of *all* human beings' response to contradiction and oppression — of men, women, working-class and affluent; of white races and black. The contradictions, the forms and extents of oppression are different for the different genders and classes and races, and the forms which accommodation and resistance take will differ.[19]

The dialectic of accommodation and resistance is manifest in the reactions of women and girls to contradictory situations that face them. Most females neither totally acquiesce in, nor totally eschew, the imperatives of 'femininity'. Rather, most females engage in daily (conscious as well as unconscious) attempts to resist the psychological degradation and low self-esteem that would result from total and exclusive application of the approved ideologies of femininity: submissiveness, dependency, domesticity, passivity, etc. Females' attempts to offset these demands with those of self-esteem (that is, to mediate the contradiction between femininity and competence as it is socially defined) exhibit both daily resistance and daily accommodation — not unlike the dialectic proposed by Genovese for blacks. Accommodation and resistance are apparent in adult women and in young girls as well.

Accommodation and Resistance by Adult Women

There are several areas of women's lives in which the dialectic of accommodation and resistance can be seen. The accommodation and resistance can be divided into two categories that, although theoretically distinct and heuristically fruitful, will be seen to be empirically overlapping. It is important to point out that not every act by a female is an instance of accommodation or resistance. Many acts (and attitudes) are neither. Indeed, an act can in *one* instance be an expression of resistance, and in *another* context or situation express accommodation. Furthermore, in the discussion of accommodation and resistance by women and girls that follows, I attempt to lay out the terrain for study, not to provide empirical 'proofs' of any sort regarding accommodation and resistance.

First, I will describe some of the discrepancies that exist between a woman's public behavior and her private thoughts and beliefs. It is often the case that while one of these expresses accommodation, the other expresses resistance. Second, I will describe some ways that women appropriate (use and shape to their own ends) the ideology of femininity and feminine sexuality. For it is often the case that a woman who exhibits femininity and apparently demure sexuality, may be using these to achieve ends which differ fundamentally from what men and the rest of society expect (or desire).

Public/Private Discrepancies

There are several kinds of discrepancies. They are often examples of rebellion that is private. One type of discrepancy was described by Doris Lessing in her novel *The Summer before the Dark*,[20] where she describes a married woman in her mid-forties who dutifully and smilingly serves coffee and cake in the garden to her husband and his male guest. Then she sits down to join them, smiles again, and turns off her mind to them — in order to think her *own* thoughts — which include how boring their conversation is. This woman's public/private behavior is an example of an apparent acquiescence in the role of dutiful, submissive wife, but is in fact an accommodation with a critical edge: it contains an internal resistance; a separateness; and an internal non-subordination.

Public/private discrepancies also include the obverse of this example. There are instances in which the public behavior of a woman is resistant to the stereotype of femininity but her private beliefs continue to hold to the ideologies that devalue women — the ideology that women are not capable of taking care of themselves, for example, and that women 'need a man to lean on'. (The argument here does not suggest that women should be completely independent from men; what it does condone is an equal relationship between a man and a woman.) One sees today professional women who have attained success in their careers. This has necessarily involved hard work, a certain amount of aggressiveness, and usually a measure of independent thought and behavior. However, many of these women continue to believe that they cannot take care of themselves — they need a Prince Charming. This feeling of dependence has been called the 'Cinderella Syndrome'.[21] While some of these women have *publicly* resisted the stereotyped expectations for them, their internal beliefs devalue themselves as women, and are thus an internal accommodation to the ideology of female helplessness and dependency.

This type of public resistance with a simultaneous private acceptance of the ideology that women's concerns are not of value is also apparent in the working-class or professional woman who has had to take on allegedly male characteristics of exploitativeness and domination in order to get where she is. And in taking on these characteristics she has treated other females as *males* have treated them: with disrespect, condescension, exploitation. Such male-identified behavior by the woman manifests her own internalization and acceptance of the dominant ideology that devalues women's abilities and motivation. She says, 'There is no social discrimination against women: *I* made it. And if other women don't, it's their own fault.'

The same phenomenon of public resistance and private accommodation is apparent in working-class women who are 'tough' and aggressive in non-domestic situations, but who are submissive with their men, and who accept this submissiveness as appropriate. In addition, one can cite the female prostitute who publicly breaks the code of femininity (by being a prostitute) but who is on the whole quite dependent on, and submissive with, her pimp.

Finally, an obverse example is the working-class woman who submits in various (demeaning) ways to the demands of her boss, in order to survive in an oppressive job situation, and who thus accommodates to the role of submissive female. However, if she resists this public degradation psychologically (that is, privately) by holding on to her own value, and 'dreams' of a better life, where such submission is not necessary, she is manifesting public/private discrepancy which is part of her simultaneous accommodation and resistance to her own exploitation.

Appropriation of Femininity and Sexuality

The second type of activity is that in which a woman appropriates the ideology of femininity or female sexuality, and shapes it to her own ends. For example, first take the appropriation of femininity. Most women who accept femininity as their natural role do not passively adopt the stereotypical set of expectations. Rather the doctrine of femininity is often used by women as Genovese argued the slaves used paternalism: to try to ensure their own protection by men, as a way of enforcing a reciprocity of duties and obligations. Femininity may become a way of gaining security against a harsher public world.

Moreover, femininity is often used to achieve power in a situation or relationship that is overtly (but only apparently) one in which the male has power. Thus, the wife, or secretary, or administrative assistant, is the real power behind the throne, and apparent submissiveness has been used (and is used) to prevent actual subordination.

A similar phenomenon is the use of femininity to convince these men who do have power that you, as a woman, are not threatening. For example, in university departments in which a female assistant professor is up for tenure or promotion, one sometimes sees her displaying apparent submissiveness or taking a demure stance *vis-à-vis* the males in her department who will vote on her. One purpose of such a display (or deception, if you will) is to convince the males that, even though you are intelligent and a scholar, you are not threatening to them. Thus, feminine 'wiles' may be used to get what is desired when other, more straightforward ways are not available or cannot ensure success. This is an example of an accommodation to the feminine role that has a large component of resistance. Indeed, it becomes its *opposite*: femininity used to fend off the discrimination of oneself as a woman.

In a related argument, Angela McRobbie[22] suggests that for some working-class women, taking on of femininity (the role of wife, marriage, and romance) is not just acquiescence in the social demands of femininity, but expresses as well an opposition to school and to male culture. It is, she argues, a form of resistance to the sexual attitudes of the working-class boys and the unrewarding demands of the school. Yet it is clearly an accommodation to the female role, and is a real contribution to reproducing the young woman's ultimate social position of working-class housewife, dependent on her husband.

There are also women who appropriate the female role in order to attempt to provide self-esteem. Thus, the woman who raises the 'best' children, who has the 'best' house, who, it is said, 'lives' through her children, her husband and her furnishings, may be taking the only legitimate or available avenue to try to achieve success and self-esteem in a society which defines success in ways that normally exclude her.

Even becoming pregnant and having a child can sometimes express accommodation and resistance. Childbearing may be fully desired; it can also be an accommodation to what women have 'always' done and is expected from them; and it can, on occasion, include a significant amount of *resistance* to the alienation and degradation of life in modern society. As one low-income woman told Robert Coles, 'Having a baby inside me is the only time I'm really alive.'[23] Another woman told an interviewer, 'The only way I can be creative in this world is by having a baby.'[24]

Child-rearing itself can entail the same resistance: the nurturing of children and the love returned can be a struggle to ward off or compensate for the dehumanization and alienation of a non-nurturing world. Indeed, I would argue that some mothers raise children in an effort to make the personal political: the resistance to a sexist, racist environment may involve bringing up children who are politically sensitive to these as social problems.

In ways similar to the appropriation of femininity, some women use the ideology of female sexuality (as passive, demure, or submissive) in order to achieve positions of non-subordination, equality, and power. The promise of sex to a male with power, the provision of sex to a boss or supervisor, is an apparent acceptance of the role of female as submissive sexual object. But it may also be a simultaneous use of, appropriation of, and resistance to, the ideology that females are powerless and passive: it may be the use by a woman of her own sexuality to attain power or status normally denied her by other, more straightforward means. The process occurs in factories and business offices, graduate and undergraduate departments of universities, and of course between husbands and wives.

Other examples of resistance to the female role by appropriation of 'feminine' characteristics are some types of sickness. Thus, as Freud argued,[25] hysteria and frigidity (and perhaps the more common 'headache') may often be somatic symptoms of inner conflicts regarding sex and sexuality. In a similar vein, alcoholism, schizophrenia and other, less drastic forms of mental illness, as well as pill dependency, may all result at least in part from unsuccessful attempts to *reconcile the contradictions of being female.*[26] As Piven and Coward have argued,[27] such illnesses are 'hidden' forms of protest, and are particularly suited to appropriation by·females. They express resistance to the female role through privatized, inwardly directed and 'quiet' and acquiescent forms, rather than through the outwardly directed, public, sociopathic forms some males utilize.

Alcoholism and schizophrenia represent extreme forms of resistance within accommodation to the female role. However, the kinds of resistance and accommodation described here are those that characterize the everyday lives of women. They attempt to reveal how, in daily interaction with men and in social institutions, women engage in a negotiation for equality, respect and power that belies a total acceptance of the stereotypical female role and characteristics. The fact that most women accommodate to and resist female stereotypes and the contradictory constraints imposed upon them does not deny that some women may genuinely and totally believe that they, as females, are inferior to their men, should be passive, submissive and dependent. And of course there are some women, perhaps some lesbians, who may totally *reject* what femininity entails, with little if any accommodation. However, what I am arguing here is that most women neither totally accept or reject femininity, but make concessions to it and the contradictory demands of femininity and self-esteem. They adapt femininity to their own ends, resist it in subtle ways, and use it to ward off its consequences.

The next section applies the concepts of accommodation and resistance to the activity of young girls, using these constructs to interpret data from a study of children in five elementary schools. The data bear on the contradiction between home and work as it was perceived by 100 girls and boys and provide examples of accommodation and resistance by some of the girls.

Accommodation and Resistance by Young Girls

As part of a larger project[28] which investigated school knowledge, work, and modes of pedagogy in five elementary schools in contrasting social class contexts, I interviewed 100 fifth-grade children. Eighty-seven per cent of the children in the study were white. The study included, in addition to these interviews, ten three-hour observations in each fifth-grade classroom (and three three-hour observations in each second-grade classroom); interviews of school personnel; and analysis of curriculum and other school materials. The schools differed by the social class composition of their students, with incomes ranging from very low (in two schools) to very high (in two schools).[29] For purposes of the present discussion I will label the populations of schools in the following way. There were three schools which I will call (blue-collar and white-collar) *working-class* — although the white-collar occupations included some firemen, technicians, clerical worker, and teacher, which are sometimes referred to as lower-middle-class or middle-class. There were two schools which I will call *upper-middle-class* affluent professional — in which the family occupations were cardiologist, corporate lawyer, professor, advertizing and banking executives, automobile dealer, etc.

The interviews were of 25 working-class girls and 25 working-class boys; and 25 upper-middle-class girls and 25 upper-middle-class boys. The interviews were wide-ranging, involving attempts to find out what the children thought about their school experiences, their teachers, their present lives, and their futures. All interviews were with fifth-grade children, aged 9–10 years. Each interview include the following questions: 'Will you get married when you grow up?'; 'Do you want to work when you grow up?' (if so, 'What kind of work do you want to do?') If the child was a girl, I asked her, 'Do you think your husband will want you to work?' And if the child was a boy, I asked, 'Will you want your wife to work?' I report the following data as interesting and suggestive, but do not regard them as definitive because of the small sample (of 100 children).

Interview Data.   The responses to the questions suggest that most of the children in the study perceived conflicts between the girls' future role as wife and her working at a job. Most children also stated that there would be a conflict between a girls' desire to work and (in many cases) her future husband's desire to have her stay at home. In all schools more girls reported a conflict than did boys; and while most of the girls stated that their husbands would *not* want them to work, only half of the boys said that they would not want their wives to wrok. The data and some of the responses, broken down by social class and gender, are as follows.

In the *working-class* schools, almost all of the girls (22 of 25) said they would work or wanted to work when they grew up. Most of them were quite emphatic about it, expressing that they would work *despite* their husbands. All but one of the girls (24) said their husbands would *not* want them to work. Some of the girls' responses are:

> 'Husbands *never* want their wives to work. They just want them to clean and clean and make food. But I *want* to work. My mother works at the diner — and she had to work at night and my father didn't want her to.'
> 'I want to be a nurse as long as I can. I don't *care* what my husband says.'
> 'I don't *want* to get married. I just want to be free. I want to have time for myself. I don't always want to be home.'
> 'Yes [I want to work]. If the husband loses his job then they'll still have the money. If he goes on strike we'll still have to support the children.'
> 'I *want* to work, but I'd have to quit [working] when I had a kid, so what's the use of starting?'
> 'Yes [I want to work]. Because I won't be rich. I don't *want* to be rich. You have everything you want and you don't have to work. They just have to stay home and have all the money. I want to *work!*'
> 'Yes — he's *gonna* let me work.' (All emphases in original statements.)

The three girls who said they would not work said,

> 'No [I won't work]. Husbands think you have to stay home. They'll think it's too hard for us. Or we'd get our hands dirty.'
>
> 'Probably not if I had kids.'
>
> 'No [I won't work]. My father doesn't want my mother to work because she's grouchy when she comes home.'

While all but one of these working-class girls expressed the belief that their husbands would *not* want them to work, the opinion was not universal among the boys. Slightly more than half of the working-class boys (15 of 25) said that they would not want their wives to work, but the rest (10 of 25) or almost half, said yes, she *should* work, (for more money). Some of the boys' responses are:

> 'No [she shouldn't work]. Not if I'm a cop. She should stay home and take care of the kids and the house.'
>
> 'Yes, if we needed the money.'
>
> 'No, I wouldn't want my wife to work. Even though women are going to get equal rights, they still have to stay in the house.'
>
> 'Not if we have kids.'
>
> 'No, because I'd be working.'
>
> 'No [she shouldn't work]. Don't take this personal, (pause) but girls are sort of dainty. They *shouldn't* work.'
>
> 'Yes, if she had to. My mother says she *wants* a job — but he [my father] doesn't want her to. And when they have a fight she says, "I'm going to get a job." And he treats her like a waitress. He just tells her to get the dinner.'

In the *upper-middle-class* schools, all but one of the girls (24 of 25) said they wanted to work, or would work (or be in the 'clubs' — the Junior League, and other upper-middle-class, lower-upper-class clubs). Many of the girls (16) volunteered the information that they would stop or would have to stop when they had children. However, in contrast to the working-class girls (all but one of whom said their husbands would *not* want them to work) only slightly more than half of the upper-middle-class girls (14 of 25) said that their husbands would not want them to work. There was not the emphatic, 'I'd work anyway!' attitude among these girls as there was among the working-class girls. Most of the upper-middle-class girls took for granted that they would work. Some of their responses are:

> 'Yes. I want to be an actress. My cousin just made a TV commercial. Her aunt is an agent.'
>
> 'Yes — but you have to go to the right college. I want to be a psychotherapist.' (Why?) 'Because I like people.'
>
> 'Yes, but women's lib and all that is dumb. No one *has* to be equal. I *want* boys to be better than me. Who *wouldn't* want that?'
>
> 'Yes, I want to be a violinist. But I don't know if he [my husband] would want me to work. Men are number one. I don't think I would *like* to be as strong as men. Strong women wouldn't be pretty.'
>
> 'Yes, if you're a wife you've got to clean and cook. And *that's* no fun. I don't want to do that. But I'll probably be a wife and I'll work too.'

'Yes — I'm not going to pick up after everyone! But fathers work to pay for us.'
'Yes — I'm going to be three things: a teacher, a ski instructor, and a mother. But my mom says that I'd probably be bored being a teacher. And teachers don't get paid that much.'
'Well, I'll be in the League, where you're known.'
'Yes — and I could do *lots* of things. (Pause) I probably couldn't be President, though.'

As noted above, slightly more than half of the upper-middle-class girls (14 of 25) said they thought their husbands would *not* want them to work. However, most of the upper-middle-class boys (20 of 25) said their wives could do what they wanted to. Most of the boys included some statement about male chauvinism or the Equal Rights Amendment in their response; and several expressed the contradictory conviction that, even though male chauvinism was wrong, *their* wives would stay home and take care of the kids. Some of the boys' responses follow:

'Yes [women should work]. I'm not a male chauvinist. My grandmother says a woman's place is in the home. But my mother owns a bookstore.'
'Yes — they [girls] have the same abilities boys do. Male chauvinism is *stupid*. It's not fair to not give women chances to do everything men do.'
'Yes! Good *idea* [for women to work]. I don't want *my* wife to work, though. I think women should work, but I want my wife to take care of the kids. Well, don't think I'm prejudiced or anything. Men and women are the same — same brains.'
'Well, women should have equal chances, but *my* wife will stay home.'
'I don't know — maybe not — it would all depend on a lot of things, if we had a kid to feed, or a job. It would all depend on what she thought.'
'If she wants to. I don't care.'
'If my wife wants to work, it's up to her — Let her *work!*'

The interview responses, taken across social class and looked at by sex, suggest that for most of the girls, and for about half of the boys, there is a perceived conflict between the girls' role as wife and mother and as a person who works outside the home. The responses of the working-class girls, who were so eager to work, and so insistent that they would work despite their husbands' objections, contrast with the memories of adult working-class women reported by Rubin in 1976 and earlier by Komarovsky (in 1962).[30] These researchers asked adult working-class women whether they had wanted to work when they had been young, and most of them reported that while they might have had a dream of being an actress or such, most remember wanting primarily to get married, rather than to work. The fact that the working-class girls I interviewed were so eager to work may have to do with cultural effects of the Women's Rights Movement or other social developments. It may also have to do with the *age* of the girls I interviewed. As fifth-graders, they had not yet reached the teenage, high school years, when they will be faced with more explicit social pressure to 'fit in' to the feminine stereotype: to look attractive to boys, to not appear unusual or too masculine, to acquire a boyfriend, and then a husband.[31] Some of these fifth-graders (as teenagers) may abandon their plans to work (and may forget that such plans existed).
As research has shown, high school is a time when many girls who had

excelled heretofore begin to decline academically.[32] They are often counseled out of demanding courses (necessary for professional careers) or they may self-select out of such courses, thinking perhaps that the courses are too difficult, or designed for boys; or the girls may reject the courses to avoid appearing overly smart and thus unattractive to boys.[33] Indeed, one researcher found that the 'fear of success' increases in high school girls. A 1974 study found that 29 per cent of the fifth-grade girls studied exhibited fear of success, while 60 per cent of the tenth-grade girls exhibited this fear.[34]

Observational Data. The processes of accommodation and resistance described earlier can be observed in elementary school girls. There are several relevant types of activity that I observed in fifth-grade (and some second-grade) girls during ten months of classroom observation.

The activity I will report seems to manifest the processes of accommodation and resistance. However, I did not do in-depth case studies of any of the girls. Thus, I do not know for certain *why* they were engaged in some of this activity. I present my own interpretation of their actions and attitudes, and not theirs. I suggest that, since almost all the girls interviewed expressed some awareness of the conflicts involved, their behavior could indeed be expressing accommodation and resistance to gender-related pressures or contradictions. The following, then, is interpretive and hypothetical: it describes possibilities for in-depth, long-term study.

I observed six types of behavior. Although (as I have said) the exact nature of the ideologies and contradictions differs in working-class and more affluent contexts, all types of behavior existed in all schools. There were, however, interesting differences in the *frequency* with which certain forms of accommodation and resistance appeared among the social classes. In addition, while girls in various social classes may resist in similar fashion, the ways these resistances are played out in adulthood will be quite different for working-class and more affluent females.[35]

Intellectual (and artistic, or athletic) achievement is the first type of behavior that I interpret as having both accommodative and resistant aspects. Many elementary school girls acquiesce in the teachers' demands for neatness, obedience, and thoroughness in tasks. This may be an accommodation on the girls' part to what is understood or felt to be how good girls act — it is in accord with approved behavior for them. However, I observed a number of girls, in all social classes, for whom hard work, diligence, and school-related achievement seemed to express more than the desire to do what was asked. For these girls it was behavior that *resisted* passivity and submissiveness. For example, attempts to excel academically and in school-related activities such as sports and musical instruments demand perseverance, aggressiveness, a measure of independence, and effort over and above obedience and neatness. That such achievement may involve conflict for the girls is possible. One girl in an upper-middle-class school who played the violin was quite talented, and her teacher told me she practised a great deal. She gave a school concert, and worked very hard to prepare for it. She was also one the highest academic achievers in the fifth grade, an extremely studious and meticulous child. Her IQ was 145. Despite her efforts to achieve, she was the child who told me in the interview that although she wanted to play the violin when she grew up she didn't know if she would, because 'men are number one' — and, she said, 'strong women wouldn't be pretty'.

Another girl in the same school was quite aggressive and assertive, very often stating her opinions forcefully in class discussions and taking a leadership role in group projects. She was also a talented creative writer; her written work was startling in its maturity and interesting use of language. Yet, despite her strength, independence and talent, she told me that she wanted boys to be 'better, who *wouldn't* want that!'

The contradiction between the potentials of these two girls and their sexist attitudes towards themselves and their futures suggests to me a process of accommodation and resistance. The attempt to excel is a resistance to the feminine stereotype, but the attitude that men are more important, and better, is an obvious accommodation of this resistance to society's sexist values.

For some of the working-class girls I observed, intense interest in, and effort to do well in, school work expressed not only their willingness to do what the teacher asked, but seemed to express a strong desire to be qualified to get a job later. As several said, 'If you don't have the skills, the boss won't hire you.' For a few, achievement at school seemed to secure their hopes to work later, to get a job. One girl seemed to use intense effort to complete her assignments as a way of screening out a very chaotic, unpleasant classroom environment. She told me that she wanted to be a veterinarian, and that she did not want to work in a factory like her mother did. I watched her persist at her desk to do her school work as the teacher screamed at other children, gave confusing directions, and belligerent boys roamed the classroom. Thus, I interpret her hard work not only as an accommodation to expectations that she do what is demanded in school, but also that through this accommodation she can resist both present and future social discomfort.

The appropriation of femininity is the second category of activity. I observed many fifth-grade girls in the working-class schools who appeared to fulfil the feminine stereotype for little girls: they wore dresses and skirts, they were not intellectually aggressive in class, they were quiet, did not often call out, and they did not engage in aggressive physical activities in the playground; instead, they stood alone or in groups and talked or played jump rope. However, there were multiple occasions in the working-class schools where I observed exaggerated feminine behavior that was used to resist the flow of work assignments, and to resist the teacher in other ways. For example, on one occasion a teacher in one of the working-class fifth grades gave the class an assignment to trace Christopher Columbus' route to the New World on a map. She told them it was something 'different' from what they usually did, and she wanted to see if they could do it. A group of the 'feminine' little girls began to giggle, blush, laugh and whisper. They were not doing their work, and were expressing their resistance to the assignment by the use of exaggerated female behavior. The teacher responded to them by saying, 'some silly little girls in the back better get to work.'

On another occasion in a second grade in one of the working-class schools, I observed that some of the girls had marked off a round table in the corner of the room as 'the girls' club'. When I asked them why they wanted a club, one girl said, 'To get away from them', and pointed to a group of boys standing at the door. The group of boys, I subsequently noticed, was usually in the library corner playing cards. They would not let the girls get books from the library corner. Moreover, some of the boys in this class engaged in repeated harassment of the girls on the playground, pulling their hair, chasing and hitting them. The girls appeared to have banded together under the banner of their sex to get the teacher to allow them to have a corner of the room to themselves.

Another example of the appropriation of femininity by fifth-grade girls in the working-class schools involved occasions on which I observed several girls being quite coy with the male fifth-grade teacher. They were using feminine 'wiles' to resist school work, to try to persuade him not to give them so much math. And finally, there was the case of a quite proper little girl in one of the working-class schools who wore clean, dainty sweaters and blouses to school and who told me with pride that *she* was going to be a *secretary*; and she patted the collar of her white sweater with apparent satisfaction. I interpret this behavior as a suggestion that for this girl femininity was a matter of pride, and that she may use it to achieve success in the world of work.

In the upper-middle-class fifth grades I, of course, also observed girls who seemed to fit the feminine stereotype, with dresses, and quiet and demure behavior. However, there were somewhat fewer of these in the upper-middle-class schools than in the working-class schools. Some girls in the upper-middle-class schools wore clothes in which they could be more active: corduroy pants or dungarees, slacks, pullovers and sweaters or shirts. Indeed, regardless of their clothes, many of the girls in these fifth grades were more assertive and intellectually aggressive in class than were the girls in the working-class schools. Indeed, two fifth-grade teachers seemed to encourage such behavior in the girls. And, despite the attitude expressed by many boys in the interviews (above) — that Equal Rights Amendment or no, their wives would stay home — some of these same boys expressed admiration for several of the girls who, they said, were 'really smart'. Girls in the upper-middle-class schools participated more in classroom discussions and projects than in the working-class schools, and a larger number of them than in the working-class schools were involved in school clubs, music events, and plays.

Because of a greater acceptance as equals in the classroom, and because they were more often encouraged to be active, there was less need for the middle-class girls to use exaggerated 'femininity' to get what they wanted; there were other, more legitimate ways that were built into the school and classroom environment.

Tomboyishness is another way that some of the girls resisted the feminine stereotype. Tomboyishness is in part a matter of taking on characteristics of dress and physical activity that are more characteristic of boys of that age. Such girls eschew the quiet, indoor activities of many girls, preferring to play outdoors, and to be active. I observed more of this in the upper-middle-class schools than in the working-class schools. In fact, in one upper-middle-class fifth grade there was a child who was a girl but whom I mistook for a boy on my first two visits. She was quite tomboyish: she dressed exactly like most of the boys; her hair was short; her features were not distinctly masculine or feminine; also, she was very active outdoors and during lessons; she called out sarcastic comments in class as often as some of the other 'discipline problems', all of whom (except for her) were boys.

A less extreme example of tomboyishness was one little girl who refused to wear skirts. She wanted to wear work overalls, and her teacher told me that her mother was quite upset about this, and was 'working on it with her'. Within several months (according to her teacher) this little girl was wearing a dress every day. It may not be necessary to point out that tomboyish behavior is resistant to the constrictions imposed on little girls in both dress and behavior. However, an interesting dialectic was involved with these two tomboyish girls. The other side of the coin of active tomboy behavior in public was an intense shyness in personal contact, such as in the interviews I conducted with them.

Appropriation of sexuality is the next type of behavior that manifested both accommodation and resistance. I observed two fifth-grade girls in the working-class schools who were using their nascent sexuality to get attention, to disrupt the class, and in one instance to turn the boys against the female teacher. One of the girls came to school with nail polish, rouge, hair that had been curled and styled, and usually *without* her homework. She had a sexual, suggestive manner with the boys in the class. The teacher was female, and the girl told me that she did not like the teacher because she 'tries to tell me what to do'. This girl was one of the very few girls (in any school) that I heard directly challenge statements a teacher had made in class. In another working-class fifth grade was a girl who had been held back. She was very attractive, and she flirted with the boys, and argued with the female teacher, whom she said she did not like. The teacher told me that she 'seems like a teenager', and that she 'gets the boys all excited' so that they do not pay attention.

Being a discipline problem is a phenomenon that, for girls, seems to express resistance not only to school, but to what is expected of them as girls. That is, they may be expressing resistance to both school *and* gender ideologies of passivity, submissiveness and acquiescence, and to their teachers as older females as well. I see their deviance from the norms of school and femininity as organized responses — as organized nonconformity. Their nonconformity is not necessarily conscious; it is *not* an *inability* to follow the rules, but may be a structured response of resistance.

Distancing and alienation, and staying home from school frequently, is a final form of resistance in accommodation. It is one that is particularly quiescent and directed against the self. As research studies have shown, boys are more likely to engage in aggressive, disruptive behavior than girls.[36] Most girls do not resist so openly, so publicly. Rather, I would argue, girls are more likely to resist the pressures of school life in ways that are internalized and not so obvious as boys' resistance. They may tune out, turn inward, and — by a psychological distancing from events that Anthony Giddens[37] rightly argues is a resistant act — effect a subtle resistance to school that is incorporated into the feminine stereotype. Some girls in the working-class schools seemed extremely removed (alienated) from their classroom surroundings; but then, so were some of the working-class boys. In-depth study is necessary here in order to assess any gender variations in this phenomenon.

Accommodation and resistance, even when it takes the form of a turning away or withdrawal, is an active process. The analysis above suggests that most girls are not passive victims of sex-role stereotypes and expectations but are active participants in their own development. Indeed, one could do an analysis of minority girls, and of boys of all races and social classes, to assess how these children react to the contradictions and pressures that confront them. I would argue that accommodation and resistance will be an integral part of the overall processes that *all* children use to construct their social identities.

Implications

This section discusses implications (of viewing gender and gender construction as involving active responses to social contradiction) for how we work towards social change for women.

Eugene Genovese[38] argued that the slaves' accommodation and resistance to paternalism allowed them to gain a measure of self-esteem and community without which their psychological survival would not have been possible. However, he also argued that this same paternalism, and the slaves' own accommodation and resistance to it, trapped them in a web of dependency:

> The legacy of paternalism, no matter how brilliantly manipulated to protect their own interests, kept the slaves and generations of later blacks from a full appreciation of their individual strength. And the intersection of paternalism with racism worked a catastrophe, for it transformed elements of personal dependency into a sense of collective weakness . . . . They could not grasp their collective strength as a people, and act like collective men [sic].[39]

Genovese goes further to argue that wherever paternalism exists, resistance tends to become a defensive action, aimed at protecting the individuals against aggression and abuse. Such resistance, as part of accommodation, does not readily pass into an effective weapon for liberation. Moreover, he argues that paternalism undermines solidarity among the oppressed, by linking them in dependency relations not to each other, but to their oppressors.

If we think about this argument in the context of the ideology of femininity for women, we can arrive at the following point: the ideology of femininity reinforces a paternalistic dependency on *men*. The accommodation and resistance to that, by individual females, is often a defensive action (no matter how creative) that is aimed *not* at transforming patriarchal or other social structures, but at gaining a measure of protection *within* these. Thus, not only femininity (as an ideological, practical limit on activity) but also the process of accommodation/resistance itself, traps women in the very contradictions they would transcend. It traps them because their daily accommodation and resistance does not seek to remove the structural causes of the contradictions. For such transformation women need collective action. That is to say, while accommodation and resistance as modes of daily activity provide most females with ways of negotiating individually felt social conflict or oppression, this individual activity of everyday life remains just that: individual, fragmented and isolated from group effort. It is thus politically weakened. While, as Anthony Giddens[40] argues, the actions of individuals do mediate immediate environments and affect them, individual women acting alone (*I* would argue) cannot reorganize or transform the legal, economic, religious or other cultural sanctions and bases on which certain men get — and attempt to keep — social power. To change these relations of power, not only is individual activity necessary, but it will be necessary for women to join together to take collective action.

To those women who say they cannot resist, who say it is too much to *ask* that we resist and take collective action against oppressive men and the machines of sexist law and tradition, I would say: but women have *always* resisted! As part of their daily efforts to attain self-esteem and survival, women have always fought back. This knowledge that we have done so should empower us. The knowledge that we are, by our past and present accommodation and resistance, already implicated in our personal development, should enable us to take the step to collective political struggle for determination of our fate.

However, women must work with men. For gender freedom is not possible without freedom from capitalist exploitation. (Although we now know that freedom from capitalist exploitation does not itself ensure female liberation.[41]) However, social transformation of a capitalist society to a society that is humane for all of its members is not possible without social change in the status and power of women; and social change for women is inextricably interwined with the liberation from exploitation of *men*.

As an example of the conjuncture of male and female liberation from *economic* exploitation, consider the fact that without sexual discrimination in the labor market, capitalistic economic exploitation of the working class as a whole would be quite difficult. If all working-class women (white and minority together) refused to be hired for low wages, or refused to replace men who were on strike, then it would be extremely difficult for management to exploit either men or women. This would be true because there would be no reserve labor pool of women to hire cheaply; and, as history shows, a labor force that is larger than the job pool is considerably easier for management to exploit and control than when workers are in demand.[42] The refusal by an individual woman to comply with her own exploitation is necessary in my scenario, but it is not sufficient; all women must refuse together. And all those men who support humanitarian social change must refuse with them.

We must nurture in females a sense of solidarity and potentiation. We must argue that females have the power to work for new, more equitable kinds of social arrangements. Moreover, we must nurture in both females *and* males the understanding that it is *legitimate* for women to engage in political struggle. For as women are currently defined by ideologies of femininity, it is not considered *feminine* for women to act together in public political protest.

Notes

1 See, for example, WALUM L.R. (1977) *The Dynamics of Sex and Gender*, London, Routledge and Kegan Paul; studies cited by WEITZMAN, L. (1979) *Sex Role Socialization*, Palo Alto, California, Mayfield Publishing Co., MACCOBY, E. and JACKLIN, C. (1974) *The Psychology of Sex Differences*, Vol. I, Stanford, California, Stanford University Press, and by SAFILIOS-ROTHSCHILD, C. (1979) *Sex Role Socialization and Sex Discrimination: A Bibliography*, National Institute of Education, US Department of Health, Education and Welfare. See also PITCHER E. and SCHULTZ L. (in press) *Boys and Girls at Play: The Development of Sex Roles*, South Hadley, Massachusetts, J.F. Bergin, Publishers.
2 See studies cited by WEITZMAN, L. *Sex Role Socialization*, Chapter 3, 'The school years', pp. 35–47; also GOODMAN, L.W. *et al.*, 'A report on children's toys', in STACEY, J., *et al.* (eds) (1974) *And Jill Came Tumbling After*, New York, Dell; also KOERBER, C. 'Television', in KING, J. and SCOTT, M. (eds) (1977) *Is This Your Life?*, London, Virago; and STERNGLANZ S. and SERBIN, L. (1974) 'Sex role stereotyping in children's television programs', *Developmental Psychology*, 10, pp. 710–15.
3 For example, CHETWYND, J. and HARTNETT, O. (1978) *The Sex-Role System*, London, Routledge and Kegan Paul, p. 18; WEITZMAN, L. *Sex Role Socialization*, p. xii; or STARK-ADAMEC, C. (Ed.) (1980) *Sex Roles: Origins, Influences, and Implications for Women*, Montreal, Eden Press, p. 6.
4 GENOVESE, E. (1972) *Roll, Jordan, Roll: The World the Slaves Made*, New York, Vintage.
5 There are various formulations of what is considered feminine. Almost all statements I have seen contain several or all of the above characteristics. See for example, CHETWYND, J. and HARTNETT, O. *The Sex Role System*, p. 20; or GARSKOF, M.H. (1971) *Roles Women Play*, California, Brooks Cole; or BROVERMAN, I.K. *et al.* (1972) 'Sex-role stereotypes: A current appraisal', *Journal of Social Issues*, 28, 2, p. 66–8.
6 For example, HORNER, M.S. 'Femininity and successful achievement: A basic inconsistency', in BARDWICK, J. *et al.* (Eds) (1971) *Feminine Personality and Conflict*, California, Brooks Cole Publishing; BROVERMAN, K. *et al.*, 'Sex-role stereotypes: A current appraisal', pp. 59–78; and BARUCH, G. and BARNETT, R. (1975) 'Implications and applications of

recent research on feminine development', *Psychiatry*, 38, pp. 318–27.

7 SEWELL, W. and SHAH, V. (1968) 'Social class, parental encouragement, and educational aspirations', *American Journal of Sociology*, 73, pp. 559–72; GOODE, W., HOPKINS, E. and McCLURE, H. (1971) *Social Systems and Family Structures*, Indianapolis, Bobbs-Merrill; RABBAN, M.L. (1950) 'Sex role identification in young children in two diverse social groups', *Genetic Psychological Monographs*, 42, pp. 81–158.

8 GOODE, W. *et al.*, *Social Systems and Family Structures*.

9 RUBIN, L. (1976) *Worlds of Pain: Life in the Working-Class Family*, New York, Basic Books, pp. 167–76.

10 *Ibid.*

11 *Ibid.*

12 GOODE, W. *et al.*, *Social Systems and Family Structures*.

13 RABBAN, M. 'Sex role identification in young children in two diverse groups'.

14 *Ibid.* Also WEITZMAN, L. *Sex Role Socialization*, p. 26.

15 GORNICK, V. 'Women as outsiders', in GORNICK V. AND MORAN, B. (Eds) (1971) *Woman in Sexist Society: Studies in Power and Powerlessness*, New York, New American Library; also WESKOTT, M. (1979) 'Feminist criticism of the social sciences', *Harvard Educational Review*, 49, pp. 422–30.

16 The following description of slave life relies on GENOVESE, E. *Roll, Jordan, Roll*.

17 *Ibid,.* p. 659.

18 *Ibid.*, p. 437.

19 I would call attention to the general similarity of the schemata implicit in my use of accommodation and resistance (that is, from acceptance to accommodation and resistance, to rejection) to the schema put forth by others who have attempted to characterize the response of people to oppressive aspects of their environment. For example, Antonio Gramsci talks about 'good sense' in a contradictory consciousness GRAMSCI, A. (1971) *Selections from the Prison Notebooks*, New York, International Publishers; and Geoff Mungham and Geoff Pearson present a schema of dominant, negotiated, and oppositional working-class responses to oppressive political changes MUNGHAM, G. and PEARSON, G. (1976) *Working-Class Youth Culture*, London, Routledge and Kegan Paul.

20 (1973) New York, Alfred A. Knopf.

21 PALM, S. and BREWER, I. (1979) *The Cinderella Syndrome*, Sarasota, Florida, Septima.

22 McROBBIE, A. 'Working-class girls and the culture of femininity', in CENTRE FOR CONTEMPORARY CULTURAL STUDIES, UNIVERISTY OF BIRMINGHAM: WOMEN'S STUDIES GROUP (1978) *Women Take Issue: Aspects of Women's Subordination*, London, Hutchinson Educational.

23 ZINN, H. (1980) *A People's History of the United States*, New York Harper and Row, p. 498.

24 Jane Califf, personal communication.

25 FREUD, S. (1925) 'Some psychical consequences of the anatomical distinctions between the sexes', *Standard Edition*, London, Hogarth Press, Vol. 19; also EYER, J. and FREUD, S. (1966) *Studies in Hysteria*, New York, Avon Books.

26 As we know, the majority of mental patients are women (and a majority of these are married) GOVE, W.R. and TUDOR, J.F. (1973) 'Adult sex roles and mental illness', *American Journal of Sociology*, 78, pp. 812–35). Women are preponderant among the enlarging category of prescription addiction as well CLOWARD, R. and FOX PIVEN, F. (1979) 'Hidden protest: The channeling of female innovation and resistance', *Signs: Journal of Women in Culture and Society*, 4, pp. 651–69 (p. 652).

27 CLOWARD, R. and FOX PIVEN, F. 'Hidden protest: The channeling of female innovation and resistance'.

28 Reported in ANYON, J. (1980) 'Social class and the hidden curriculum of work', *Journal of Education*, 162, pp. 67–92; ANYON, J. (1981) 'Social class and school knowledge', *Curriculum Inquiry*, 11, pp. 3–42; ANYON, J. (1981) 'Elementary schooling and distinctions of social class', *Interchange*, 12, 2–3, pp. 118–32; and ANYON, J. (1981) 'Schools as agencies of social legitimation', *International Journal of Political Education*, 4, pp. 195–218.

29 Data on family occupations and income are reported in detail in ANYON, J. 'Social class and the hidden curriculum of work', and ANYON, J. 'Social class and school knowledge'.

30 RUBIN, L. *Worlds of Pain: Life in the Working-Class Family*; KOMAROVSKY, M. (1962) *Blue-Collar Marriage*, New York, Vintage.

31 KENISTON, K. and KENISTON, E. (1964) 'An American anachronism: The image of women and work', *The American Scholar*, 33, pp. 355–75; KAGAN, J. 'Acquisition and significance of sex typing and sex-role identity', in HOFFMAN, M. and HOFFMAN, L. (Eds) (1964) *Review of Child Development Research*, New York, Russell Sage Foundation, pp. 137–67.

32 MACCOBY, E. 'Sex differences in intellectual functioning', in MACCOBY, E. (Ed.) (1966) *The Development of Sex Differences*, Stanford, California, Stanford University Press.

33 KELLY, A. (1981) *The Missing Half*, Manchester, England, Manchester University Press; SARIO, T., JACKLIN, C. and TITTLE, C. (1973) 'Sex role stereotyping in the public schools', *Harvard Educational Review*, 43, pp. 386–404.

34 BARUCH, G. 'Sex-role attitudes of fifth grade girls', in STACEY J. *et al.* (Eds), *And Jill Came Tumbling After*.

35 I would like to thank Nancy R. King for making this point to me.

36 JACKLIN, C. 'Sex differences and their relationship to sex equity in learning and teaching', paper prepared for the National Institute of Education, September 1977, p. 3. Cited by WEITZMAN, L. *Sex Role Socialization*, p. 21; also, SHORTELL, J.R. and BILLER H.B. (1970) 'Aggression in children as a function of sex of object and sex of opponent', *Developmental Psychology*, 3, pp. 143–44.

37 GIDDENS, A. (1979) *Central Problems in Social Theory: Action, Structure and Contradiction in Social Analysis*, Berkeley, California, University of California Press.

38 GENOVESE, E. *Roll, Jordan, Roll*.

39 *Ibid.*, p. 149.

40 GIDDENS, A. *Central Problems in Social Theory*.

41 LAPIDUS, G. (1978) *Women in Soviet Society*, Berkeley, California, University of California Press; MURRAY, N. (1979) 'Socialism and feminism: Women and the Cuban revolution', *Feminist Review*, 2, pp. 57–71, and *Feminist Review*, 3, pp. 99–108. For a good discussion of this, see ARNOT, M. (1981) *Class, Gender and Education*, Milton Keynes; Open University Press.

Acknowledgement

*Part of this chapter will appear in the author's *Social Class and Gender in US Education* (forthcoming), London, Routledge.& Kegan Paul.

3.   Gender, Resistance and Power

Lynn Davies, University of Birmingham

'Mr Clayton, you can have a laugh with him, cos you can get him mad,
just like that, you've only got to say "I ain't doing my work", he'll say
"GET outside, GET to Mrs Ingram, GO here...."'   (Donna, 5F)

The aim of this chapter is to move on from the frequent portrayal of the female as
subordinate and oppressed, towards a demonstration of the creative possibilities in
female resistance. Thus a central theme is that of power, a concept which will first
require a definition. Elaborations on power are commonplace in discussions of the
teacher's role — particularly the 'nice' distinctions between power and authority.
Power is usually seen as 'the capacity .... to mobilise resources for the attainment
of goals' (Musgrove, 1971); but because I am equally interested in pupil power, I
find a broader definition is needed. Power has to be more than the ability to make
others do what you want, or permit *you* to do what you want, for pupils may not
necessarily be consciously aware of precisely what they want teachers or others to
do, although the reverse *may* be true. In its widest sense, power is the ability to
alter or influence the course of events, to create a happening, *whether or not a
particular goal is in view*. A teenage mother was quoted in a Sunday paper recently:

'Some of the girls won't use any sort of contraception, just for the thrill.
It's like when we were kids running across the road in front of the cars,
it's like breaking a school rule, like jumping down the corridors and
screaming something rude ...'   (*The Observer*, 16 August 1981)

The concept of power being goal-directed does not somehow capture the flavour of
this type of Russian Roulette. Here power is the creation of possibilities where
none existed before, and it is this meaning, the creation of possibilities, that I shall
be referring to when I claim that boys and girls *may* seek to exercise power in
different ways in the classroom. My argument will be that school resistance should
be capitalized upon — not in order to make all girls, or all pupils troublesome, but
in order to provide them with a recognition of their own power which they may be
able to transfer to other forms of efficacy in their lives.
   There is an obvious initial difficulty in attempting to isolate gender as an area
of concern. To emphasize the multi-faceted nature of school interaction, I shall
start with a model, derived from Lenski (1966), of the basic dimensions of
institutionalized power. Lenski drew a series of adjacent boxes to demonstrate how
different societies are stratified on a range of parallel dimensions, which may
include class, sex, ethnicity, education, property, political power and wealth
hierarchies. Each individual holds simultaneous membership in each 'system' of
power, and the systems do not always correlate perfectly. (Examples of non-
correlations in this country would be the West Indian doctor, or the female MP.)

The weighting accorded to each of these dimensions in terms of the allocation of resources to an individual will vary between cultures and over time: the sex attribute which is a totally limiting factor in one culture may be secondary to an ethnic or class dimension in another. Social change can be explained not just by shifts in power within one dimension (with, for example, some occupational groups gaining ascendancy over others), but also by alterations in the weightings attached to the relative importance of, say, wealth or education. Struggles for power involve not only struggles between individuals and classes, but also competition between the systems, and thus between different principles of distribution.

If we transfer Lenski's analysis to the micro-society of the school, we arrive at the possible model shown in Figure 1.

	Rank/Role	Ability	Gender	Social class	Race
Weighting	10	8	5	5	3
	Head Deputy House Heads Teachers	'Intelligent' (A)	(A) Male	Socio-economic class I II (A) III	(A) White
	Prefects Sixth form (A) -------- Fifth form (B)		(B) Female	IV	
	First form	(B) 'Remedial'		V (B)	Asian -------- West Indian (B)

Fig. 1 Model of the basic dimensions of institutionalized power: the school

Just as Lenski could forecast the probability of an individual acquiring scarce resources by plotting his (sic) position on all dimensions (and thus almost according him a 'score'), one could plot a member's position on the school's various hierarchical distributive systems of rank/role, ability, gender, social class and race, and arrive at an institutionally derived 'status score'. While individual *A* scores highly on many dimensions, individual *B* does not. *A* is likely to be a 'well-behaved' pupil; *B* is likely to be a representative of the group I was researching in my study of deviant girls (for a fuller discussion, see Davies, 1979; 1980). My argument is that a pupil who is accorded few official sources of power and privilege by the controlling agents will have to find other ways of establishing identity and efficacy. One of these ways is to stand the model on its head and *use* the lowly position as a source of control. Much has been written on polarization — the maintenance of 'low ability' cultures by pupils as a means of identification and group status (Hargreaves, 1967; Lacey, 1970); Willis has explained how social class styles come to be translated into school resistance; an ethnicity example would be the specific display of West Indian culture in school as a means of group signification and strength. I shall look at how the gender dimension may also be upturned to provide a powerful avenue for bargaining and exchange.

My observation of the girls found them having access to a variety of 'scripts' through which they countered power scenarios from teachers. Many of these were, of course, common to pupils to both sexes, in that pupils in general share commonalities with regard to lack of rights and freedoms, and hence may perfect the 'underdog' style to preserve self-respect. The strategies include playing dumb; injured innocence; exaggerating the pupil role to make a mockery of it; withdrawal into strategic silence. But I noted that the girls would use a particular range of styles which I put under the general heading of 'female acculturation'. Again some explication of terms is necessary. The old notion of 'socialization' into sex roles may lead to problems of determinism and the ignoring of the immediacy of social contexts which influence the choice of behavioural stances. I prefer Lacey's (1977) definition of socialization (which he used with regard to new teachers) as 'the adoption or creation of appropriate social strategies', because it makes the issue of internalization problematic, and indicates a range of possible behaviours. Ultimately, however, I am selecting the term 'acculturation': this was forged to describe colonial contact between cultures, and (as distinct from 'enculturation') has adaptive, accommodatory connotations. It has the advantage of reinstating 'the socialized' as active participants rather than objects of repression or domination, and brings into focus socialization as a relationship *between* people, rather than an unchallenged, unidirectional process (Gomm, 1978). A culture contact framework implies the need for a study of those being socialized (the cultures of children, student teachers, mental patients), and forces a consideration of differential power between those who aim to shape others and those who are the targets. The 'female role' is not, therefore, something merely transmitted or passed on by the family or the media, but instead is seen as a combination of *reactive* responses to repeated situations, conflicts and relationships.

There is no one 'female sex role' in contemporary British society. We must look at the combination of patriarchy, capitalism and advanced industrialization to discover the range of 'official' type-scripts available for females.[1] Under patriarchy, the female role is explicitly a relational one, with female status deriving from a woman's position *vis-à-vis* a man, whether as marriageable prospect, wife, property, or mother of his children. That 'mother' is not sufficient status on its own is clear from the low prestige and financial support still accorded to unmarried mothers. The 'spinster' — the woman who has no official relation with a man — is a term to evoke pity or disparagement, in a way 'bachelor' is not (and the girls in my study wanted to avoid both these non-relational female roles). There is no masculine equivalent for the word 'mistress', with all its ownership connotations. In some ways all the girls' concerns and accounts of action could be said to derive from relationships: their identity could be established only by how others were seen to 'treat' them, whether teachers, boyfriends or parents. Even aggressiveness was derived from this dependency, for the girls' strongest reactions were to threats to how they might be perceived by men, not insults to their intelligence, activity, prowess. As I taped their conversations, they would enquire:

Julie: . Do you ever play this back to your husband?
LD: Why?
Julie: Just wondered. Case he wondered, who's this girl carrying on.

> *Debbie*: Does he ever talk about some of we? Like does he say, who's that?

The irony was that, although it was in my interests as objective listener that they did not care what I thought of them, their concern about what my husband thought confirmed my own mere intermediary status. Many female teachers in the school had to be acknowledged as women on their own; but the popular female teachers were those who revealed aspects of their relationships with husbands, or were thought to have menfriends.

Capitalism added to patriarchy defines the relational and secondary status of women still further, but in a changing economy also throws up contradictions. While patriarchal socialism could work within a collective or kibbutz system, the nuclear family and its concomitant sexual division of labour perform key consumer functions for a capitalist economy, so that the resultant domestic, privatized type-script for women is a pervasive one. The scripts for inevitable romance and fulfilling motherhood are literally written and acted out by the media and advertizing daily; there are few female type-scripts that give alternative scenarios to love, marriage and producing children, few status type-scripts written for solo women performers or groups of women. Hence, in spite of often harrowing family experiences, most of the 'wenches' had no alternative long-term lines to the marital dialogue. It was easier to embrace a romantic or 'magical' female script, in the same way that Cohen (1972) describes the working-class boys' limited and 'magical' attempt to restore working-class community.

Advanced industrial society also, however, benefits from a certain number of women in the labour market. The passive female type-script generates less union activity and confrontation than with male workers; the masculine breadwinner role means that women make fewer wage demands for themselves. They form a useful low-paid subsidiary sector in productive industry; or their domestic lines can be easily translated into other caring and service roles supportive of the male labour market. The problem for capitalism of simultaneously maintaining domestic and wage labour scripts for women is managed by a fine series of balances: in war-time the patriotic script took precedence, and encouraged women into munitions factories and agriculture; in a time of economic recession and a depressed labour market, we are seeing a re-emergence of the 'first-five-years-of-life' maternal deprivation tragedy, with both Conservative and Liberal parties stressing the need for mothers to remain at home with young children to combat social evils such as juvenile crime. The type-script has the dual latent function of facilitating closure of expensive nursery education, and releasing jobs for male workers, thus alleviating to some extent the eventual threat to the system of massive unemployment. Current type-scripts encompassing 'community care' have also been analyzed by the Equal Opportunities Commission as being in fact a euphemism for 'female responsibility', that is, it will be individual women who eventually take the burden of the old and the handicapped, not men or the State (EOC, 1982). Soviet Russia also has had to re-introduce family type-scripts, when women too enthusiastically learnt their employment and career lines after the Revolution; not only were they not producing enough new workers, they were undermining the family unit now seen to be as essential to State capitalism as to private sector capitalism.

However, official type-scripts are not limiting or all-pervasive. Combinations of working and motherhood scripts for women have particular temporal, regional and ethnic variations. Driver, for example, attributes his controversial finding of

West Indian girls doing better in school than West Indian boys to the traditional concentration of power, property and prestige in the hands of women, 'the unspoken assumption among many West Indian women that they, rather than their husbands and brothers, are the guardians of their family's good name and the providers of its stable income' (1980). The women in the area of my study (which I refer to as Scrapton) were not necessarily solely responsible for the family's subsistence, but there was nonetheless a long tradition of married women working, often in heavy industry such as foundries, sometimes twilight shifts, sometimes in what were termed 'dirty' or 'unpleasant' surroundings. Teachers described Scrapton as 'matriarchal', and this may be related to the female experience of heavy work, and also to a local scripting of the domestic dialogue. Female type-scripts are only probabilities for action; not only can women extemporize around the themes, but they can, and do, create forceful and substantive parts for themselves within what might appear to be supporting roles. The domestic script is appropriated as a power scenario, where the woman is dominant, literally the producer — of children, food and other services — and director of the whole play, as well as acting the key part. Daughters are understudies for the central role, looking after younger siblings, babysitting in the evening, or being kept away from school to care for new babies. The male may provide the financial backing for this drama, but the woman is central, simultaneously powerful in this role and progressively limited by its type-casting.

The women's collective drama group, provided by the extended family typical of Scrapton, is an even more influential and self-sufficient venture. It provides a pool of actors who can step in at short notice to 'help out'. While this provides opportunities for women to practise other work or leisure scripts, it means that their domestic part can never be completely filed away, but has to be reserved because of the need for reciprocal understudying elsewhere. It also means that the male has fewer opportunities or incentives to learn the domestic script: there will always be somebody from the agency to outshine him.

The male working-class script, on the other hand, justifies, or even celebrates manual labour in its themes of toughness or machismo (Miller, 1958; Willis, 1977). This may mean that physical action is as important as the lines men speak. The ritual aggression at football matches documented by Marsh *et al.* (1978) demonstrates how carefully stage-managed this action is; but the availability of a physical rather than a verbal retort means the possible transformation of self-projection into violence in and out of the home. The female reaction to violence can be manifold: there is avoidance; or there is the 'weakness' script which portrays the woman as so fragile as to denigrate the man that strikes her (and neither of these two scripts is available to men); or there is the incorporation of reciprocal violence into the female scripts, as seen in Scrapton. Girls were deemed to 'fight much dirtier', for there are no Queensberry rules in female fighting scripts: the powerless can afford no such luxuries. As the Newsons discovered:

When girls do fight, we might expect the exchange to be more vicious on average, especially in view of the fact that there are few socially prescribed rules for physical combat and its resolution between girls as opposed to between boys. (Newson and Newson, 1978).

The script is largely an improvised one.

Paradoxically, female scripts may be temporarily more powerful because they derive from the culture of powerlessness. Women have had centuries to perfect scripts to counter power, to protect their status against male dominance. They are practised martial arts experts — using the strength of the opponents to resist and overcome. If men treat them as helpless, then a script for helplessness will enable them to exert their will in other spheres. If they are relegated to the home, they will make that a locus of control. If they are handled as sex objects, they will use their virginity or sexuality to bargain with, making themselves 'cost' something, and upgrade their value once more. Moves towards equality, but where women will simply have to compete with men, lose and form a subsidiary class (rather than maintaining a *separate* status system) may find women reviving the untouchable script. A bargaining model of sexual stratification is one used recently showing how the resources and trading of income and sexuality between men and women change over time, with women in an advanced economy increasingly using income as a resource (Collins, 1971). Alternatively, women may win power and value by stressing differences, establishing their own society: there are women's collectives, or women's cooperatives in the Third World; or women may use sexuality, as in a brothel, or purity, as in a nunnery. As well as having different resources for bargaining, women apparently use very different bargaining strategies (Tedeschi *et al.*, 1973). They are more concerned with presentation of self, and take cues from both the situation and the behaviour of other people to draw inferences about what conduct would look best in the eyes of others. They prefer 'accommodative' solutions (again the culture contact pattern) and will respond more cooperatively to cooperation; but if others exploit them, or seek competitive advantage, they are more concerned with saving face, and hence react in such situations with greater retaliation and vindictiveness than men. This certainly accords with both teachers' and pupils' perceptions (in my research) of girls being 'bitchier', using more foul language, being more aggressive when they did fight. The native may be on the surface accommodating, but revolt can never be ruled out as a possibility.

If we take the culture contact model further into the school, the colonial analogy seems yet more apt. In my study, the school type-script for teachers was that of colonial administrator — on the surface benevolent, but using the ancient principle of divide and rule. District officers (the teachers) had their own jurisdiction, but could refer dissenters to regional capitals (Heads of House) for justice. The teachers interpreted their colonizing role in divergent ways, however, and tended towards either warfare or infiltration techniques. The warfare men (and they were all men) I called 'territorials'. They wanted tougher discipline. Their actual phraseology gives the best flavour of this:

> 'I know what I want from a system — hard treatment . . . no good being soft.'
> 'At the beginning of the term pretend to smash hell out of them . . . have the different years coming in separately in the morning and smash them one by one . . . just to show . . .'

They thought the 'shopfloor' teacher should be allowed to cane.

> 'Kids in this particular culture expect corporal punishment. Respect stems from fear.'
> 'Easy to say motivate them, all this load of rubbish.'

'I think what they could do is these punishment rooms. Put a kid in there for a week, and he must go to that room, must be in solitary, must work, and that's it.'

All these extreme hardliners seemed to see school therefore as a battlefield, with tactics (surprise early attacks), hand-to-hand combat (might is right) and prisoners of war (solitary confinement). The campaign areas are crucial for territorial advantage:

'If you can control the corridors, that's where the power is . . . if you can go down a corridor and pick out five kids doing something wrong, that's five different classes you've got that know Mr Grant has got this . . . he's a bloke not to tangle with.'

Battles, of course, require a strong general, and the territorials thought the Head should be seen to be, literally, a 'hard man'.

In contrast to the territorials were the 'communicators'. These were the teachers (equally men and women) who saw it as important to get to know the children well, who wanted more individual, humane treatment of pupils. They wanted to 'make relationships with them'.

'So many people forget that kids are young people, they have the same emotions and hang-ups as we do.'
'I always try to treat every class I take as potential adults . . . I expect them to take certain degrees of responsibility within that age range . . . then I will readjust my concept and my attitude towards individuals within that class according to how they do behave.'

In other words, these teachers would treat children as cooperators *until proved otherwise*, rather than 'smash' them from the beginning, *expecting* deviance. They avoided 'confrontation situations'. They would not 'waste their time' on uniform harangues, did not see wearing jewellery as 'the end of Western civilization', did not see their refusal to police the corridors as resulting in chaos. They thus wanted the school to spend more time on personalized pupil contact, less on power confrontations and rule enforcement. Some teachers focussed this particularly on the girls, who, they felt, would benefit from the pastoral side, from feeling able to discuss problems, from being permitted to dress in an adult manner.

Predictably, the teachers whom the 'difficult' girls accepted and would even work for, all fell into the 'communicator' category. If we recall Durkheim's concept of social solidarity, it was, he thought, best achieved by rational means, including a rational view of control, authority and punishment. Teachers saw girls especially as needing to have 'reasons' for behaviour before they would conform. The territorials, however, wanted unquestioning obedience from the native troops; yet many pupils, and in particular the 5F girls, lacked the spirit of Empire, and took every situation on its merits. For such pupils elect their leaders; their political instincts undermine a totalitarian regime at every point. One might want to argue that the communicator teachers were in fact merely using a more subtle and ultimately more efficient form of social control; but, as intimated earlier, I want to get away from the idea of the school 'socializing' pupils into roles, whether sex roles or deference roles. What emerges from the comparison of teacher types is not so much differences in *control* as differences in *negotiation*; with resistant girls especialy, one is never quite sure who is controlling whom — and this applies to both types of teacher. In trying to analyze the interactions, I became particularly interested in the strategies brought into the school from the local female culture, in the use made by the girls of local adaptations from the culture of powerlessness; such scripts were in turn to shape *teachers* into particular adaptive strategies. Hence I want to examine five themes specifically: bargaining; matriarchy; humour; femininity and individuation.

Bargaining

What the girls could offer teachers was some sort of allegiance to the pupil role — but in return they demanded recognition as young women with taste and refinement. It was a double game that everyone played — for the successful, communicator teacher intimated, 'Look, I know that you're mature and responsible, but I have to treat you on the surface as a pupil.' Small instances best demonstrate the nuances of this interaction. The biology teacher is leading a practical session on mouth-to-mouth resuscitation. 'I don't want to breathe into anyone else', announces Dawn. 'You don't want to do it? We'll go onto something else then', says the teacher. 'No, it's all right, we'll do it', says Dawn, magnanimously. In the middle of a maths lesson, Debbie would enquire, 'How many eye-shadows you got on?' 'Two', says the teacher, as if this were a routine question. 'Looks nice', acknowledges Debbie, 'I'll get you to come round and do my make-up tonight.' The girls would, with mock seriousness, advise such teachers on their boyfriends or on other relationships, and the teachers would not take offence. In return they would confide in the girls about their private lives: one particular teacher impressed the girls by telling them she was pregnant before even telling other members of staff. Consultation and communication as if to adults seem a small price to pay for fewer 'discipline' problems, yet it is surprising how many teachers appear threatened by such possibilities and refuse to contemplate the seemingly desultory conversational exchanges which in fact give important messages about female status and worth.

For these are Goffman's 'character contests', and the script is about honour, not just amusement. It has been established that rather than there being universal sex role differences, status is the crucial concept to explain situations where sex differences do appear (Meeker *et al.*, 1977). In task behaviour, for example, differences are minimized when equal status, leadership and respect are positively and overtly established between the sexes. In a similar way, it has been found that concern for what others think of oneself is connected with differences in classroom behaviour for girls but not for boys (Lahaderne and Jackson, 1970). Thus, giving status to pupils, especially to girls, may be an integral component of the successful classroom bargain.

Matriarchy

As mentioned, the local area was seen as matriarchal, with women as the dominant figures (as an extreme example, teachers attributed girls' loud voices to the fact that their mothers shouted in the factories). Certainly it seemed to be the mothers who came up to the school if there were trouble; who sorted out the Education Welfare

Officer; who defended their children's rights against the police or other agents of social control — and not necessarily because they had more time than their husbands. The scripts for such confrontations, and the accompanying 'language', were clearly transported into the school by the girls; in addition they had access to what can only be described as a 'mother' script: talking to the (usually male) teachers as if they were small boys. They would display mild irritation if interrupted in private conversation in the middle of lessons. They could destroy the teacher's power lines by patronizing repetition: 'He says, you'll have to have the cane. I says, I'll have to have the cane then, won't I?' The implication is that they have more important things to think about than these childish pursuits (and their own experience of violence in and out of the home means that the cane is indeed of marginal significance). A perceptive remark one day by Terri provided a clue to the basis of the girls' interpretations of teachers:

'. . . but when you see some of the teachers, you wish you'd played them up worser. They're so bigheaded, they're like they're kids an' all. The way they say, here you, come here — you say, wait, you don't say that to me. Who do you think you're talking to? They say it as though they're kids to other kids.'

No only was the girls' 'mother' script a useful ploy, but it was reinforced by their perception of teachers as behaving like children, with bad manners and impetuous inroads into privacy. Such teachers it was clear had to be socialized by the girls into adulthood.

Humour

Humour is, of course, another way to defuse, debunk or control. This is not just the cracking of jokes in the classroom, but the creation of absurd or inappropriate roles and relationships. Walker and Adelman give a nice example here:

'What strikes us about the relationship between Colin and Karen is the way she seems to be constantly playing minor variations on the theme of him as likeable but inefficient. It is as though she is able to create an individual identity for herself out of the stream of classroom events by the use of fluent repartee to manage incidents in a way that keeps Colin within the image she has defined for him. She therefore creates an identity for herself, not as a public figure in the class, but through her ability to use talk to maintain her definition of the situation and so sustain a unique relationship with Colin (Walker and Adelman, 1976).

Similarly, the girls in my study would tease a young female teacher about the invented troubles she has with her private life. 'You've gotta get it sorted out, Miss', says Linda with much gravity. Each week they would expand the scenario, using the sitcom dialogue technique: 'She invited him home for tea, you know.' 'Never!' 'She did.' 'Snot right, is it.' The aim was to 'make the teacher go red', which she invariably did, although laughing the while.

Anthropologists see jokes as the management of 'ungrammatical' identity relationships; in a later article, Walker and Goodson however claim the converse, that those with the most power in a situation tell the most jokes: 'Humour, and especially wit, are basically of an aggressive nature and threaten the stability of the institution. The result is a norm for the use of humour to follow the distribution of power' (1977). Perhaps both are true. Undoubtedly humour is seen as threatening: an interesting incident occurred when on the last day of lessons before their examinations about a dozen fifth-year girls were 'caught with chalking all over their skirts', having inscribed messages such as 'Goodbye teacher'. After being made to stand in silence for an hour, the girls were all sent home with letters to their parents, excluded from school, and not permitted to return until their examinations; the offence was to remain on their record cards. One has to examine why this apparently victimless crime of skirt-chalking received such extortionate and escalatory treatment. One reason would relate to the violation of the female image, for 'they looked an unholy mess . . . they looked a sight', commented the Deputy Headmistress. The other reason would be their temporary control over the school 'ethos': 'The school was literally having a good giggle, a good laugh, you could feel the atmosphere, the temperature rise.' Certainly it is a well-known educational fact that teachers' jokes are funny and pupils' jokes are not; but this also means that pupil humour is doubly sacrilegious and can be doubly effective.

Shared jokes are of course part of the pupil sub-culture which gives status and identification to its members; and both sexes I found would delight in 'dirty' stories, in innuendo, in deliberately taking teachers' statements 'the wrong way'. A photography lesson found the class convulsed at having to 'fiddle about' in the dark bag. 'Get in the bag!' says Debbie to Robert, with heavy double entendre. Much of this joking relies on past shared language experiences, and may be only partially intended for the teacher; it demonstrates both group membership and personal sophistication at the same time. But rather than simply using the authority figure as a 'fall guy', jokes are also a key component in relationships *with* teachers. They reduce social distance, and establish in the end no subject as sacrosanct. Musgrove is interesting here:

> Sex and humour may take the power out of schools as social and educational systems, but both may promote an extension of communication to difficult or risky topics and across age and status barriers. Jesters can make suggestions about dangerous and normally forbidden issues to their superiors; girls can often do likewise (when the superior is male) (Musgrove 1971).

The notion of the creative 'jester' role having particular salience for girls is an appealing one, and might be worth some more participant observation.

Femininity

The power here takes two forms. One is the immediate use of feminine 'wiles' or ploys — what teachers referred to as 'fluttering the eyelashes', or 'turning on the waterworks'. This places teachers in a double-bind: if they negotiate with the girls as they would with boys (with, for example, the use of caning) they face outrage because of the violations against sex role expectations; if they admit the girls as representatives of a female sex role ideology they may undermine their own control because of the concessions they have to make to resultant strategies.

The second angle of femininity is the use of the objectified position of the female. Whereas boys were unofficially slapped by teachers of both sexes, girls were never struck by a male teacher 'for obvious reasons'.

> I mean male members of staff find it difficult because they can't hit a girl. I mean none of us is supposed to, but they can't because it's going to be even more difficult if they do get into trouble. They might shout — I won't say they shout rape, but the fact that a man has handled a girl in some way. . . .

This is the crux of the distinction: a female teacher hitting a boy is acceptable, or has maternal/familial connotations; a male teacher hitting a girl is unacceptable because of sexual connotations. The male teacher is *not* seen as acting 'in loco parentis'; this is related to the double standard operating in society whereby more girls are locked up as 'being in need of care and attention' — they are potentially sexual beings and must be protected from themselves. A girl will *use* this objectifying, however: she would 'have her father or mother up to the school' immediately, as soon as she was 'handled' by a male teacher. The objectifying of women (that any interaction must be sexual) may be in the interests of patriarchy, but it is in fact a contradiction which the school has to cope with, and presents particular problems for male teachers which the girls are quick to capitalize upon. Another female teacher commented: 'There's nobody as hard on a girl as a woman is. And there's nobody can show sympathy when she needs it, as a woman. Because it can be misconstrued if it comes from a man.' Although girls may respond well to personalized interactions, men have to be wary. If they cannot touch them, and they cannot be concerned about them, it is unsurprising that boys are preferred for classroom interaction (for discussion and evidence of such preference, see Davies, 1973 and 1980; Fuller, 1979). The only safe role is the familial one of 'uncle' or 'grandfather'; and even this may not be accepted by the girls. 'He treats me like a kid of five. "I treat you like an uncle, don't I?" I says, ugh, he thinks he's our uncle, shows me up ....' Relegating girls to the status of small children is unacceptable; but equally problematic is negotiating with them as adult women.

Individuation

Teachers comment on the fact that girls are 'more sensitive to their rights'. This 'sensitivity' is not a passive Victorian stance, but demonstrates itself in particular behavioural postures agreed upon by teachers and pupils of both sexes. Girls are 'quicker to take offence', more reactive to personal remarks. They bear grudges, they flare up. Whether this 'taking things personally' relates to the privatization of the home can only be surmised; certainly those with the fewest rights are likely to be the most concerned to protect them. But whatever its source, it is an important way to create impetus from the slightest teacher remark. In the short term it is also effective because teachers become wary of girls, and practise 'avoidance' techniques for fear of confrontation; in the long term, of course, it is counter-productive because the teaching-learning relationship is underdeveloped through fewer interactions. In all the self-concept schedules, which were backed up by teacher perceptions, I found girls more individualized, less predictable, more concerned about presentation of self, about their image in the classroom. Boys emerged as more enthusiastic, taking their punishment better. They may thus be seen as more sycophantic, more ready to enter and conclude classroom negotiations on the teacher's terms. Literature on managerial styles suggests men succeed partly because socialization into group or team considerations, rather than privatized concerns, means that they can be aware of and use people in their work and friendship groups, but also be tolerant of weakness (Hennig and Jardin, 1976). Women managers are more likely to be concerned about day-to-day competence, and to take matters on principle, thus being intolerant of hypocrisy or inefficiency. (I certainly saw this critical stance in the girls' views of contradictions in teachers.) Male managers apparently recognize the need to work out team strategies to win, and the need for a leader or coach. We may find here both a clue to, and a critique of, the 'correspondence principle', that the social relations of schooling correspond to and replicate the social relations of the workplace. The acceptance of hierarchies and tolerance of authority may be, paradoxically, more salient for male pupils and workers than for female, in spite of the formers' outward themes of toughness and independence. A distinctive attitude towards supervisory authority was noted in Jephcott's early study *Married Women Working*, where women rejected 'democratic leadership' in favour of 'an efficient organiser whose skilful management was their direct gain and who would be considerate and flexible in meeting their individual needs' (Jephcott, 1962). I found teachers admitting knowing the girls less well, and hence ironically, more prone to assertive stereotypes — often contradictory ones at that. Girls were apathetic and yet at the same time aggressive; they accepted everything you said but they argued too much; they were less easy to put down but they were more submissive. They ended up in tears for every little bruise while managing to be more placid. They were more frivolous yet they thought more deeply. The teachers may well have had less knowledge of the girls, but also, I think, the contradictions stem from the greater range of scripts which the girls bring to a situation: their acculturation to powerlessness may mean a potentiality to spot just the right stance to bring home an advantage.

Conclusions

While highlighting certain aspects of 'the feminine wile', I would not necessarily want to endorse them as ploys to be perfected in the education of girls. They are, by definition, short-term strategies to cope with immediate status threats, and as such bear little relationship to long-term control over events. Yet they have symbolic importance in terms of consciousness raising. There was an interesting staffroom discussion one day about girls' 'smiling'. A House Head related how periodically he would find himself saying to a girl after he had reprimanded her, 'Come on, you wouldn't get a boy smiling like that.' The boys would understand the implication and be amused — they would be a poof with such a smile — but the girl would flush and be embarrassed. The teacher thus implies to the girls that he is too old to be taken in by such ploys; he also felt it was 'not fair', that some male teachers did not know how to cope with it. In that he felt it was only semi-conscious, he would often deliberately draw attention to sex role behaviour in this way in the classroom, or would make the boys go out first; he attempted, by always using their Christian names, to undermine what he saw as the 'brutalization' of boys. But it is not enough, as he realized, to make teachers aware of their 'sex-typing' stances; pupils must also be made conscious of their sex-typed counter-strategies. One way to enhance the capacities of girls to take charge of their lives is to show them that they already have (albeit unconscious) ways to influence people, to change events, to create possibilities. At the same time, they must realize that the display of these particular resistances only confirms them in officially subordinate roles, and that alternatives might be found.

I am increasingly unhappy with deterministic Marxist models which relate school action directly to the capitalist order, or even to patriarchal capitalism. The staff balance of, for example, territorials and communicators, and resistant teachers together with resistant pupils, will engender an enormous variety of strategies for the survival of the school economy. And while the official type-scripts for women outlined earlier do provide a framework for behaviour, it is the women and girls themselves who create the accommodatory solutions and styles. That these are self-reinforcing and short-term there is no doubt; but seeing them as creative and adaptive to context means that there are the seeds there for mutant plant life. I like Kelly's idea of 'behaviour as an experiment':

> 'Behaviour is indeed a question posed in such a way as to commit man to the role and obligations of an experimenter ... when we see behaviour that distresses us, we will spend less time wondering what conditioned it, and ask instead, what is the experiment that is being performed, what hypotheses are being tested, how the outcomes are to be assessed, and whether it opens the door to any man's further adventure' (Kelly 1970).

The transformation of experiment to routine is what Kelly calls 'repeating what seems promising': I would hold that schools are not places where teachers and pupils bombard each other with 'learned' or 'socialized' role styles, but places where people experiment with each other, trying this, trying that, until a 'promising' line, some semi-serious repartee coalesces to become a preferred script. The usefulness of female strategies means that they will often be repeated, and the girls will condition themselves; but it might be productive for both sexes to be made aware of what they are experimenting with, and to deliberately 'play' at other postures and stances to gauge effect and counter-effect. Even more important would be for pupils to discuss the *reasons* for their power experiments, that is, to analyze power differentials both within and outside school. There is nothing new in a call for more, rather than less, official power for pupils, or for more dignity and humanity: I have attempted to outline some of the resources pupils may use if status is *not* accorded by the school. Immediate confrontation can be avoided by more efficient colonization, by more 'communication'; but peaceful independence requires in the end a handing over of responsibility. One girl, one vote?

Notes

1 Throughout, 'type-script' will refer to societal ideologies for the sexes, while 'script' is the individual creation or appropriation of a stance. Again, for a fuller discussion of scripts, and the use of the television metaphor, see Davies, 1979 or 1980.

References

COHEN, P. (1972) 'Sub-cultural conflict and working-class community', University of

Birmingham, CCCS, *Working Papers in Cultural Studies*, No. 2.

COLLINS, R. (1971) 'A conflict theory of sexual stratification', *Social Problems*, 19, pp. 3–21.

DAVIES, L. (1973) 'The contribution of the secondary school to the sex-typing of girls', unpublished MEd dissertation, University of Birmingham.

————— (1979) 'Deadlier than the male? Girls' conformity and deviance in school', BARTON, L. and MEIGHAN, R. *Schools, Pupils and Deviance*, Nafferton.

—————(1980) 'Deviance and sex roles in school', unpublished PhD thesis, University of Birmingham.

DRIVER, G. (1980) 'How West Indians do better at school (especially the girls)', *New Society*, 17 January, pp. 111–14.

EQUAL OPPORTUNITIES COMMISSION (1981) 'Caring for the handicapped: Community policies and women's lives'.

FULLER, M. (1979) 'Dimensions of gender in a school', unpublished PhD thesis, University of Bristol.

GOMM, R. (1978) 'Perspectives on socialization', *The Social Science Teacher*, 8, 2, p. 51.

HARGREAVES, D. (1968) *Social Relations in a Secondary School*, London, Routledge and Kegan Paul.

HENNIG, M. and JARDIN, A. (1978) *The Managerial Woman*, London, M. Boyars.

JEPHCOTT, P. (1962) *Married Women Working*, London, George Allen and Unwin.

KELLY, G. (1970) 'Behaviour is an experiment', BANNISTER, D. (Ed.), *Perspectives in Personal Construct Theory*, London, Academic Press.

LACEY, C. (1970) *Hightown Grammar*, Manchester University Press.

————— (1977) *The Socialisation of Teachers*, London, Methuen.

LAHADERNE, H. and JACKSON, P. (1970) 'Withdrawal in the classroom: A note on some educational correlates of social desirability among school children', *Journal of Educational Psychology*, 61, 2, pp. 97–101.

LENSKI, G. (1966) *Power and Privilege: A Theory of Social Stratification*, New York, McGraw Hill.

MARSH, P., ROSSER E. and HARRE, R. (1978) *The Rules of Disorder*, London Routledge and Kegan Paul.

MEEKER, B. and WEITZEL-O'NEILL, P. (1977) 'Sex roles and interpersonal behaviour in task-oriented groups', *American Sociological Review*, 42, pp. 91–105.

MILLER, W. (1958) 'Lower class culture as a generating milieu of gang delinquency', *Journal of Social Issues*, 14, 3, pp. 5–19.

MUSGROVE, F. (1971) *Patterns of Power and Authority in English Education*, London, Methuen.

NEWSON, J. and NEWSON, E. (1976) *Seven Years Old in the Home Environment*, London, Allen and Unwin.

TEDESCHI, J., SCHLENKER, B. and BONOMA, V. (1973) *Conflict, Power and Games*, Chicago, Aldine Publishing Co.

WALKER, R. and ADELMAN, C. (1976) 'Strawberries', in STUBBS, M. and DELAMONT, S. (Eds) *Explorations in Classroom Observation*, London, Wiley.

WALKER, R. and GOODSON, I. (1977) 'Humour in the classroom', in WOODS, P. and HAMMERSLEY, M. (Eds) *School Experience*, London, Croom Helm.

WILLIS, P. (1977) *Learning to Labour*, Farnborough, Saxon House.

4.   Work, Class and Teaching

Michael W. Apple, University of Wisconsin

Proletarianization: Class and Gender

An examination of changes in class composition over the past two decades points out something quite dramatically. The process of proletarianization has had both a large and consistent effect. There has been a systematic tendency for those positions with relatively little control over their labor process to expand; at the same time, there has been a decline in positions with high levels of autonomy.[1]

This should not surprise us. In fact, it would be unusual if this did not occur, especially now. In a time of general stagnation and of crises in accumulation and legitimation, we should expect that there will be attempts to further rationalize managerial structures and increase the pressure to proletarianize the labor process. This pressure is not inconsequential to educators, not only in regard to the kinds of positions students will find available (or not available) after completing (or not completing) schooling, but also in regard to the very conditions of working within education itself. The labor of what might be called 'semi-autonomous employees' will certainly feel the impact of this. Given the fiscal crisis of the state, this impact will be felt more directly among state employees such as teachers. One should expect to see a rapid growth of plans and pressures for the rationalization of administration and labor within the state itself.[2] This is one of the times when one's expectations will not be disappointed

In earlier work, I argued that teachers have been involved in a long but now steadily increasing restructuring of their jobs. I claimed that they were faced more and more with the prospect of being deskilled because of the encroachment of technical control procedures into the curriculum in schools. The integration of management systems, reductive behaviorally based curricula, pre-specified teaching procedures and student responses, and pre- and post-testing was leading to a loss of control and a separation of conception from execution. In sum, the labor process of teaching was becoming susceptible to processes similar to those that had led to the proletarianization of many other blue, pink, and white collar jobs. I suggested that this restructuring of teaching had important implications given the contradictory class location of teachers.[3]

When I say that teachers have a contradictory class location, I am *not* implying that they are by definition within the middle classes, or that they are in an ambiguous position somehow 'between' classes. Instead, along with Wright, I am saying that it is wise to think of them as located simultaneously in two classes. Thus, they share the interests of both the petty bourgeoisie and the working class.[4] Hence, when there is a fiscal crisis where many teachers are faced with worsening working conditions, lay-offs, and even months without being paid — as has been the case in a number of urban areas in the United States — and when their labor is restructured so that they lose control, it is possible that these contradictory interests will move closer to those of other workers and people of color who have historically been faced with the use of similar procedures by capital and the state.[5]

Yet, teachers are not only classed actors, but also gendered actors, something that is too often neglected by many investigators. This is a significant omission. A striking conclusion is evident from the analyses of proletarianization. In every occupational category, *women* are more apt to be proletarianized than men. This could be because of sexist practices of recruitment and promotion, the general tendency to care less about the conditions under which women labor, the way capital has historically colonized patriarchal relations, and so on. Whatever the reason, it is clear that a given position may be more or less proletarianized depending on its relationship to the sexual division of labor.[6]

In the United States, it is estimated that over 90 per cent of women's (paid) work falls into four basic categories: (1) employment in 'peripheral' manufacturing industries and retail trades, and particularly in the expanding but low-paid service sector of the economy; (2) clerical work; (3) health and education; and (4) domestic service. Most women in, say, the United States and the United Kingdom are concentrated in either the lowest-paid positions in these areas or at the bottom of the middle pay grades when there has been some mobility.[7] One commentator puts it both bluntly and honestly. 'The evidence of discrimination against women in the labour market is considerable and reading it is a wearing experience.'[8]

This pattern is, of course, largely reproduced within education. Even given the years of struggle by progressive women and men, the figures — most of which will be quite familiar — are depressing. While the overwhelming majority of school teachers are women (a figure that becomes even higher in the primary and elementary schools), many more men are heads or principals of primary and elementary schools, despite the proportion of women teachers.[9] As the vertical segregation of the workforce increased, this proportion actually increased in inequality. In the United States, in 1928 women accounted for 55 per cent of the elementary school principalships. Today, with nearly 90 per cent of the teaching force in elementary schools being women, they account for only 20 per cent.[10] This pattern has strong historical roots, which cannot be separated from the larger structures of class and patriarchy outside the school.

I shall argue that unless we see the connections between these two dynamics — class and gender — we cannot understand the history of and current attempts at rationalizing education or the roots and effects of proletarianization on teaching itself. Not all teaching can be unpacked by examining it as a labor process or as a class phenomenon, though as I have tried to demonstrate in my own work much of it is made clearer when we integrate it into theories of and changes in class position and the labor process. Neither can all of teaching be understood as totally related to patriarchy, though an immense amount of why it is structured the way it is due to the history of male dominance and gender struggles.[11] These two dynamics (with race, of course) are not reducible to each other, but interwine, work off, and co-determine the terrain on which each operates. It is at the intersection of these two dynamics that one can begin to unravel some of the reasons why procedures for rationalizing the work of teachers have evolved. As we shall see, the ultimate effects of these procedures, with the loss of control that accompanies them, can bear in important ways on how we think about the 'reform' of teaching and curriculum and the state's role in it.

Academic Knowledge and Curricular Control

So far I have made a number of general claims about the relationship between proletarianization and patriarchy in the constitution of teaching. I want to go on to suggest ways we can begin to see this relationship in operation. Some sense of the recent past of the state's role in sponsoring changes in curricular and teaching practice is essential here.

The fact that schools have tended to be largely organized around male leadership and female teachers is simply that, a social fact, unless one realizes that this means that educational authority relations have been formally patriarchal. Like the home and the office, male dominance is there; but teachers — like wives, mothers, and clerical workers — have carved out spheres of power and control in their long struggle to gain some autonomy. This autonomy only becomes a problem for capital and the state when what education is for needs revision.

To take one example outside education, in offices clerical work is in the process of being radically transformed with the introduction of word processing technologies, video display terminals, and so on. Traditional forms of control — usually based on the dominance of the male boss — are being altered. Technical control, where one's work is de-skilled and intensified by the 'impersonal' machinery in the office, has made significant inroads. While certainly not eliminating patriarchal domination, it has in fact provided a major shift in the terrain on which it operates. Capital has found more efficient modes of control than overt patriarchal authority.[12]

Similar changes have occurred in schools. In a time when the needs of industry for technical knowledge and technically trained personnel intersect with the growth in power of the new petty bourgeoisie and the re-assertion of academic dominance in the curriculum, pressures for curricular reform can become quite intense. Patience over traditional forms of control will lessen.

Patriarchal relations of power, therefore, organized around the male principal's relations to a largely female teaching staff, will not necessarily be progressive for capital or the state. While it once served certain educational and ideological ends, it is less efficient than what has been required recently. Gender relations must be partly subverted to create a more efficient institution. Techniques of control drawn from industry will tend to replace older styles which depended more on a sexual division of power and labor within the school itself.

An example will document the long and continuing history of these altered relationships. In the United States, for instance, during the late 1950s and 1960s, there was rather strong pressure from academics, capital, and the state to re-institute academic disciplinary knowledge as the most 'legitimate' content for schools. In the areas of mathematics and science especially, it was feared that 'real' knowledge was not being taught. A good deal of effort was given to producing curricular programs that were systematic, based on rigorous academic foundations, and, in the elementary school material in particular, teacher proof. Everything a teacher was to deal with was provided and pre-specified. The cost of the development of such programs was socialized by the state (that is, subsidized by tax dollars). The chances of their being adopted by local school districts were heightened by the National Defense Education Act, which reimbursed school districts for a large portion of the purchase cost. That is, if a school system purchased new material of this type and the technology which supported it, the relative cost was minimal. The bulk of the expense was repaid by the state. Hence, it would have seemed irrational not to buy the material — irrational in two ways: (1) the chance of getting new curricula at low cost is clearly a rational management decision within industrial logic, and (2) given its imprimatur of science and efficiency, the material itself seemed rational.

All of this is no doubt familiar to anyone who lived through the early years of this movement, and who sees the later, somewhat less powerful, effects it had in, say, England and elsewhere. Yet this is not only the history of increasing state sponsorship of and state intervention in teaching, curriculum development and adoption. *It is the history of the state, in concert with capital and a largely male academic body of consultants and developers, intervening at the level of practice in the work of a largely female work force.* That is, ideologies of gender, of sex appropriate knowledge, need to be seen as having possibly played a significant part. The loss of control and rationalization of one's work forms part of a state/class/gender 'couplet' that works its way out in the following ways. Mathematics and science teaching are seen as abysmal. 'We' need rapid change in our economic responsiveness and in 'our' emerging ideological and economic struggle with the Soviet Union.[13] Teachers (who just happen to be almost all women at the elementary level) are not sophisticated enough. Former ways of curricular and teaching control are neither powerful nor efficient enough for this situation. Provide both teacher proof materials and financial incentives to make certain that these sets of curricula actually reach the classroom.

One must integrate an analysis of the state, changes in the labor process of state employees, and the politics of patriarchy to comprehend the dynamics of this history of curriculum. It is not a random fact that one of the most massive attempts at rationalizing curricula and teaching had as its target a group of teachers who were largely women. I believe that one cannot separate out the fact of a sexual division of labor and the vision of who has what kinds of competence from the state's attempts to revamp and make more 'productive' its educational apparatus. In so doing, by seeing these structurally generated relationships, we can begin to open up a door to understanding part of the reasons behind what happened to these curriculum materials when they were in fact introduced.

As numerous studies have shown, when the material was introduced into many schools, it was not unusual for the 'new' math and 'new' science to be taught in much the same manner as the old math and old science. It was altered so that it would fit into both the existing regularities of the institution and the prior practices that had proven successful in teaching.[14] It is probably wise to see this as not only the result of a slow-to-change bureaucracy or a group of consistently conservative administrators and teachers. Rather, I think it may be just as helpful to think of this more structurally in labor process and gender terms. The supposed immobility of the institution, its lack of significant change in the face of the initial onslaught of such material, is at least partly tied to the resistances of a female work force against external incursions into the practices they had evolved over years of labor. It is in fact more than a little similar to the history of ways in which other women employees in the state and industry have reacted to past attempts at altering traditional modes of control of their own labor.[15]

A Note on the State

These points about the resistances of the people who actually work in the institutions, about women teachers confronted by external control, may seem straightforward. However, these basic arguments have very important implications not only about how we think about the history of curriculum reform and control, but more importantly about how many educators and political theorists have pictured the larger issue of the state's role in supporting capital. In the historical example I gave, state intervention on the side of capital and for 'defence' is in opposition to other positions within the state itself. The day-to-day interests of one occupational position (teachers) contradict the larger interests of the state in efficient production.[16] Because of instances such as this, it is probably inappropriate to see the state as a homogeneous entity, standing above day-to-day conflicts.

Since schools *are* state apparatuses, we should expect them to be under intense pressure to act in certain ways, especially in times of both fiscal and ideological crises. Even with this said, though, this does not mean that people employed in them are passive followers of policies laid down from above. As Roger Dale has noted:

> Teachers are not merely 'state functionaries' but do have some degree of autonomy, and [this] autonomy will not necessarily be used to further the proclaimed ends of the state apparatus. Rather than those who work there fitting themselves to the requirements of the institutions, there are a number of very important ways in which the institution has to take account of the interests of the employees and fit itself to them. It is here, for instance, that we may begin to look for the sources of the alleged inertia of educational systems and schools, that is to say what appears as inertia is not some immutable characteristic of bureaucracies but is due to various groups within them having more immediate interests than the pursuit of the organization's goals.[17]

Thus, the 'mere' fact that the state wishes to find 'more efficient' ways to organize teaching does not guarantee this will be acted upon by teachers who have a long history of work practices and self-organization once the doors to their rooms are closed. However, the fact that these are primarily women employees who have faced these forms of rationalization has meant that the actual outcomes of these attempts to retain control of one's pedagogic work can lead to rather contradictory ideological results.

Legitimating Intervention

While these initial attempts to rationalize teaching and curricula did not always produce the results that were anticipated by their academic, industrial, and governmental proponents, they did other things that were, and are, of considerable import. The situation is actually quite similar to the effects of the use of Tayloristic management strategies in industry. As a management technology for deskilling workers and separating conception from execution, Taylorism was less than fully successful. It often generated slowdowns and strikes, exacerbated tensions, and created new forms of overt and covert resistance. Yet, its ultimate effect was to legitimate a particular ideology of management and control both to the public and to employers and workers.[18] Even though it did not succeed as a set of techniques, it ushered in and finally brought acceptance of a larger body of ideological practices

to deskill pink, white, and blue collar workers and to rationalize and intensify their labor.

This too was one of the lasting consequences of these earlier curriculum 'reform' movements. While they did not completely transform the practice of teaching, while patriarchal relations of authority which gave teachers some measure of freedom were not totally replaced by more efficient forms of organizing and controlling their day-to-day activity, they legitimated both new forms of control and greater state intervention using industrial and technical models and brought about a new generation of more sophisticated attempts at overcoming teacher 'resistance'. Thus, this new generation of techniques — from systematic integration of testing, behavioral goals and curriculum, competency based instruction and pre-packaged curricula to management by objectives, and so forth — has not sprung out of nowhere, but — like the history of Taylorism — has grown out of the failures, partial successes, and resistances that accompanied the earlier approaches to control. This is not only the history of the control of state employees to bring about efficient teaching, but a re-articulation of the dynamics of patriarchy and class in one site, the school.

Intensification and Teaching

Having paid particular attention to the historical dynamics operating in the schools, I shall now focus on more current outgrowths of this earlier history of rationalization and control.

The earlier attempts by state bureaucrats, industry and others to gain greater control of day-to-day classroom operation and its 'output' did not die. They have had more than a decade to grow, experiment, and become more sophisticated. While gender will be less visible in the current strategies (in much the same way that the growth of management strategies in industry slowly covered the real basis of power in factories and offices), it will be present in important ways once we look at changes in the labor process of teaching, how some teachers respond to current strategies, and how they interpret their own work.

In previous work I have focussed on a number of elements through which curricula and teaching are controlled (aspects of deskilling and reskilling of labor and the separation of conception from execution in teachers' work); here I shall concentrate on something which accompanies these historically evolving processes: what I shall call *intensification*.

Intensification 'represents one of the most tangible ways in which the work privileges of educational workers are eroded.' It has many symptoms from the trivial to the more complex — from no time at all to even go to the bathroom, have a cup of coffee or relax, to having a total absence of time to keep up with one's field. We can see intensification most visibly in mental labor in the chronic sense of work overload that has escalated over time.[19]

This has had notable effects outside education. In the newspaper industry, for example, because of financial pressures and the increased need for efficiency in operation, reporters have had their story quotas raised substantially. Hence the possibility of doing non-routine investigative reporting is lessened considerably. This has had the effect of increasing their dependence 'on prescheduled, proformulated events' in which they rely more and more on bureaucratic rules and surface accounts of news provided by official spokespersons.[20]

Intensification also acts to destroy the sociability of non-manual workers. Leisure and self-direction tend to be lost. Community tends to be redefined around the needs of the labor process. And, since both time and interaction are at a premium, the risk of isolation grows.[21]

Intensification by itself 'does not necessarily reduce the range of skills applied or possessed by educated workers.' It may, in fact, cause them to 'cut corners' by eliminating what seems to be inconsequential to the task at hand. This has occurred with doctors, for instance, where many examinations now concentrate only on what seems critical. The chronic work overload has also caused some non-manual workers to learn or relearn skills. The financial crisis has led to shortages of personnel in a number of areas. Thus, a more diverse array of jobs must be done that used to be covered by other people, people who simply no longer exist within the institution.[22]

While this leads to a broader range of skills having to be learned or relearned, it can lead to something mentioned earlier — the loss of time to keep up with one's field. That is, what might be called 'skill diversification' has contradictions built into it. It is also part of a dynamic of intellectual deskilling[23] in which mental workers are cut off from their own fields and again must rely even more heavily on ideas and processes provided by 'experts'.

While these effects are important, one of the most significant impacts of intensification may be in reducing the *quality*, not the quantity, of service provided to people. While traditionally 'human service professionals' have equated doing good work with the interests of their clients or students, intensification tends to contradict the traditional interest in work well done, in both a quality product and process.[24] *Getting* done becomes more important than what was done or how one got there.

Some of these aspects of intensification are increasingly found in teaching, especially in schools dominated by behaviorally pre-specified curricula, repeated testing, and strict and reductive accountability systems. To make this clear, I shall draw on data from recent research on the effects of these procedures on the structure of teachers' work.

I have argued here and elsewhere that there has been a rapid growth in curricular 'systems' in the United States, one that is now spreading to other countries.[25] These curricula have goals, strategies, tests, textbooks, worksheets, appropriate student response, etc. integrated together. In schools where this is taken seriously,[26] what impact has this been having? We have sufficient evidence from ethnographic studies of the labor process of teaching to be able to begin to point to what is going on. For example, in one school where the curriculum was heavily based on a sequential list of behaviorally defined objectives, multiple worksheets on skills which the students were to complete, with pre-tests to measure 'readiness' and 'skill level' and post-tests to measure 'achievement' that were given often and regularly, the intensification of teacher work is quite visible.

In this school, such curricular practice required that teachers spend a large portion of their time evaluating student 'mastery' of each of the various objectives and recording the results of these multiple evaluations for later discussions with parents or decisions on whether or not the student could 'go on' to another set of skill-based worksheets. The recording and evaluation made it imperative that a significant amount of time be spent on administrative arrangements for giving tests, and then grading them, organizing lessons (which were quite often pre-packaged), and so on. One also found teachers busy with these tasks before and after school and, very often, during their lunch hour. Teachers began to come in at 7:15 in the morning and leave at 4:30 in the afternoon. Two hours more work at home each night were not unusual.[27]

Here too getting done became the norm. There is so much to do that simply accomplishing what is specified requires nearly all of one's efforts. 'The challenge of the work day (or week) was to accomplish the required number of objectives.' As one teacher put it, 'I just want to get this done. I don't have time to be creative or imaginative.'[28] We should not blame the teacher here. In mathematics, for example, teachers typically had to spend nearly half of the allotted time correcting and recording the worksheets the students completed each day.[29] The situation seemed to continually push up the work load of these teachers. Thus, even though they tended to complain at times about the long hours, the intensification and the time spent on technical tasks such as grading and record keeping, the amount of time spent doing these things grew inexorably.[30]

Few of the teachers were passive in the face of this. Even though the elements of curricular control were effective in structuring major aspects of their practice, teachers often responded in a variety of ways. They subtly changed the pre-specified objectives at times, thereby attempting to overcome the separation of conception from execution. They sometimes simply informally refused to teach certain objectives because they could not see their relevance. They tried to resist the intensification as well: first, by trying to find some space during the day for doing slower paced activities; and second, by actually calling a halt temporarily to the frequent pre- and post-tests, worksheets and the like and merely having 'relaxed discussions with students on topics of their own choosing'.[31]

This, of course, is quite contradictory. While these examples document the active role of teachers in attempting to win back some time, to resist the loss of control of their own work, and to slow down the pace at which students and they were to proceed, the way this is done is not necessarily very powerful. In these instances, time was fought for simply to relax, if only for a few minutes. The process of control, the increasing technicization and intensification of the teaching act, the proletarianization of their work — all of this was an absent presence. It was misrecognized as a symbol of their increased *professionalism*.

Profession and Gender

We cannot understand why teachers interpreted what was happening to them as the professionalization of their jobs unless we see how the ideology of professionalism works as part of both a class and gender dynamic in education. For example, while reliance on 'experts' to create curricular and teaching goals and procedures grew in this kind of situation, a wider range of technical skills had to be mastered by these teachers. Becoming adept at grading all those tests and worksheets quickly, deciding on which specific skill group to put a student in, learning how to 'efficiently manage' the many different groups based on the tests, and more, all became important skills. As responsibility for designing one's own curricula and one's own teaching decreased, responsibility over technical and management concerns came to the fore.

Professionalism and increased responsibility tend to go hand in hand here. The situation is more than a little paradoxical. There is so much responsibility placed on teachers for technical decisions that they actually work harder. They feel that since they constantly make decisions based on the outcomes of these multiple pre- and post-tests, the longer hours are evidence of their enlarged professional status.

> One reason the work is harder is we have a lot of responsibility in decision-making. There's no reason not to work hard, because you want to be darn sure that those decisions you made are something that might be helpful.... So you work hard to be successful at these decisions so you look like a good decision maker.[32]

It is here that the concept of professionalism seemed to have one of its major impacts. Since the teachers thought of themselves as being more professional to the extent that they employed technical criteria and tests, they also basically accepted the longer hours and the intensification of their work that accompanied the program. To do a 'good job', you needed to be as 'rational' as possible.[33]

We should not scoff at these perceptions on the part of the teachers. First, the very notion of professionalization has been important not only to teachers in general but to women in particular. It has provided a contradictory yet powerful barrier against interference by the state; and just as critically, in the struggle over male dominance, it has been part of a complex attempt to win equal treatment, pay, and control over the day-to-day work of a largely female labor force.[34]

Second, while we need to remember that professionalism as a social goal grew at the same time and was justified by the 'project and practice of the market professions during the liberal phase of capitalism',[35] the strategy of professionalism has historically been used to set up 'effective defenses against proletarianization'.[36] Given that I said earlier about the strong relationship between the sexual division of labor and proletarianization, it would be not only ahistorical but perhaps even a bit sexist as well to wholly blame teachers for employing a professional strategy.

Hence, the emphasis on increasing professionalism by learning new management skills and so on and its partial acceptance by elementary school teachers can best be understood not only as an attempt by state bureaucrats to deskill and reskill teachers, but also as part of a much larger historical dynamic in which gender politics have played a significant role.

Yet the acceptance of certain aspects of intensification is not only due to the history of how professionalism has worked in class and gender struggles. It is heightened by a number of internal factors, as well. For example, in the school referred to earlier, while a number of teachers believed that the rigorous specification of objectives and teaching procedures actually helped free them to become more creative, it was clear that subtle pressures existed to meet the priorities established by the specified objectives. Even though in some subject areas they had a choice of how they were to meet the objectives, the objectives themselves usually remained unchallenged. The perceived interests of parents and the establishment of routines helped assure this. Here is one teacher's assessment of how this occurs.

> Occasionally you're looking at the end of the book at what the unit is going to be, these are the goals that you have to obtain, that the children are going to be tested on. That may affect your teaching in some way in that you may by-pass other learning experiences simply to obtain the goal. These goals are going home to parents. It's a terrible thing to do but parents like to see 90's and 100's rather than 60's on skills.[37]

In discussing the use of the skills program, another teacher points out the other element that was mentioned. 'It's got a manual and you follow the manual and the kids know the directions and it gets to be routine.'[38]

Coupled with perceived parental pressure and the sheer power of routine is something else, the employment practices surrounding teaching. In many schools, one of the main criteria for the hiring of teachers is their agreement with the overall curricular, pedagogic, and evaluative framework which organizes the day-to-day practice. Such was the case in this study. Beyond this, even though some investigators have found that people who tend to react negatively to these pre-packaged and systematized curricular forms often leave teaching,[39] given the depressed market for new teachers, and the conscious decision by school districts to hire fewer teachers and increase class size, fewer jobs are available. The option of leaving or even protesting seems romantic.

Gendered Resistance

To return to a claim I made earlier: teachers have not stood by and accepted all this. In fact, our perception that they have been and are passive in the face of these pressures may reflect our own tacit beliefs in the relative passivity of women workers. This would be an unfortunate characterization. Historically, for example, in Britain and the United States, the picture of women teachers as non-militant and middle-class in orientation is not wholly accurate. There have been periods of exceptional militancy and clear political commitment.[40] However, militancy and political commitment are but one set of ways in which control is contested. It is also fought for on the job itself in subtle and even 'unconscious' (one might say 'cultural') ways, ways which will be contradictory as we shall now see. Once again, gender is of prime import.

In my own interviews with teachers it has become clear that many of them feel rather uncomfortable with their role as managers. Many others are less than happy with the emphasis on programs which they feel often 'lock them into a rigid system'. Here the resistance to rationalization and the loss of historically important forms of self-control of one's labor has very contradictory outcomes, partly as a result of sexual divisions in society. Thus, a teacher using a curricular program in reading and language arts that is very highly structured and test based states:

> While it's really important for the children to learn these skills, right now it's more important for them to learn to feel good about themselves. That's my role, getting them to feel good. That's more important than tests right now.

Another primary grade teacher, confronted by a rationalized curriculum program where students move from classroom to classroom for 'skill groups', put it this way:

> Kids are too young to travel between classrooms all the time. They need someone there that they can always go to, who's close to them. Anyway, subjects are less important than their feelings.

In these quotes, resistance to the administrative design is certainly evident.

There is a clear sense that something is being lost. Yet the discomfort with the process is coded around the traditional distinctions that organize the sexual division of labor both within the family and the larger society. The *woman's* sphere is that of providing emotional security, caring for feelings, and so on.

Do not misconstrue my points here. Teachers should care for the feelings and emotional security of their students. However, while these teachers fight on a cultural level against what they perceive to be the ill effects of their loss of control and both the division and intensification of their labor, they do so at the expense of re-instituting categories that partly reproduce other divisions that have historically grown out of patriarchal relations.[41]

This raises a significant point. Much of the recent literature on the role of the school in the reproduction of class, sex, and race domination has directed our attention to the existence of resistances. This realization was not inconsequential and was certainly needed to enable us to go further than the overly deterministic models of explanation that had been employed to unpack what schools do. However, at the same time, this literature has run the risk of romanticizing such resistances. The fact that they exist does not guarantee that they will necessarily be progressive at each and every moment. Only by uncovering the contradictions within and between the dynamics of the labor process *and* gender can we begin to see what effects such resistances may actually have.

Labor, Gender and Teaching

I have paid particular attention here to the effects of the restructuring of teachers' work in the school. I have claimed that we simply cannot understand what is happening to teaching and curriculum without placing it in a framework which integrates class (and its accompanying process of proletarianization) and gender. The impact of deskilling and intensification occurs on a terrain and in an institution that is populated primarily by women teachers and male administrators, a fact that needs to be recognized as being historically articulated with both the social and sexual divisions of labor, knowledge, and power in our society.

Yet, since teachers are primarily women, we must also look beyond the school to get a fuller comprehension of the impact of these changes and the responses of teachers to them. We need to remember that women teachers often work in *two* sites — the school and then the home. Given the modification of patriarchal relations and the intensification of labor in teaching, what impact might this have outside the school? If so much time is spent on technical tasks at school and home, it is possible that less time may be available for domestic labor in the home? Other people in the family may have to take up the slack, thereby partly challenging the sexual division of household labor. On the other hand, the intensification of teachers' work, and the work overload that may result from it, may have exactly the opposite effect. It may increase the exploitation of unpaid work in the home by merely adding more to do without initially altering conditions in the family. In either case, such conditions will lead to changes, tensions, and conflicts outside the sphere where women engage in paid work.[42] It is worth thinking very carefully about the effects that working in one site will have on the other. The fact that this dual exploitation exists is quite consequential in another way. It opens up possible new avenues for political intervention by socialist feminists. Showing the relationship between the home and the job, and the intensification growing in both, may provide for a way of demonstrating the ties between both of these spheres and between class and gender.

Thinking about such issues has actually provided the organizing framework for my analysis. The key to my investigation has been reflecting about changes in *how* work is organized over time and, just as significantly, *who* is doing the work. A clearer sense of both of these — how and who — can enable us to see similarities and differences between the world of work in our factories and offices and that of semi-autonomous state employees such as teachers.

What does this mean? Historically the major struggles labor engaged in at the beginning of the use of systematic management concerned resistance to speed-ups.[43] That is, the intensification of production, the pressure to produce more work in a given period, led to all kinds of interesting responses. Craft workers, for example, often simply refused to do more. Pressure was put on co-workers who went too fast (or too slow). Breaks were extended. Tools and machines suddenly developed 'problems'.

Teachers — given their contradictory class location, their relationship to the history of patriarchal control and the sexual division of labor, and the actual conditions of their work — will find it difficult to respond in the same way. They are usually isolated during their work, and perhaps more so now given the intensification of their labor. Further, machinery and tools in the usual sense of these terms are not visible. And just as importantly, the perception of oneself as professional means that the pressures of intensification and the loss of control will be coded and dealt with in ways that are specific to that workplace and its own history. The ultimate effects will be very contradictory.

In essence, therefore, while similar labor processes may be working through institutions within industry and the state which have a major impact on women's paid work, these processes will be responded to differently by different classes and class segments. The ideology of professional discretion will lead to a partial acceptance of, say, intensification by teachers on one level, and will generate a different kind of resistance, one specific to the actual work circumstances in which they have historically found themselves. The fact that these changes in the labor process of teaching occur on a terrain that has been a site of patriarchal relations plays a major part.

I do not want to suggest that once you have realized the place of teaching in the sexual division of labor, you have thoroughly understood deskilling and reskilling, intensification and loss of control, or the countervailing pressures of professionalism and proletarianization in teachers' work. Obviously, this is a very complex issue in which the internal histories of bureaucracies, the larger role of the state in a time of economic and ideological crisis,[44] and the local political economy and power relations of each school play a part. What I do want to argue quite strongly, however, is the utter import of gendered labor as a constitutive aspect of the way management and the state have approached teaching and curricular control. It is the absent presence behind all of our work.

Acknowledgement

I would like to thank the following people for their comments and suggestions on the ideas expressed in various drafts of this chapter: Sandra Acker, Rima D. Apple, Madeleine Arnot, Shigeru Asanuma, Ann Becker, Mimi Bloch, Linda

Christian, Miriam David, Andrew Gitlin, Esteban De La Torre, Glenn Hudak, Sue Carl Kaestle, Ki Seok Kim, Dan Liston, John Novak, Leslie Rothhaus, Ken Teitelbaum, Geoff Whitty, and Ann Marie Wolpe.

Notes

1 WRIGHT, E.O. and SINGELMANN, J. (1981) 'The proletarianization of work in American capitalism', University of Wisconsin-Madison Institute for Research on Poverty, *Discussion Paper*, 647–81, p.38.

2 *Ibid.*, p. 43. See also APPLE, M.W. (1981) 'State, bureaucracy and curriculum control', *Curriculum Inquiry*, 11, 4, pp. 379–88. For a discussion that rejects part of the argument about proletarianization, see KELLY, M. (1980) *White Collar Proletariat*, Routledge and Kegan Paul.

3 APPLE, M.W. (1981) 'Curricular form and the logic of technical control', in BARTON, L., MEIGHAN, R. and WALKER, S. (Eds), *Schooling, Ideology and the Curriculum*, Falmer Press, pp. 11–27. This argument is expanded considerably in APPLE, M.W. (1982) *Education and Power*, Routledge and Kegan Paul.

4 WRIGHT, E.J. (1980) 'Class and occupation', *Theory and Society*, 9, 2, pp. 182–3.

5 APPLE, M.W. (1982) *op. cit.* (Note 2).

6 WRIGHT, E.J. (1980) *op. cit.*, p. (Note 4) 188. Clearly, race plays an important part here too. See REICH, M. (1981) *Racial Inequality*, Princeton University Press and BARRERA, M. (1979) *Race and Class in the Southwest: A Theory of Racial Inequality*, Notre Dame Press.

7 HOLLAND, J. (1980) 'Women's occupational choice: The impact of sexual divisions in society', Stockholm Institute of Education, Department of Educational Research, *Reports on Education and Psychology*, p. 7.

8 *Ibid.*, p. 27.

9 *Ibid.*, p. 45.

10 KELLY, G. and NIHLEN, A. (1982) 'Schooling and the reproduction of patriarchy', in APPLE, M.W. (Ed.), *Cultural and Economic Reproduction in Education: Essays on Class, Ideology and the State*, Routledge and Kegan Paul, pp. 167–8. One cannot fully understand the history of the relationship between women and teaching without tracing the complex connections among the family, domesticity, child care, and the policies of and employment within the state. See especially DAVID, M. (1980) *The State, the Family and Education*, Routledge and Kegan Paul.

11 For an interesting history of the relationship among class, gender, and teaching, see PURVIS, J. (1981) 'Women and teaching in the nineteenth century', in DALE, R., ESLAND, G., FERGUSSON, R. and MACDONALD, M. (Eds), *Education and the State Vol. 2: Politics, Patriarchy and Practice*, Falmer Press, pp. 359–75. I am wary of using a concept such as patriarchy since its very status is problematic. As Rowbotham notes, 'patriarchy suggests a fatalistic submission which allows no space for the complexities of women's defiance.' Quoted in DAVIS, T. (1981) 'Stand by your men? Feminism and socialism in the eighties', in BRIDGES, G. and BRUNT, R. (Eds), *Silver Linings: Some Strategies for the Eighties*, Lawrence and Wishart, p. 14. A history of women's day-to-day struggles falsifies any such theory of 'fatalistic submission'.

12 BARKER, J. and DOWNING, H. (1981) 'Word processing and the transformation of the patriarchal relations of control in the office', in DALE, R., ESLAND, G., FERGUSSON, R. and MACDONALD, M. (Eds), *Education and the State Vol. 1: Schooling and the National Interest*, Falmer Press, pp. 229–56. See also the discussion of deskilling in EDWARDS, R. (1979) *Contested Terrain*, Basic Books.

13 For an analysis of how such language has been employed by the state, see APPLE, M.W. (1982) *op. cit.* (Note 3), APPLE, M.W., in press, 'Common curriculum and state control', *Discourse*, and DONALD, J. (1979) 'Green paper: Noise of a crisis', *Screen Education*, 30 (Spring).

14 See, for example, SARASON, S. (1971) *The Culture of the School and the Problem of Change*, Allyn and Bacon.
15 APPLE, M.W. (1982) *op. cit.* (Note 3), BENSON, S.P. (1978) 'The clerking sisterhood: Rationalization and the work culture of saleswomen in American department stores', *Radical America*, 12, (March/April), pp. 41–5.
16 Roger Dale's discussion of contradictions between elements within the state is quite interesting in this regard. See DALE, R. (1981) 'The State and education: Some theoretical approaches', in *The State and the Politics of Education*, The Open University Press, E 353, Block 1, Part 2, Units 3–4, and DALE, R. (1982) 'Education and the capitalist State: Contributions and contradictions', in APPLE, M.W. (Ed.), *Cultural and Economic Reproduction in Education: Essays on Class, Ideology and the State*, Routledge and Kegan Paul, pp. 127–61.
17 DALE, R. (1981) *op. cit.* (Note 16), p. 13.
18 I have examined this in greater detail in APPLE, M.W. (1982) *op. cit.* (Note 3). See also EDWARDS, R. (1979) *op. cit.* (Note 12), and CLAWSON, D. (1980) *Bureaucracy and the Labor Process*, Monthly Review Press.
19 LARSON, M. (1980) 'Proletarianization and educated labor', *Theory and Society*, 2, p. 166.
20 *Ibid.*, p. 167.
21 *Ibid.* Larson points out that these problems related to intensification are often central grievances even among doctors.
22 *Ibid.*, p. 168.
23 *Ibid.*, p. 169.
23 *Ibid.*, p. 167.
25 APPLE, M.W. (1982) *op. cit.* (Note 3). See also BUSWELL, C. (1980) 'Pedagogic change and social change', *British Journal of Sociology of Education*, 3, pp. 293–306.
26 The question of just how seriously schools take this, the variability of their response, is not unimportant. As Popkewitz, Tabachnick and Wehlage demonstrate in their interesting ethnographic study of school reform, not all schools use materials of this sort alike. See POPKEWITZ, T., TABACHNICK, B.R. and WEHLAGE, G. (1982) *The Myth of Educational Reform*, University of Wisconsin Press.
27 This section of my analysis is based largely on research carried out by Andrew Gitlin. See GITLIN, A. (1980) 'Understanding the work of teachers', unpublished PhD thesis, University of Wisconsin, Madison.
28 *Ibid.*, p. 208.
29 *Ibid.*
30 *Ibid.*, p. 197.
31 *Ibid.*, p. 237.
32 *Ibid.*, p. 125.
33 *Ibid.*, p. 197.
34 This is similar to the use of liberal discourse by popular classes to struggle for person rights against established property rights over the past 100 years. See GINTIS, H. (1980) 'Communication and politics', *Socialist Review*, 10, 2/3 pp. 189–232.
35 LARSON, M. (1981) 'Monopolies of competence and bourgeois ideology', in DALE, R., ESLAND, G., FERGUSSON, R. and MACDONALD, M. (eds), *Education and the State Volume 2: Politics, Patriarchy and Practice*, Falmer Press, p. 332.
36 LARSON, M. (1980) *op. cit.* (Note 19), p. 152.
37 GITLIN, A. (1980) *op. cit.* (Note 27), p. 128.
38 *Ibid.*
39 LAWN, M.A. and OZGA, J.T. (1981) 'Teachers: Professionalism, class and proletarianization', unpublished paper, p. 15 in mimeo.
40 OZGA, J.T. (1981) 'The politics of the teaching profession', in *The Politics of Schools and Teaching*, The Open University Press, E 353, Block 6, Units 14–15, p. 24.
41 We need to be very careful here, of course. Certainly, not all teachers will respond in this way. That some will not points to the partial and important fracturing of dominant

gender and class ideologies in ways that signal significant alterations in the consciousness of teachers. Whether these alterations are always progressive is an interesting question.

42   While I have focussed here on the possible impacts in the school and the home on women teachers, a similar analysis needs to be done on men. What changes, conflicts, and tensions will evolve, say, in the patriarchal authority structures of the home, given the intensification of men's labor? I would like to thank Sandra Acker for raising this critically important point.

43   CLAWSON, D. (1980) *op. cit.* (Note 18), pp. 152–3.

44   APPLE, M.W. (1981) *op. cit.* (Note 2).

5.   A Cloud over Co-Education: An Analysis of the Forms of Transmission of Class and Gender Relations

Madeleine Arnot, The Open University

In 1948 John Newsom,[1] then a school inspector, in his book *The Education of Girls* expounded the view that girls' education should reflect the fact that,

> Women possess certain particular needs based on their particular psychology, physiology and their social and economic position.... The fundamental common experience is the fact that the vast majority of them will become the makers of homes, and that to do this successfully requires the proper development of many talents.[2]

Girls, according to Newsom, constituted a single and more or less homogeneous group since they shared a common interest and a main vocation in domesticity. The ideals of education should therefore reflect this future destination of women and stress the *complementarity* yet *differences* between the sexes. Schooling for girls and boys should be, in the rhetoric of the 1940s, 'equal but different', and should stress the development of individual talents and interests. As Bland, McCabe and Mort have pointed out, Newsom's book provided an early example of the attempt to overcome the contradiction between an ideology of child-centred education with its progressive ideals of individual development and the assumption that all girls were destined to a collective and identical future as 'homemakers'.[3] Yet the book is also an interesting example of yet another problem which has faced educationalists in the nineteenth and twentieth centuries. In his book, Newsom reaches a point where, having demarcated the necessary division between the sexes, he has to recommend a school structure which would fulfil the conditions for the reproduction of such a sexual division of labour. He asks the question: should boys and girls in the heterogeneity be educated together, or should they be separated during school life? He concludes:

> As far as the children are concerned there is no satisfactory evidence from which to deduce whether co-education is more generally suitable than segregation. It is a matter of opinion rather than exact knowledge. True it is rarely contended that children of primary age should be separated according to sex, but at the secondary stage there is no generally accepted theory on the subject. If there are enough boys and girls to establish separate schools, then that course is followed; if there are not sufficient for proper organization then a mixed school is provided. In certain circles, however, a cloud 'no bigger than a man's hand' [sic] is forming, a cloud whose contention is that between twelve and fifteen boys and girls are better apart. Puberty comes earlier to girls and they are already 'interested in boys' when boys are still going through the last happy period of barbarism when they regard girls as a nuisance if not with

positive distaste. Once the change from childhood to physical maturity is accomplished, it is held that they can be brought together again with profit. I do not know how far this theory is supported but it presents a fascinating field for detailed research.... If there were any possibility of the main contention of this book becoming operative, that of planning of girls' education according to their needs instead of slavishly copying the education of their brothers, there would be an additional reason for temporary segregation. It is all very difficult.[4]

In this chapter I shall show that there is just as much confusion today and just as little research on this issue as in the 1940s. It is still 'all very difficult'. Newsom's indecision about the merits of co-education is representative of the general indecision of policy-makers. For example, in 1945 the Ministry of Education's pamphlet *The Nation's Schools* could not recommend a fixed doctrine as to the provision of mixed or single-sex schools.[5] As it was desirable and advantageous for boys and girls to learn 'to know and respect each other's point of view', co-education was desirable within primary education. But in the area of secondary education, there were the rival advantages of single-sex schools. Since it was already agreed that at adolescence boys and girls *should* be separated for physical training and major games and that at this age their needs and interests ran further apart, single-sex schooling appeared to be the most logical structure. At the level of further education, the mixing of the sexes was again desirable. Therefore, the recommended form of reproduction of the division of the sexes through education was to vary according to the different *age* of the pupils and the different types of schooling offered in the primary, secondary and tertiary sectors. One might explain this by noticing that in the primary schools the gender divisions to be reproduced were those found within the domestic sphere where brothers and sisters mix together freely; whilst in the secondary schools the preparation was for the sexual division of labour found within paid employment and a gender-divided labour market. By the time students reached further education, they could be safely brought together since the patterns of gender differentiation would be largely settled.

The debate over the relative merits of each type of school has a long and forgotten history, forgotten perhaps because it is an issue that appears only to concern women. This is especially the case today since it is only feminists and those agencies concerned with the equality of the sexes which have become involved in the discussions as to the advantages and disadvantages of each form of schooling. The traditional and the socialist histories of education have marginalized women's educational experiences and have assumed that the discussion of female education is something which can occur without reference to, or influence upon, male or class histories of education. Thus the issue of what Weinberg[6] called the 'sex structure' of schools is an absent or well-hidden aspect of these accounts. However, if we are not to treat gender categories as natural organizing principles of educational research and gender relations as only referring to female education, then we have to investigate the sets of gender relations made available, through a class determined educational system, to *both* men and women. Thus what I would like to show in this chapter is that the issue of whether to support single-sex or co-educational schools is broader than the current feminist concern of attempting to help girls study science subjects, to help them compete as equals with boys, or to help girls enter university and male occupations. It is an issue which involves analyzing the differences between class-based notions of education in the state and private sector and the reproduction of the socio-sexual division of labour under capitalism.

I shall trace the outlines of what I have called the 'hidden' history of co-education, in the context of a pattern of educational policy-making which assumed that boys' and girls' education should be different. In a patriarchal society, such a pattern of policy-making was hardly surprising. However, it also led to various problems in the nineteenth century and in this century since it posed the question: how does one place two different types of education (one for each sex) within *one* state system of education? Secondly, how does one locate female class differences in an educational system designed to reproduce the seemingly more important set of class relations — those of men and male occupational hierarchies? The solutions to such policy dilemmas were to utilize the ideology of *female domesticity*, as female historians have shown.[7] Where the two processes of class and gender reproduction collude historically is in the attempted imposition through schooling of a bourgeois family form that entailed the social construction of the female housekeeping wife dependent upon a wage- or salary-earning husband. Secondly, it involved the development of the *myth of female classlessness* which blurred or covered over the differences of educational provision for girls of different social classes.[8]

The dual impact of these two ideological aspects of the processes of reproducing dominant class and gender relations led not to a single educational structure but to a variety of school structures. The history of schooling reveals the range of alternative 'sex structures' available at any one time, as well as the class factors involved in their provision. Thus whilst one might want to talk about a dominant *gender code* in education,[9] reproducing dominant bourgeois gender relations, one must also be aware that in different historical periods and for different social classes there may be a variety of *modalities of transmission* of those gender relations.

In the context of the English state system of education, the most influential modality of transmission of class and gender relations has been that exemplified by the private single-sex grammar school. However by the late 1960s the two systems of education had diverged significantly, with the majority of state comprehensive schools offering co-education, and the majority of private secondary schools retaining their single-sex status. I shall argue that the development of such co-educational comprehensive schools did not represent, despite its progressive image, a challenge to the reproduction of dominant gender relations but rather a modification of the *form* of its transmission. In the second part of the chapter, therefore, I look at the critiques and defence of co-education and the ways in which class factors have become submerged in the debate over the merits or disadvantages of mixed schooling. It is no surprise to me, for instance, given the history of co-education, that as Jenny Shaw points out the paradox of the British model of mixed comprehensive secondary school is that 'by its own criteria of success its most promising pupils persistently underachieve'.[10] 'How is it', she asks, 'that girls, who begin their school career with what appears to be a flying start over boys, being as much as two years ahead in reading and in physical and psychological maturity, come to leave school with far fewer qualifications?'[11] The suggestion here is that such schools do not offer equality of opportunity to boys and girls alike, but rather that they actually close the door or 'harm' girls[12] by their detrimental effects.

Co-educational comprehensives historically were meant to reproduce life within a 'normal' bisexual world, and it is the reproduction of this world that feminists have responded to. In the final part of the chapter I look very briefly at the various responses of feminists to the nature of such an educational goal. I look at the critiques they offer to mixed schooling and the implications of each perspective in terms of how far they may realistically expect to break down gender inequality by the educational reforms they suggest.

The Hidden History of Co-Education

It is generally assumed that co-educational schools only became an issue in the 1970s especially after the report of the Department of Education and Science on *Curricular Differences for Boys and Girls* found that girls were more likely to achieve a broader education and make less sex-stereotyped decisions of subject choice in single-sex schools than in mixed ones.[13] Certainly that report can be seen as the contemporary catalyst to much more interest being taken in the advantages and disadvantages of mixed schools. However, the relative merits of this form of schooling had been challenged as early as the 1920s when women teachers realized that mixed schools might well involve a reduction of their promotion prospects, especially since most mixed schools had a male head, and female teachers were generally limited to teaching infants, girls and specialist domestic-type classes.[14] As it is impossible to trace the intricacies of this history of co-educational schools without more research and more space, I will therefore confine myself here to the broadest of patterns which appear to be significant.

The development of co-educational schools had been patchy in the nineteenth century, and to a large extent was determined by the social class clientele of the pupils.[15] The increasing provision of girls' private schools, both day schools and boarding schools, repeated in many ways the style and ethos of boys' schools. They attempted to emulate their academic norms as well as provide for the distinctive requirements of middle-class and aristocratic girls. In 1864 the Taunton Commission recommended that the proper development of middle-class girls' character was provided by the establishment of girls' day schools, even though a Mr Hammond who gave evidence to them reported that he had found no noticeable difference of attainment in the two sexes when taught in mixed schools. During the nineteenth century several notable girls-only public schools were set up, modelled upon the boys' public boarding schools; for example, St. Leonards, St. Andrews (1877), Roedean (1885), Godolphin School (1886), Wycombe Abbey (1896) and Sherborne (1899).[16] These schools restricted their entry to girls of specific social class (through the procedures of social selection and the setting of high fees) to a greater extent than the girls' day-schools under the aegis of the Girls' Public Day Schools Company. The main pattern of education of the bourgeoisie was therefore largely that of single-sex education which entailed a segregation of the sexes based upon a differentiation of the roles of men and women of that social strata.

Certainly, at one level, it was convenient to establish single-sex girls' schools since the boys' schools were already so well-developed. On the other hand, single-sex schooling more easily catered for the reproduction of the bourgeois gender relations in which, as Judith Okeley argues,[17] girls were prepared more for the marriage market than the labour market.

> ... girls are protected for a future marriage contract within an elite whose biological and social reproduction they ensure. They have no economic and political power independent of males such as their fathers, and later their husbands and sons.[18]

Thus the advantages of attending a public school for girls are not found in the economic advantages of access to the high status professions, nor indeed necessarily access to universities. Rather, they lie in the acquisition of the cultural capital of that social class and of maintaining the possibility of marrying into it, through the social network the schools give access to. Thus as Okeley writes, in this social strata:

> ... boys' and girls' educations are not symmetrical but they are *ideologically interdependent*. That considered female is partly defined by its opposite: that which is considered to be male. The characteristics of one institution are strengthened by their absence in the other. Qualities primarily reserved for one gender will have a different meaning in the institution of the opposing gender. The two educations are also linked in practice since, in adulthood, individuals from the separate institutions will be united in marriage for the consolidation of their class. As members of the same social class the girls and boys may share similar educational experiences but as members of different gender categories some of their educational experiences may differ.[19] (my emphasis)

What single-sex schools offered to the bourgeoisie was the chance to provide *different but equally privileged* educations for its sons and daughters, maintaining the appropriateness of a rigid sexual division of labour between public and private worlds, between male paid employment and female family responsibilities. Further, single-sex schools by their physical segregation of the sexes provided the conditions for the maintenance of female adolescent virginity and the preservation of the concept of bourgeois marriage. The reproduction of heterosexuality as the norm of sexual relations ironically required the setting up of single-sex environments, which always contained the dangers of sponsoring homosexual relations amongst staff and pupils. Yet while homosexuality amongst boys in particular was a well known occurrence in boys' public schools, it did not appear to threaten the stability of the bourgeois family form, in a way that mixing of the sexes at adolescence might have implied. As Turner argues, 'the reason why the middle class insisted on a social and educational barrier between boys and girls was because they feared that sexual misbehaviour was an inevitable consequence of co-education'.[20] Thus while the dominant form of transmission of the sexual division of labour amongst the bourgeoisie — single-sex schools — allowed for the reproduction of class cultural unity, it also provided for the reproduction of intra-class gender differentiation which maintained the notion of the bourgeois family form of salary-earning husband, and a dependent housekeeping wife who would provide the only legitimate heirs to the economic and cultural wealth of that social class.[21] However, the development of co-educational schools was beginning to be officially encouraged for the middle classes; for example, the Bryce Commission in 1895 took the view that there were too few endowed and proprietory schools which were mixed. The commission used the experience of the United States where co-education had been flourishing to argue that:

> this system has been tried with so much success in other countries, and to some extent in Great Britain itself, that we feel sure its use may be extended without fear of any undersirable consequences, and probably with some special advantages for the formation of character and general stimulus to intellectual activity.[22]

By 1898 the most famous co-educational boarding school, Bedales, had opened its door to girls. However the popularity of single-sex schools in the private fee-paying sector was to hold its own well into the latter part of the twentieth century. By 1968 the Public Schools Commission found that out of 273 public schools in England and Wales there were only three mixed public schools, accounting for 1162 out of 105,000 pupils.[23] In the maintained sector, in contrast 58 per cent of secondary schools were co-educational, catering for 60 per cent of secondary pupils. The commission felt that the high number of single-sex private schools were more a reflection of the 'intentions of their founders and the conventions of their day' than the current parental attitudes in the late 1960s. They suggested that

> many parents would welcome co-education either for its own sake or so that brothers and sisters may attend the same school where this would be more convenient than attending separate schools.[24]

The objection to co-education they saw as linked to boarding education and the fear of sexual relationships developing between male and female pupils. Such fear they felt to be exaggerated and argued instead that if girls were to have equal opportunities with boys, they could only receive these through co-educational schools.

Today there are many more mixed private secondary schools. Some boys' schools have brought girls into all 'forms' and other have let girls into the sixth form only.[25] However, as a recent report in *The Sunday Times* showed,[26] the introduction of mixing in these schools has not threatened the reproduction of gender relations at either the academic or sexual level. Girls are being recruited either to take the arts subjects which boys do not choose to study particularly at advanced levels, or to provide entertainment for boys who also might be distracted from their homosexual activities. Interestingly the penalty for a boy and girl found in bed together is expulsion whilst a lenient view tends to be taken of homosexual activities in such schools. As *The Sunday Times* reporter commented:

> This puts the schools in the curious position of turning a blind eye to an illegal activity (homosexual relations between persons under 21) while maintaining severe sanctions against a perfectly legal one (heterosexual relations between persons over 16).[27]

Male teachers also felt the advantages of the presence of girls in such mixed public schools. One, for example, claimed that the major benefit of introducing girls into previously boys-only private schools was a 'rediscovery of a relaxed normality'. Unfortunately the nature of this 'normality' can be seen in the following statement of another teacher:

> 'I couldn't face going back to the intensity of a single sex school. I'd rather leave teaching. Did you notice this morning? I went into the classroom and the girls saw straight away that I'd had a haircut and they commented on it. They'll mention your tie as well. It keeps you on your toes: in the old days masters wore the same ties for the whole term.'[28]

The dominant form of reproduction of bourgeois gender relations (until recently when it has been modified) has been that of single-sex schools which were based upon the principle of children's exclusion and protection from contact with other social classes and from contact with the opposite sex. Education was meant to train boys for their future roles as leaders of the country and as patriarchs, and to train girls for their future roles as wives and mothers of the members of that social class. In this way single-sex schools made possible a division of labour which gave both boys and girls of that social class privileges, as well as ensuring the re-production of the gender hierarchy specific to that social class. In this context a specifically bourgeois notion of femininity was transmitted to the girls that differed from those aspects of femininity taught within state secondary schools. Whilst to the outsider, the concepts of femininity in the private and state sector schools may appear to be very similar, as Lucy Blandford found, ex-public school girls in 1977 were acutely sensitive to the signs of class difference between themselves and girls from state grammar schools. These differences can be seen in the following extracts from Blandford's interviews:

> At ten a public school girl has already learned how to handle servants: that particular distance that the upper classes keep from inferiors and each other, is imbibed early. At school a girl soon learns that one doesn't talk to the kitchen staff: in the hols she learns how much to tip staff and how to do it unselfconsciously when she goes away (and these days, how not to register surprise if there's no staff to tip, times being what they are). As one grander type puts it 'You can always tell a grammar school girl who has married well by the fact that she's a fraction too familiar with her servants and rather uncomfortable with yours.'[29]
>
> Can a state-school girl pass herself off as The Real Thing? There's a moment of embarrassed surprise. 'When she's young', says Sal ... 'any pretty woman with a good figure can dress herself up and pass herself off as anything. But when she gets older, she inevitably reverts to type'. Nicki describes a well-turned-out, well-educated and ambitious state-school girl as a 'cultured pearl, not a real pearl'.[30]

In contrast to this history, many co-educational schools were available to the children of the working classes by the mid-nineteenth century. The early charity schools set up by the bourgeoisie to educate poor children in the 'rudiments' of education and to provide a training in 'morals and good conduct' were often mixed. June Purvis has documented the variety of forms of educational provision available to working-class girls from 1800 to 1870, noticing that a large number of National Society schools were mixed.[31] The evidence she collected suggested that girls attained a higher academic standard in the 3Rs especially in arithmetic when in mixed schools and taught by male teachers. Problems arose if girls were in mixed schools with infants since female pupils might be asked to help care for and teach the younger children as unpaid helpers. In 1858 the Newcastle Commission reported that of the 1895 schools they inspected nearly half were mixed, of which 10 per cent were mixed infant schools. Only 18.1 per cent were girls' schools and 22.2 per cent were boys' schools.[32] With the passing of the 1870 Education Act, a state system of national elementary schools became established, bringing together, as Purvis has pointed out, not just the fragmented system of educational provision but also the principles of class and gender differentiation and controls which had characterized the voluntary schools run by the bourgeoisie for the working classes. This Act did not attempt to establish the principle of equal education for all social classes; nor did it attempt to establish an equal education for boys and girls.

> For working class girls ... the provision of a state system of national
> education meant a renewed emphasis on education for motherhood rather
> than education for employment, a renewed emphasis that was especially
> pronounced in the latter decades of the century when grants were made
> for the teaching of cookery and laundry work. But not all working class
> girls experienced such a state system since school attendance was not
> made compulsory until 1880 and not made free until 1891.[33]

Thus despite the fact that many elementary schools were co-educational,
(about half in 1900) gender differentiation in the working classes was not seriously
challenged. As Purvis' research shows, whatever the form of schooling it was
always assumed that the female sex should be prepared for the private sphere of the
home, while boys would be prepared primarily for activities outside the home, in
paid employment. Separate schools, separate departments or separate classes were
established for boys and girls and in each type of school *gender-specific curricula*
were taught. Therefore, a range of alternative school sex-structures was offered to
the working classes; the choice being affected to a certain extent by the regional
catchment area since single-sex schools were more likely to flourish in towns, while
mixed schools were needed in the scattered populations of rural areas. However, it
is important that behind the pragmatics of policy decisions, there was little
identification of the concept of gender *mixing* with that of *identity of training* for
boys and girls. Co-educational schools generally meant that the different educations for boys and girls were 'mixed together' rather than integrated into a common
form of schooling.

Sex-segregation could involve the physical separation of boys and girls
through total exclusion in boarding schools such as those provided by and for the
middle classes, or it could involve the separation of day schools by sex, or it could
involve the separation of teaching classes and subjects for boys and girls *within* one
building. For example, the 1903 Code set up, according to David,[34] separate
'classes' in different school subjects. The basis was set for the unity and diversity of
male and female working-class education within one type of school. The production of class identity was provided through the common courses that boys and girls
took as a 'preparation for adult life', which was generally referred to by the
'neutral' concept of 'citizenship'. In the higher elementary schools these were
English language and literature, elementary maths, history and geography.
Separate courses, on the other hand, could then reproduce the sexual division of
labour. Boys were trained for their futures not just as manual workers through
such vocational courses as technical drawing and woodwork but also for their role
as future fathers, that is, wage earners and heads of households. Girls were
prepared for their future roles as economically dependent mothers and domestics
within the working class.

The growth of secondary schools involved the financial necessity of producing
larger schools. This led, according to David, to more mixed secondary grammar
schools, where women teachers tended to be excluded from headships and the
teaching of male adolescents. Not surprisingly many women teachers were in
favour of single-sex schools and a differentiation of curricula for boys and girls,
since it was in this sort of educational provision that they stood any chance of
promotion, a career, responsibilities and control over education. The numbers of
mixed secondary schools, however, were still small.

By 1919 only 224 out of 1080 secondary schools recognized as efficient were co-educational.[35] The motto 'education for one's station in life' involved class and gendered concepts of adult destiny that did not easily lead to co-education as a progressive ideal, but rather accepted it as a pragmatic necessity in certain circumstances. Put another way, the protection that upper-middle-class girls had from contact with the male sex was a possible sacrifice in the development of a sparsely funded state educational system. The compromise was to make sure that the sexes did not mix physically in any sports and to provide a range of separate classes for boys and girls within secondary schools. In the development of secondary education, what we can find is a diluted and modified version of the reproduction of bourgeois gender relations for those who could not afford the full cost of private education.

Concern over co-education was shown in the Report of the Consultative Committee of the Board of Education on the *Differentiation of the Curriculum for Boys and Girls Respectively in Secondary Schools* in 1923.[36] This report did not see the issue of co-education as part of its brief; nevertheless, in an appendix it collected the views of its witnesses upon this topic. Significantly, criticism of co-educational schools came largely from women witnesses. They argued that mixed schools were in fact boys' schools with girls in them, that women teachers and girls had no chance to get involved in the running of the school, that girls were shy in the presence of boys and that girls in girls' schools reached a higher standard than in co-educational schools. Sexual attachments were also a problem between male teachers and female pupils. (All these criticisms, interestingly, are the same as those made of mixed schools today.)

Whilst the issue was not resolved in this Report, what was evident was the tension between a desire to maintain the internal *unity* of class experience as well as the *diversity* of different sexes and different social classes. Were the sons and daughters of the working class to receive broadly similar educational experiences or would boys receive an education in common with boys of another social class, and working-class girls with their counterparts in the bourgeoisie? This tension and its resolution is still a matter of contention. Socialist historians emphasize the collective 'lived experience' of the working class in contrast with that of the bourgeoisie. On the other hand, feminists have stressed the differences between boys' and girls' schooling. While identifying class differences, they have, nevertheless, talked of a *domestic ideology* which, within a patriarchal context, has displaced class differences and *united* the subordination of daughters of the bourgeoisie and working classes. The impact of an educational ideology which is *familial* in orientation and domestic in practice (across the divide of state and private education) is supposed to have reduced the effect of class divisions amongst women to the extent that gender is primary.

My own view is that the *ideology of femininity, of family and domesticity has hidden the female class divisions within education*.[37] Whilst vocational ideology, that is, an education for different occupational statuses reveals, in far more explicit form, *male* class differentiation within state schooling, domestic ideology has more successfully involved a 'misrecognition' of the action of state and class power. In this sense, one reading the history of female education could assume that women were untouched by the class nature of society, except insofar as they married into different social classes. There is a danger that in focussing too exclusively upon gender divisions, apart from the class history of education, the *myth of female classlessness* will be perpetuated. This myth is one found in state policy. As a result, within government reports, one can find the variety of ideological solutions found to the problem of positioning a specifically 'female' education within the *structure of male class relations* within education, especially within those dealing with the tripartite division of secondary schools. The underlying ideological premise was that schools should prepare boys in different ways for their future places within the occupational hierarchy; meanwhile girls of different social classes were being prepared in different ways in different types of school for that other hierarchy — the sexual hierarchy of family life. Thus working-class girls received a diet of cookery, sewing and domestic science courses and middle-class grammar school girls learnt the range of languages, literature, history and artistic accomplishments necessary for a future marital life.

The new rhetoric of 'social engineering' by the 1970s changed the focus of girls' education somewhat since it recognized that girls were indeed likely to go into paid employment especially when single. The co-educational comprehensive school in many ways represented a new solution to the problem of class and gender inequalities in society, in that it placed all pupils in one school and theoretically encouraged children to follow courses according to their own 'interests and needs'. Pupil freedom of choice now seemed to be the way to alleviate class and gender inequalities. In this context co-educational schools acquired a new 'progressive' image which was not really challenged until the 1970s.

Historically, as we have seen, at no point and in no social class were boys and girls offered a *common curriculum* since the premise of educational policy-makers and schools was that girls should receive a different education from boys. It was hardly surprising, therefore, that when the programme of comprehensivation was developed, encouraging co-educational schools, the assumption of gender differentiation was retained underneath the new ideology of free choice and pupil needs. Instead of explicitly identifying all girls as a homogeneous group with identical needs, the reproduction of gender divisions could be left to the now historically internalized attitudes and gender ideologies of parents, teachers, careers officers, employers and finally the students themselves. In this sense the assumptions of male superiority and female domesticity (being unchallenged) were encouraged, albeit more implicitly, to prevail. The form of reproduction of gender relations became therefore more hidden and less conscious, surrounded as it was by the ideology of ability, 'achievement-motivation' and individual freedom of choice.

Critiques and Defence of Co-Education

I shall now discuss the contemporary debate over co-education which has many similarities with the views expressed in the 1920s by female witnesses to the Report of the Consultative Committee of the Board of Education.[38] The catalyst for recent discussion of the value of co-education was the 1975 Sex Discrimination Act which attempted to eliminate discrimination on the grounds of sex in areas where women have been prevented from achieving social and economic equality with men, as well as the DES survey on the *Curricular Differences for Boys and Girls* published in the same year.[39] The latter, conducted by the HM Inspectorate on primary, middle and secondary schools, revealed the extent of gender differentiation practised in schools. There was a variety of discriminatory practises based upon the assumption that boys and girls had different interests, abilities and futures. Schools were shown to be structured in such a way that children of different sexes were prepared for different roles in adult life and were encouraged to expect gender differentiation as normal. The reason given for such differentiation was not academic but that it was 'normal practice' (that is, it was a convenient long-standing organization, or it was financially necessitated). The most important effect of such practices was found in the pattern of boys' and girls' curricula — the subjects they were offered, those they chose to study and those taken by boys and girls for examination. Curricular options were offered differentially for boys and girls, especially in secondary schools. These included physical education, crafts (such as home economics, needlework, woodwork and metalwork) and the more academic subjects such as languages, physics and chemistry. The effect of such differentiation was that girls could be found clustered in the arts subjects, leaving boys in the majority in the 'hard sciences'.

However, the important revelation of this report was that the *provision* of different curricular subjects did not determine *choice*. What appeared to be important in affecting choice of subjects was whether the school was mixed or single-sex. Thus in single-sex schools, girls were more likely to take science subjects and boys were more likely to choose languages and the arts than in mixed schools. The choice of 'academic' subjects was also affected at 'A' levels where 'any correlation between the sex of the pupil and the popularity of a subject is markedly greater in mixed schools than in single sex schools'.[40] The tendency was of single-sex schools to weaken the gender patterns of subject choice, particularly as far as girls and science were concerned. These findings were supported by other pieces of research such as King's study of mathematics teaching in mixed and single sex schools,[41] and Omerod's on subject choice.[42] However, despite this evidence that girls and boys received less stereotyped educations in single-sex schools, the DES survey did not argue that boys and girls *should* be educated separately or together. It argued that '*the findings would be misinterpreted if used to argue the case for either single sex or mixed schools*', and advised a reconsideration of the curricular programmes of 12 to 16-year-olds to ensure that 'the principal areas of the curriculum are open to all boys and girls in whatever kind of school they happen to be'.[43]

The report's hesitancy to recommend single-sex education may have been affected by the other findings which, to a large extent, have been ignored by recent commentators. In almost all single-sex schools there is very little variety for the non-academically oriented pupil. Craft and practical subjects follow very traditional patterns. As Eileen Byrne has pointed out this lack of free access of girls to handicrafts and of boys to homecraft has important vocational effects.[44] Domestic economy has meant that girls are taught cookery and needlework as preparation for the home and not employment, whilst boys are taught handicrafts such as woodwork, metalwork and technical drawing which have more 'transfer value', and more conceptual elements than homecraft.

> The technical craft subjects ... unquestionably have a major educative value in their own right. Regardless of whether boys later became welders or craftsmen, woodwork, metalwork and technical drawing have several foundation and transfer values not characteristic of domestic economy. They reinforce spatial development and numerical concepts, involving mensuration and spatial relationships from the outset — the very areas in which girls are alleged to be innately weaker than boys and in which girls therefore need early reinforcement, not further deprivation.... There is a clear causal relationship between girls' exclusion from the technical

crafts and their almost total under-recruitment in the training and employment fields of construction, metal trades, electrical engineering, maintenance engineering.[45]

As Byrne pointed out, the exclusion from these subjects means that girls are most likely to see skilled work in these areas as masculine. The recent concern over the academic advantages of single-sex schools has generally been limited to a concern for girls taking 'O' and 'A' levels and for those who might attend university, rather than enter skilled apprenticeships or further training in the engineering sciences. Yet the extent of gender differences in these craft subjects at CSE can be seen in the statistics. In 1978, for example, only 540 girls passed CSE in metalwork compared with 50,493 boys; and 2126 girls took technical drawing compared with 73,461 boys.[46]

Secondly, the emphasis upon the gender differentiation of academic subjects covers the class bias of the school system, which is hidden within the findings of the report. All girls are treated as identical, as are all boys. The only other factor referred to is that of the type of school, but the main body of the report does not discuss the differences between them. In the appendices the DES report shows that physics was offered to 90–100 per cent of grammar school girls (mixed and single sex) but only 37 per cent of mixed secondary modern and 11 per cent of single-sex secondary modern school girls. While 33 per cent of girls in single-sex grammar schools and 29 per cent of mixed grammar school girls took physics, a paltry 3 and 4 per cent of girls in mixed and single-sex secondary modern schools did. The differences regarding *type of school* attended are critical to subject choice especially in subjects such as physics, chemistry and other high status 'academic' subjects. The greatest advantage of single-sex over mixed schools is in the comprehensive school group, and that difference is only 5 per cent more girls taking physics and 6 per cent more girls taking chemistry. Yet the differences regarding types of schools were not used in the report except as a means of statistically adjusting the data since most of the single-sex schools in the sample were grammar schools.

The differential impact of single-sex schooling on different social classes in different types of schools was investigated by Douglas and Ross using the National Survey of Health and Development data.[47] Here they found that the majority of middle-class children in their sample attended single-sex grammar schools whilst over half the manual working class attended secondary modern mixed schools. The sex-segregated grammar schools had the advantages of having small class sizes, more resources and high school leaving age with more of the pupils coming from middle-class homes than the mixed grammar schools. This applied especially to the boys' schools. Using class origins, type of school and the results of reading and mathematics tests administered at 11 and 15 years, what Douglas and Ross discovered was that middle-class boys, and both boys and girls of the manual working classes stayed on longer and got better 'O' level results if they attended single-sex rather than mixed grammar schools. Middle-class girls, in contrast, were at a considerable advantage at mixed grammar schools, which might be because girls' grammar schools were under-resourced and the curricular options were limited. At grammar school level therefore, the interests of middle-class girls opposed those of working-class girls. In the secondary modern schools again the middle-class girls stayed on longer in mixed schools than in single-sex schools, while for all other pupils there was no difference between co-educational or single-sex schools. Douglas and Ross leave the reader to decide whether the academic advantages of co-education for middle-class girls outweigh the disadvantages of mixed schools for all boys and working-class girls at grammar school level. Certainly there does seem to be a conflict between the results obtained here and those offered later in the DES survey. Unfortunately Douglas and Ross could not study the impact of comprehensive schools. The growth of co-educational comprehensive schools in contrast to the single-sex grammar school has certainly contributed to what Glennerster called the 'snob value' of single sex schooling,[48] because if anything the single-sex direct grant schools had become even more restricted in social class intake educating a very 'special elite'. The data are totally insufficient to make an adequate assessment of the *academic* or the *class* advantages and disadvantages of co-education and single sex schooling.[49]

Nevertheless, the concern for the academic disadvantages of co-education represents a re-evaluation of the operation of the ideology of equality of opportunity and its application to girls. More than that, it represents a challenge to the major premises of educational planning since the 1960s, especially since the growth of co-educational schools was accelerated by the re-organization of schooling along comprehensive lines. In 1975 some 87 per cent of state comprehensive schools were mixed and in contrast 74 per cent state grammar schools were single-sex. All but 3 of the 174 direct grant schools were single-sex. (In Scotland, by contrast, only 4.8 per cent of all pupils in educational authority secondary schools were in single-sex schools.) By 1978 the pattern of English and Welsh educational provision in the maintained sector was as shown in Table 1.[50]

Table 1   English and Welsh educational provision in the maintained sector, 1978

	Boys	Girls	Mixed	Total
Primary	33	31	20,577	20,641
All middle schools	7	7	1,289	1,303
All secondary schools (excluding middle)	472	482	3,156	4,110
Modern	93	95	451	639
Grammar	114	118	73	305
Technical	6	7	6	19
Comprehensive	235	248	2,594	3,077
Other secondary	24	14	32	70

Needless to say, the opposition to the comprehensive ideal was sometimes fought by attacking its co-educational status. For example in the *Bristol Evening Post* in 1964 the concern for sexual promiscuity, so feared by the middle classes, again reared its head.

One London co-education school headmaster considered his figures 'greatly improved' with only 16 pregnancies in a year among his 15 and 16 year old girls. The authorities at a large comprehensive co-educational school were shocked to discover that the babies of a number of girls found to be pregnant were actually conceived on the premises — at break times. Co-education brings sex right into the classroom.[51]

Yet according to Benn and Simon, in their study *Half Way There*,[52] there was no evidence of increased sexual promiscuity in mixed comprehensive schools. What they did find was a wide range of discriminatory practices restricting the principle of comprehensivation — the freedom of pupils to choose those subjects that suited their interests. They were particularly concerned to discover the lack of access for girls to engineering subjects such as building, woodwork, navigation, physics with chemistry, surveying, and technology courses. Half of the mixed schools limited some subjects to boys only and 49 per cent limited subjects such as catering, nursing, pottery, hygiene, jewellery making, domestic science and dancing to girls only. The future of effective comprehensivation in their view, was to *eliminate* such gender differentiation.

Support for genuinely co-educational schools came from a range of sources. The NUT, for example, stated in 1975:

> The Union recognises that the origins of separate education for boys and girls lie in the history and evolution of education. Schools traditionally educated boys and girls in ways which were intended to prepare them for quite separate and distinct roles in society as men and women: roles which were so different that the teaching methods and curricula were incompatible. Society has changed radically, however, and the pressures to give full equality to men and women in their work, their places in society and their responsibilities and commitments they face should be reflected in and catered for by the schools. To educate children in groups, segregated on the basis of difference of sex, is to effect an artificial separation which bears little or no relation to life at home or to society in general.... A pattern of education based on such separation and founded on concepts of allegedly distinguishable and incompatible needs of boys and girls no longer serves the interests either of society or of children.[53]

Thus while the current academic disadvantages of boys and girls within co-educational comprehensive schools might be recognized, the belief in the *transformative potential* of such schools (with, as Benn and Simon put it, an active attempt to change and improve those schools) was sufficient for some to continue to believe in the principle of mixing, albeit within a society still structured through class and gender inequality.

Yet support for the principle of mixing boys and girls in school came from other rather embarrassing quarters. Dale is famous for his three-volume study of the advantages of mixed and single-sex schools as seen by pupils and ex-pupils who were trainee teachers.[54] He stresses more than anything the social rather than the academic advantages of co-education since mixed schools more effectively reproduce what he calls 'normal life'; boys and girls get to know each other; they are less likely to suffer from the extremes of character defects such as the aggression of boys and the 'cattiness' or 'bitchiness' of girls. Less harsh discipline and more friendly relations exist within the happy family atmosphere of such schools. Overall, he argues, co-education leads to greater happiness since it is a less 'unnatural' or distorted educational experience. As in all such studies, Dale is careful to refer continuously to the 'objectivity' of his research even though a good deal of his analysis rests upon interpretation of interview material. The concern for 'performance' is again the criterion of assessment, except in this case it refers to social behaviour and attitudes.

His interpretation of his research data, as well as the limitations of his sample and style of inquiry, has been challenged by quite a few.[55] Perhaps the more sceptical response has been that offered by feminists who are aware of the conservative view Dale holds as to the differences between the sexes. In one paper he uses an analogy which he knew would infuriate 'members of the Women's Liberation Movement'.[56] He argues that men and women are biologically different not just in physiology but in temperament. Thus the aggression of men is compared with the 'bull who is master and defender of the herd while the cows peacefully graze and look after their offspring'. He argues:

> That men and women are complementary is a biological fact — that they also influence each other's conduct from the gift of flowers to the hurling of the kitchen utensils — is an inevitable accompaniment of life in a bi-sexual world. A family has a father and a mother; lacking one of these each member feels incomplete and unsatisfied, ... So it is with other institutions when they are one-sex — as we know from the homosexual activities in Public School and armed forces ... both the father figure and the mother figure are needed in our schools.[57]

For Dale, the advantage of mixed schools can be found precisely in their reproduction of life in a bisexual heterosexual world, in which men dominate and women learn to complement and subordinate themselves to men. With this image of 'normality' in mind, it is hardly surprising that co-educational schools are seen as nowhere near the ideal from a feminist position. The research of Michelle Stanworth, for example, confirms that it is the worst aspects of patriarchal relations which are reproduced within the mixed educational setting.[58] Girls have to cope with *devaluation* by teachers and by boys — teachers who cannot remember their names, who expect them to leave school and become good wives and mothers, or in the short term secretaries and nurses, and boys who see themselves as superior to the girls, who attract most of the teacher's attention, who ridicule the more academic girls and chase after the more amenable.

'Feminist' Responses to Co-Education

I shall now look briefly at three different responses to the data and arguments collected so far. The 'feminist' responses have not been unified; they comprise what I see as three strands each of which represents a different political position and a different concept of what education can do to reform or change gender relations. These three strands have the following features in common.
(1) They seek an educational programme of reform which will lead to the *equality of the sexes*. They argue for the importance of education and its potential to change attitudes and behaviour. However, the nature of the goal differs. For some equality of the sexes means equality of power sharing, for others it means equality in difference, or equality of opportunity. The actual *elimination* of gender as a category in education as an overall goal is not really discussed by any of the three groups, and yet it is the one goal which Eileen Byrne argues (and I would agree with her) will challenge women's subordinate position at a fundamental level.[59]
(2) All the various perspectives simplify the argument to its most essential features — that of mixed versus single sex schools. This is given legitimacy by the DES statistics which only use these two categories; yet as we have seen historically

there is a wide range of difference in the type of gender differentiation in available forms of secondary schooling. Today we can find schools with boarding provision for both sexes or one sex only; schools with two sexes mixed together in the sixth form only; schools that are paired on one site; or mixed schools in which leisure activities are divided and curricular options are gender differentiated. Rather than discuss the different *levels of degrees* or mixing and sex segregation, what characterizes nearly all the recent articles on this issue is their narrowing down of the discussion to the question: should boys be present or absent in the educational lives of girls? Physical segregation is the main issue rather than an overall assessment of when, where and how boys and girls are and could usefully be brought together or separated. Given the desire to change the sexist attitudes and practices of teachers, male pupils' behaviour and the stereotypical ambitions and self-evaluations of female pupils, the question needs to be asked: would a conscious explicit attack upon segregation, and a real attempt to reform teacher's ideology and practice, be more effective than increased or renewed sex segregation?

(3) There is more a concern to change the form of *female* education than to restructure boys' education in such a way as to 'interrupt' the socialization of boys into prejudiced men. In this sense, co-education versus sex segregation remains a feminist issue without challenging, in the present, the attitudes of men. Gender relations become identified as a *female* rather than a male problem, and one which appears to have had no historical basis within the development of a capitalist and patriarchal society.

(1) The liberal reformist perspective

The emphasis of this perspective (which is currently the most popular)[60] is on the academic failure of girls to achieve in science subjects, to get to universities and to receive a broadly based education. The assumption is that girls lack the motivation, the encouragement and the opportunity to break from the stereotyped notions of femininity and women's occupational futures. The attitudes of teachers, careers advisers, curricular texts and the pupils themselves must be challenged and opened out so that there is no division between female and male subjects, no association of non-femininity with academic success. The problem of girls' failure to enter any other than the most stereotypically female jobs is referred to as an 'educational problem' since if girls would only seize the opportunities offered in comprehensive schools, they could compete as equals with boys and men. Within this perspective is a belief in the individual nature of social mobility, of achievement and ambition. The problem for reformers, therefore, becomes one of breaking the hold of myths about women's role in society, of breaking the circulation of a sex role ideology which is seen as both the *cause* and *effect* of women's inferior position. The solution to such female underachievement is to sponsor single-sex classes in a compensatory fashion, giving girls a chance to develop for themselves their spatial and mathematical abilities, without the competition of boys, and to encourage them to see science and technology as female occupational areas.

Such a perspective offers considerable optimism to teachers and educational planners since it gives practical and 'do-able' advice at the classroom level. Yet there are several difficulties in this viewpoint. The first is obvious: *does the separation of girls from boys actually change patriarchal relations* or does it merely give girls access to the male world of science in which they still might only become technicians and laboratory assistants? Even if girls were to receive identical qualifications to boys there is no guarantee that they will obtain the same jobs as boys. As Wolpe has pointed out,[61] qualifications do not guarantee occupational entry especially in an occupational world in which male skills are defined as superior to women's and there is resistance from male dominated employers and trade unions.

The idea of compensatory education for girls in single-sex classes has been taken up by the Equal Opportunities Commission, and by ILEA educational officers. Further, it receives support from the various schools which are already trying it out. What is not yet clear is which category of pupil is to be encouraged to attend single-sex classes (that is, 'A', 'O' level or CSE candidates). There also seems to be an assumption that if the pattern of boys' and girls' examination passes, subject choice and entry rates into further training and higher education matched, then equality of the sexes would be achieved. However, the problem here is that such a view ignores the *class inequalities* of education and tends to assume that class oppression should be shared equally. The school is left in a social and political vacuum with none of its history of educational provision that constructed the problem of educational gender differentiation in the first place. Paradoxically the school is expected to challenge the reproduction of gender relations even though it itself was set up precisely to reinforce this. The limits of any compensatory programme need to be recognized at the outset.

(2) The Conservative Perspective

This position is most similar to that which has underpinned educational policy-making since the nineteenth century. Support for single-sex schools was justified, according to this perspective, because of the special role which women have as mothers and wives, which differentiates them from men. The ideology of equality of the sexes in this context has meant that boys' and girls' education should be different but equal. According to Sarah Delamont,[62] in the nineteenth century feminists were divided into two camps — which she called the 'separatists' and the 'uncompromising'. The analogy here is with the separatists who argued for a special education for girls to prepare them for their uniquely feminine futures. The most recent example of this view is to be found in Barbara Cowell's article.[63] She writes, 'if society is to benefit from the intellectual and emotional potential of women, we shall have to ensure that they retain without shame their different qualities', and this may well be achieved by a period of separate education. The conservatism of her view is best shown in the following quotation:

> There are few more grotesque sights than that of the supposedly intelligent women who neglects her children, in that short period when they really need her care in order to foster her own ambitions. Such neglect . . . breeds immense resentment in the next generation. Children with the resulting sense of deprivation spend the rest of their lives wresting from society, from their unfortunate partners, the special attention denied them in infancy.[64]

Girls, according to Cowell, should not be encouraged to *envy* men, just as the working class should not envy those with privilege. Further, they should not aim to study science since that is just helping to 'propel our civilization down the slippery slope into a completely materialistic way of life'. The tendency of girls to copy boys, and the tendency of women to aspire to the male world only leads, according to her, to unhappiness, high divorce rates and the too high expectations and vast disillusionment of women. In contrast, an emphasis upon gender specialities and differences would allow women to find solidarity amongst other women. This *solidarity* and the *polarity* it produces *between* men and women should be encouraged, in Cowell's view, through single-sex schools during adolescence when the physical, emotional and mental development of girls and boys differs.

What this position represents is a concern to reproduce the dominant set of gender relations through traditional forms of schooling, although Cowell is prepared to compromise with separate schools being on the same campus or very close together so that facilities for joint social functions can be held. The model school for her is the old single-sex grammar school since what was reproduced in such schools were traditional gender differences.

(3) The Radical Perspective

The most radical feminist position has recently been put in Sarah, Scott and Spender's article in *Learning to Lose*.[65] Using much the same data on mixed schools as the liberal reformist and conservative perspectives, these authors argue very forcefully against mixed schools on the basis that they are the main means of reproducing the patriarchal relations of domination. The academic and social relations of schooling, the atmosphere, the ideology of teachers and pupils all contribute to the subordination of girls. In their view it is the presence of boys which affects girls' low self-perception, low academic performance and narrow traditional feminine interests after school. The only way they can suggest to prevent such gender reproduction is through single-sex schools where the 'subversive potential' of schools can be appropriated for feminist practice. With an all-female teaching staff and a female head, girls will perceive that it is not impossible for women to hold power, and to enter the male world of science. They will learn to appreciate feminine friendships and a sense of solidarity with each other. Through the cultivation of 'sisterhood' girls will be able to 'grow and develop their human potential, they will be in a much stronger position to resist oppression in the wider society'.[66] Further, single-sex schools could attempt to counteract the traditional patterns of socialization the girls will have experienced in their homes. As Rosemary Deem summarizes their case:

> the emphasis on academic learning in a single sex school is not likely to convey to girls the impression that it is unimportant whether girls do well at school or not, a message which may already be conveyed to girls by their socialization and culture and not always contradicted in mixed schools.[67]

Sex segregation through schooling will not blur or eliminate the boundary between girls and boys but will allow girls to 'find their self confidence and to learn how to challenge patriarchal relations'. On the one hand, the absence of boys and their jokes, their ridicule of girls, their absorption of the teachers' energy, their competitive spirit and their aggression, and, on the other hand, the cultivation of a feminist consciousness within all-girls' schools leads the authors to support the principle of sex segregation, without reference to the impact this might have upon boys. They recognize that what they are suggesting is radical, but do not think they are being utopian:

> We are assuming that universal single sex education for girls would completely resolve the problem of sexism in education but in an age where co-education is heralded as a symbol of progress, it must be made clear that while it may represent progress for boys, for girls it represents a defeat rather than an advance.[68]

Conclusion

I have tried to show that the issue of co-education and single-sex schools is not just a contemporary but also a historical debate which has involved notions of what the relations between the sexes should be in an educational system which was already class divided. The use of single-sex schooling had been the major form of reproduction of gender relations — relations that constituted the bourgeois ideal of the family form, of male hierarchy and female dependency and subordination. Co-education represented a variation on that form of reproduction — never a radical alternative to the nature of the relations between the sexes. The pattern of educational provision was, therefore, essentially one of gender segregation and differentiation either physically or through the provision of separate classes, activities and curricular options. The nature of differentiation between boys and girls differed between social classes in terms of the type of subjects to be studied. For the working classes, the differentiation is most acute in the craft subjects studied; in the middle classes the science and arts split ws the most significant aspect of the gender divide. At no point historically was there an attempt to set up an equal (that is, identical) education for boys and girls.

The evidence for the impact of single-sex and mixed-sex schools must be taken in the context of the type of school discussed, the types of school subjects and the social class origins of pupils before we can adequately decide on the basis of evidence rather than political perspective which type of schooling would benefit girls. Yet even then what will we say about the *education of boys*? The feminist ideals for girls' education, of whatever variety, do not leave a clear strategy as to how to overcome *male prejudicial attitudes* to women. The question remains, are patriarchal and sexist attitudes a female or a male problem? A separate strategy for one sex does not, in my view, challenge the overall reproduction of dominant gender relations. We may merely *interrupt* it by using, for our own purposes, a pre-existing form of schooling. Gender as a basis for allocating individuals will not disappear as an educational or a social variable if schools or classes are allocated to one or other sex, nor will the inequalities of social class, which distinguish the educational experiences and future work lives of working-class and middle-class girls. What the three perspectives offer are ways to change the *form* of reproduction of gender relations: they do not challenge the *causes* of what it is that is reproduced. In other words, they focus on changing the modality of transmission of gender relations without changing *what* should be reproduced. We do not surely want to change the nature of 'femininity' as a concept but rather to abolish it as a social construct into which children are socialized. But we can only do this by understanding the meaning and significance the concepts of gender have within patriarchal relations in the family and the waged labour process in advanced capitalism. There is a danger if we do not understand the location of schooling within this political and economic context that we will be naively optimistic in believing that educational reform can change society.

As a political strategy, the support for single-sex education should recognize that small single-sex schools are unlikely to receive resources equal to those of the larger mixed schools in the current climate, especially when it comes to the funding of expensive science, technology and craft courses. Nor are girls' schools likely ever to achieve equal status to boys' schools unless the economic and political basis of patriarchal relations is challenged, since within such relations what is 'female' will always be defined as inferior. Similarly, compensatory educational programmes will run into conflict with the closed nature of the labour market and its gendered structures.

The implications of feminist struggles over sex segregation for class struggles over education cannot be ignored, or seen as separate. Single-sex schooling was part of the reproduction of class relations, in just as significant a way as were the different types of school and curricula provided through secondary schooling. The history of class reproduction, of class relations and bourgeois privilege includes, not as a marginal but as an integral feature, the reproduction of bourgeois family forms (of the norms of heterosexuality, female virginity, and marriage) as well as particular concepts of masculinity and femininity which held together the gender division of labour within paid employment and family life. Support for single-sex schools or sex segregation, therefore, has class connotations. In particular, we may find ourselves pushed into a position of supporting the private single-sex schools against state comprehensives, irrespective of the class selection and privilege involved. Further, we have to be careful that we do not attack comprehensive schools for failing to achieve a programme of reform which, in my view, they were never designed to do, that is, restructure the relations between the sexes in such a way as to eliminate gender as an educational discriminator. Their historical role so far has been to facilitate different 'interests' and 'needs' without taking on the reform of those 'needs' and 'interests'.

Genuine equality of the sexes has not yet been an educational goal and if it is now to become one, should we not, first of all, set up major educational reforms in teacher education, in in-service training programmes to reshape teachers' classroom practice, redesign the curricula and rewrite text books, etc. Should we not try to re-educate parents and employers? Should we not try to uncover the hidden forms of reproduction of gender relations, especially those which underpin the ideologies of parental freedom of choice (which led middle-class parents to choose single-sex schools), of student freedom of choice and of teacher neutrality. In the context of such a programme of educational reform, in my view it will be the co-educational comprehensive schools that will have the resources to offer a more equal education to boys and girls and will have the facility for bringing to the fore the issue of gender discrimination and prejudice, for both male and female pupils and teachers.

Notes

1 NEWSOM, J. (1948) *The Education of Girls*, London, Faber and Faber.
2 *Ibid*, p. 110.

3 BLAND, L., McCABE, T. and MORT, F. (1979) 'Sexuality and reproduction: Three 'official' instances', in BARRETT, M., CORRIGAN, P., KUHN, A. and WOLFF, J. (Eds) (1979) *Ideology and Cultural Production*, London, Croom Helm.

4 NEWSOM, J., *op. cit.* (Note 1) pp. 158–9.

5 MINISTRY OF EDUCATION (1945) 'The nation's schools: Their plan and purpose', Pamphlet No. 1, London, HMSO.

6 WEINBERG, A. (1981) 'Non-decision making in English education: The case of single sex secondary schooling', paper presented at the British Sociological Association Conference, Aberystwyth.

7 DAVID, M.E. (1980) *The State, Family and Education*, London, Routledge and Kegan Paul; DYEHOUSE, C. (1981) *Girls Growing Up in Late Victorian and Edwardian England*, London, Routledge and Kegan Paul; BURSTYN, J.N. (1980) *Victorian Education and the Ideal of Womanhood*, London, Croom Helm; PURVIS, J. (1980) 'Working class women and adult education in nineteenth century Britain', *History of Education*, 9, 3, pp. 193–212; PURVIS, J. (1981) 'The double burden of class and gender in the schooling of working class girls in nineteenth century England, 1800–1870', in BARTON, L. and WALKER, S. (Eds) (1981) *Schools, Teachers and Teaching*, Barcombe, Falmer Press.

8 These points are more fully developed in ARNOT, M. (1981) 'Towards a political economy of women's education', paper presented at The Political Economy of Gender Relations in Education Conference, OISE, Toronto. ARNOT, M. (1982) 'Male hegemony, social class and women's education', *Journal of Education*, 164, I, pp. 64–89.

9 See MACDONALD, M. (1980a) 'Socio-cultural reproduction and women's education', in DEEM, R. (Ed.) (1980) *Schooling for Women's Work*, London, Routledge and Kegan Paul; MACDONALD, M. (1980b) 'Schooling and the reproduction of class and gender relations', in BARTON, L., MEIGHAN, R. and WALKER, S. (Eds) (1981) *Schooling, Ideology and the Curriculum*, Barcombe, Falmer Press.

10 SHAW, J. (1974) 'Finishing school: Some implications of sex-segregated education', in LEONARD BARKER, D. and ALLEN, S. (Eds) (1976) *Sexual Divisions and Society: Process and Change*, London, Tavistock.

11 *Ibid.*, p. 134.

12 See also SHAW, J. (1980) 'Education and the individual. Schooling for girls, or mixed schooling — a mixed blessing?', in DEEM, R. (Ed.) (1980) *op. cit.* (Note 9).

13 DES (1975) 'Curricular differences for boys and girls', *Educational Survey No. 21*, London, HMSO.

14 DAVID, M.E., *op. cit.* (Note 7).

15 Other factors included religion since several mixed schools were set up by religious foundations (such as the Quakers) or by individual philanthropists. See TURNER, B. (1974) *Equality for Some*, London, Ward Lock.

16 For a brief review of information on girls' schools, see Report of the Committee on Public Schools appointed by the President of the Board of Education (1942) *The Public Schools and the General Education System*, Chapter 8, HMSO.

17 OKELEY, J. (1978) 'Privileged, schooled and finished: Boarding education for girls', in ARDENER, S. (Ed.) (1978) *Defining Females*, London, Croom Helm.

18 *Ibid.*, p. 109.

19 *Ibid.*, p. 110.

20 TURNER, B., *op. cit.* (Note 15) p. 182.

21 This argument ties into that presented in ENGELS, F. (1972 edition) *The Origin of the Family, Private Property and the State*, London, Lawrence and Wishart.

22 Quoted in LAWSON, J. and SILVER, H. (1973) *A Social History of Education in England*, London, Methuen and Co., p. 344.

23 PUBLIC SCHOOLS COMMISSION (1968) *First Report Vol 1*, London, HMSO, para. 64.

24 *Ibid.*, para. 301.

25 RAE, J. (1981) *The Public School Revolution*, London, Faber and Faber, suggests that 60 out of 210 Headmasters Conference Schools had admitted girls, of which 26 were fully co-educational. These figures have been challenged by WALFORD, G. (1982), 'The "dual

student market" and public schools', paper presented at the BSA conference, Manchester. He suggests that of 211 HMC schools in Great Britain and Northern Ireland in 1981, 46 were fully co-educational and at least 72 admitted some girls at sixth form only.

26 WILBY, P. (1981) 'A parent's guide to private education', *The Sunday Times Supplement*, 22 and 29 November.

27 *Ibid.*, pp. 54–5.

28 *Ibid.*, p. 53.

29 BLANDFORD, L. (1977) 'The making of a lady', in MACDONALD-FRASER, G. (Ed.) (1977) *The World of the Public School*, London, Weidenfeld and Nicolson, p. 204.

30 *Ibid.*, p. 198.

31 PURVIS, J. (1981) *op. cit.* (Note 7).

32 DAVID, M.E. *op. cit.* (Note 7) p. 36.

33 PURVIS, J. (1981) *op. cit.* (Note 7) p. 111.

34 DAVID, M.E., *op. cit.* (Note 7) p. 137.

35 TURNER, B., *op. cit.* (Note 15) p. 182.

36 BOARD OF EDUCATION (1923) *Report of the Consultative Committee on Differentiation of the Curriculum for Boys and Girls Respectively in Secondary Schools*, Second Impression, London, HMSO.

37 ARNOT, M., *op. cit.* (Note 8).

38 BOARD OF EDUCATION, *loc. cit.* (Note 36).

39 DES, *op. cit.* (Note 13).

40 *Ibid.*, p. 16.

41 KING, W.H. (1965) 'Experimental evidence on comparative attainment in mathematics in single sex and co-educational secondary schools', *Educational Research*, 8, pp. 155–60.

42 OMEROD, M.B. (1975) 'Subject preference and choice in co-educational and single sex secondary schools', *British Journal of Educational Psychology*, 45, pp. 257–67.

43 DES, *op. cit.* (Note 13) p. 22.

44 COMMISSION OF THE EUROPEAN COMMUNITIES (1978) 'Equality of education and training for girls (10–18 years)' by BYRNE, E.M. *Education Series*, No. 9, Brussels.

45 *Ibid.*, p. 42.

46 DES (1976) *Statistics of Education*, Vol. 2, School Leavers CSE or GCE.

47 DOUGLAS, J.W.B. and ROSS, J.M. (1966) 'Single sex or co-ed? The academic consequences', *Where*, 25 (May) pp. 5–8.

48 GLENNERSTER, A. (1966) 'Comprehensive reorganization — will there be more co-ed schools?' *Where*, 26, (July) pp. 16–18.

49 For further confusing and inconclusive data, see SUTHERLAND, M.B. (1961) 'Co-education and school attainment', *British Journal of Educational Psychology*, 31, 2, pp. 158–69; WOOD, R. and FERGUSSON, C. (1974) 'Unproved case for co-education', *The Times Educational Supplement*, 4 October, p. 22.

50 Source: DES (1978) *Statistics of Education*, Vol. 1, Schools. In contrast, 1046 independent schools were single-sex out of 2220 such schools.

51 Quoted in HANSARD, (1964) Debate on Grammar Schools, 27 November.

52 BENN, C. and SIMON, B. (1972) *Half Way There*, Harmondsworth, Penguin.

53 Quoted in LAVIGUEUR, J. (1977) 'Co-education and the tradition of separate needs', in SPENDER, D. and SARAH, E. (Eds) (1980) *Learning to Lose*, London, The Women's Press.

54 DALE, R.R. (1969) *Mixed or Single Sex School*, Vol. 1 (1971); *Mixed or Single Sex School: Some Social Aspects*, Vol. 2; (1974) *Mixed or Single Sex School: Attainment, Attitudes and Over-view*, Vol. 3, London, Routledge and Kegan Paul.

55 See DEEM, R. (1978) *Women and Schooling*, London, Routledge and Kegan Paul; SHAW, J., *op. cit.* (Notes 10 and 12), and SARAH, E., SCOTT, M. and SPENDER, D. (1980) 'The education of feminists: The case for single sex schools', in SPENDER, D. and SARAH, E. (Eds) (1980) *Learning to Lose*, London, The Women's Press.

56 DALE, R.R. (1975) 'Education and sex roles', *Educational Review*, 27, 3, pp. 240–8.

57 DALE, R.R. Vol. 1, *op. cit.* (Note 54) p. 114.

58 STANWORTH, M. (1981) *Gender and Schooling*, Women's Research and Resource

Centre, London, Pamphlet No. 7.
59 BYRNE, E. (1978) *Women and Education*, London, Tavistock.
60 See ARNOT, M. (1981) 'Cultural and political economy: Dual perspectives in the sociology of women's education', *Educational Analysis*, 3, 1, pp. 97–116 for further discussion of this perspective which I call the 'culture perspective' in sociology of education.
61 WOLPE, A.M. (1978) 'Girls and economic survival', *British Journal of Educational Studies*, 26, 2, pp. 150–62.
62 DELAMONT, S. (1978) 'The contradictions in ladies' education', in DELAMONT, S. and DUFFIN, L. (Eds) (1978) *The Nineteenth Century Women*, London, Croom Helm.
63 COWELL, B. (1981) 'Mixed and single sex grouping in secondary schools', *Oxford Review of Education*, 7, 2, pp. 165–72.
64 *Ibid.*, p. 166.
65 SARAH, E., SCOTT., M. and SPENDER, D., *op. cit.* (Note 55).
66 *Ibid.* p. 65.
67 DEEM, R., *op. cit.* (Note 55) p. 75.
68 SARAH, E., SCOTT, M. and SPENDER, D., *op. cit.* (Note 55) p. 70.

6.   The Conservative School? Sex Roles at Home, at Work and at School

Sara Delamont, University College, Cardiff

> In assembly the lower school is addressed by the Senior Mistress, Mrs Marks. Pupils are told they will soon be given a form to take home — school wants the phone number of where mother works. Mrs Marks says that if they are ill or have an accident, school tries to get mother. The school try not to bother father, because he is the head of the family, his wage keeps the family while mother's is only for luxuries, so try to contact mother. They are not to go home alone. They must report to the Deputy Head and they will probably be taken home. They are too young to decide if they are too ill to manage. If there is no-one at home — mum, granny or auntie — they will be put to bed at school.

This homily was recorded in a comprehensive in a northern city in 1978.[1] This chapter uses such data to argue that in the past decade schools have shown themselves to be more conservative about sex roles than either homes or wider society. This argument is crystallized in that homily. The official voice of the school is claiming that male work is economically crucial and female work is frivolous, in a city where women's labour force participation is high, and in a neighbourhood where one-income families are poor families. Local employers make extensive use of female labour and the pupils in the audience know their mother's wages are not for luxuries, yet the school harks back to some golden age when mothers were always at home to care for ailing offspring.

The chapter begins with some evidence of the conservative sex-role ideologies offered by schools in Britain and the US. Material on childrearing and the world beyond schools is then presented to reveal some of the contrasts with schools. The third section offers one possible explanation for the current conservatism in schools, relating it to my notion of the 'double conformity' trap (Delamont and Duffin, 1978). The chapter relies on data different from those in Delamont (1980) and shows that the argument can be sustained from other researchers' findings as well as the author's.

Conservative Schools?

The argument that schools are presenting pupils with a more conservative, and indeed an out-of-date, view of male and female roles has been made in more detail elsewhere (Delamont, 1980) than is possible here. The claim that schools are conservative where sex roles are concerned depends on one's definition of conservatism. In this chapter conservatism means that schools are treating males and females as much more different than the outside world does. In particular, schools are seen as conservative because they:

1   segregate the sexes very rigidly;
2   steer boys and girls to different curricular areas;
3   offer outdated role models, emphasizing males as breadwinners and
     females as unemployed housewives;
4   fail to challenge pupils' *own* sex-role stereotypes;
5   enforce exaggeratedly different clothes, demeanours, language uses
     and activities.

These five areas of sex segregation will be shown in outline. The rationale here is
that while the sexes may be differentiated in all these ways in wider society, schools
are more rigid in their enforcement. For example, Katherine Clarricoates (1980)
observed a school's reaction to a 7-year-old boy who preferred dolls to cars and
baking to football. She reports:

> Mrs T . . . reads Michael's 'diary' for the morning: 'On Saturday I helped
> my Mum bake a cake and I made a dress for my doll'. The teacher
> despairs: 'Couldn't you play football or something?'

This shows a *mother* allowing a boy to enjoy cooking and sewing, while the school
objects to it. The teacher is more conventional than the outside world where male
chefs and male clothing designers are highly paid, highly acclaimed and even
knighted. (*The Sunday Times Magazine* of 17 January 1982, for example, was
devoted to five leading chefs, four of whom were men.) Schools which reject males
who desire to cook or girls who fight have fallen behind the outside world in their
attitudes to sex roles. The education system's rejection of sexual equality is
illustrated here with data on interaction inside schools; the effects of the rejection
are well-documented (for example, Sutherland, 1981).
    Everyday life in schools can be analyzed in many ways. Here five aspects are
separated, for clarity:

1   formal organization of schools;
2   management and disciplinary strategies;
3   content and strategies of teaching;
4   socializing and sociability;
5   pupils' attitudes and behaviours.

These are generalized headings which separate different aspects of school life to
enable us to scrutinize them for stereotyped sex roles being perpetuated.

Formal Organization

Under this heading there is evidence that most schools segregate the sexes as a
normal part of their organizational arrangements. Typically lavatories, changing
rooms, cloakrooms and even playgrounds are sex-specific. Class lists and registers,
record cards and sports facilities are usually separate. For example, Carol Buswell
(1981) writing of a comprehensive school in the north of England says:

> Most of the daily routines of the school revolved around, and underlined
> the pupils' sex . . . the registers were not alphabetical but divided into

girls' names and boys' names. Several teachers had boxes for work labelled 'Boys' and 'Girls' and, of course, record cards in the pastoral offices were pink and blue.... In the school a pupil could be classified by sex up to *twenty* times in a day — day after day.

Similarly Katherine Clarricoates (1980) reports that at Dock Side primary school: 'separation begins in early infancy with separate playgrounds, separate toilets, separate lines, even separate lists on registers.' These segregations are taken for granted. Yet there would be an outcry if schools listed 'black' children separately from whites on registers or assigned different school entrances. Separation of playgrounds by sex is reported by Harman (1978) and Wolpe (1977), coloured record cards by King (1978), and differential registration listing was found in all six ORACLE schools (Delamont, 1980).

Pupils in schools are frequently required to dress differently by sex. Ninety per cent of secondary schools have uniforms, and these clothe the sexes differently — usually skirts for girls and ties and blazers for boys. Many schools forbid not only female pupils but also women teachers to wear slacks (King, 1978; Delamont, 1980). For example, at one 9–13 middle school studied during the ORACLE project we heard the following staffroom conversation: 'about whether the women teachers could wear trousers. Apparently Miss Tyree won't have the staff wear them and when she was asked by the Deputy before she said: 'No' and then 'Are they all transvestites?' Skirts restrict girls' activities, while boys are made uncomfortable by blazers and ties. New boys at secondary and middle schools observed during the ORACLE project were reminded to wear both, and forced to keep them on during most school activities. Improperly knotted ties were a source of friction, not suffered by girls in these six schools because they did not have to wear ties. For example, at Kenilworth 11–14 school in September we observed new 11-year-old pupils arrive for an English lesson with Mr Gordon:

> He began the lesson by sending one or two of the boys out because their ties weren't tied properly. He said that he was getting very fed up with the way he could always see the boys' top buttons and could very rarely see the tips of their ties as they had them so short. He warned them that next time he wouldn't just send them out to re-do them he would give them a punishment as well.

Clothing rules are one visible way of dividing males and females in school: track suits would be much more practical than school uniforms and would emphasize similarities.

Another aspect of the formal organization of the school which emphasizes sex differences is the staffing structure. Males hold the positions of authority (heads, heads of departments, caretakers), while women occupy subordinate roles (class teachers, secretaries, dinner ladies, cleaners, playground attendants) as Keith Scribbins (1977) has shown. Buswell (1981) says girls only saw a senior woman teacher when they had personal problems.

Children see an exaggerated sexual division of labour in the schools, the effects of which have not been investigated yet. While the organizational separations may be trivial in their effects, they are one aspect of sex-role stereotyping. The management and disciplining of pupils are equally divisive.

Management and Discipline

Stressing differences and rivalries between males and females is one common teacher strategy to manage and discipline pupils. For example, Buswell (1981) reports that in 'more than half' the classes she studied 'teachers requested pupils to line up and enter and leave the room by sex'. Ridiculing one sex or the other, or labelling the activities of either males or females, is equally common. Buswell (1981) recorded one teacher saying: 'If the ladies would put away their combs, we'll begin.' King (1978, p. 52) offers some nice examples of one teacher strategy for organizing and controlling pupils, such as the teacher saying, 'Boys close your eyes. Girls creep out, quietly get your coats. Don't let the boys hear you!' This shows a teacher using sex segregation to motivate and to control children, a combination which is extremely common. Later King (1978: 68) quotes the use of ridiculing a child as a disciplinary strategy with the comment, 'Oh, Phillip is a little girl. He's in the wrong queue', again a very common teacher usage. Katherine Clarricoates (1980) quotes teachers saying: 'Why don't you boys do as you're told; you don't find the girls behaving like that', and 'Let's have a game of general knowledge: boys against girls.' Teachers in the two 11–14 schools studied during the ORACLE project also resorted to gender comparisons to try to motivate boys. For example, at Kenilworth in the A form's French lesson with Miss Stockton, there was an oral, informal vocabulary drill. The observer noted: 'The girls particularly seemed to enjoy this and to have remembered the vocabulary . . . . This provoked a comment from Miss Stockton to the effect that "Are the girls the only brainy ones?"' At Waverley School too, teachers tried to motivate boys by comparing them to girls. For example, one class was in the school library with Miss Southey, one of the English staff. We recorded: 'Most of the girls have chosen to take books out. The teacher says: "All the girls are taking out books, but not one boy yet. Can't the boys read in this class?" A few boys take books out.' Whether these comments are as effective as they are common is unclear.

Contents and Strategies of Teaching

This heading covers the actual teaching which is the official *raison d'être* of schooling. Analysis of the content of the curriculum, in terms of syllabuses, textbooks, worksheets, exam papers, and other written materials and of the spoken academic content of lessons shows that there is a great deal of implicit and explicit sexism. One striking example of the explicit sexism in the US comes from Mary Lee Smith's (1978) research in Fall River, Colorado. In a social studies lesson she recorded a teacher of American History saying:

> I'm glad to see you people are really thinking about these issues. Some of you chose to talk about women's lib. Equal pay for equal work is OK, but we all know that if the woman works, that means that some-one else has got to take care of the kids, and that means day care centers, and then we've got the government controlling the development of our kids, and then what happens to the family? (1978, pp. 12–13)

This is perhaps an extreme example of teacher prejudice being presented as facts.
While that discourse is peculiarly American in its content, British versions of

the underlying sentiments are not hard to find. For example, Carol Buswell's (1981) research in a comprehensive school included an analysis of the humanities curriculum in the lower school. She found that in 326 pages of text, 'man' was used to mean male 252 times. There were 169 pictures of males and only 21 of women; 102 individual men were covered but only 14 women. Among the pupil tasks were the following:

> Look at the pictures of the clothes the Romans wore. Would they be easy for your mother to wash if you were a Roman?
> Find the name of this make of car. Your father or brother will probably know. Ask them.
> Make up a poem about a very rich man or a very poor man.

Similarly 9-year-olds in one middle school were told that when they got a new book they should examine the title page. The name and status of the author would be informative. A chemistry book whose author is head of science in a big grammar school will be acceptable 'but if the author is just a housewife — *well!*'

The collection of papers on women and science education edited by Alison Kelly (1981) contains several papers which analyze the sexual biases of science curricula in schools. Jan Harding (1981), for example, reports that girls seem to do worse than boys in science exams when multiple-choice questions are used. Judy Samuel (1981) has analyzed the text and illustrations in school science books and argues that too many of them show males engaged in doing science while women watch.

The author has only once seen a teacher deliberately teach something non-sexist. In one German lesson:

> Mr Baden goes over Frau/Fraulein, says he does not know if the Germans have a word for Ms now. Asks what 'Ms' means. Pupils volunteer 'Miss' and 'Mrs', no one knows. He explains how Ms is deliberately designed to avoid the distinction.

During the ORACLE research, I found that the more the teachers tried to 'humanize' lesson content, or relate academic topics to homely, familiar things, the more likely sex stereotyping was to creep in. Perhaps the most extreme example came in a music lesson for 11-year-olds:

> The children are to draw some instruments. Mr Tippett began by saying that violins were like young ladies. They are fairly big at the top, they are small-waisted, and they have got ... er.
> 'Big Bums!' came a suggestion.
> 'Yes that is right — large bottoms' said Mr Tippett.

Such 'teaching' carries over into the next category — socializing and sociability.

Socializing and Sociability

Several researchers have noted how praise for personal appearance and clothing is more frequently aimed at girls than boys — but that girls only receive compliments when they wear dresses rather than trousers. Girls' personal appearances are a legitimate subject for comment: 'Girls are told "You've done enough fussing. I know you're all filmstars." Miss Tweed asked about the school photographer, "Did he faint with delight at such loveliness?"' Similarly, at the beginning of an English lesson for 11-year-olds:

> The children come in from hockey or PE with their hair wet, and the lesson begins with a good deal of cheerful chatter about how the whole place looked like a ladies' hairdresser.

All the children have wet hair, but it looks like a ladies' hairdresser, not a barber's.

Another aspect of this 'banter' is the way in which many teachers joke about hostility between boys and girls, and so do not make it problematic. The French teacher who asks how many siblings pupils have, and replies 'Poor Lad' to the boy with four sisters is lightening the tone of French classes, but 'Lucky Thing' would serve as well and challenge pupils' own stereotypes. The acceptance of pupil hostilities typically arose when a boy had to take a seat near girls, or vice versa. For example, in two different French lessons for 11-year-olds, a similar remark was made.

> Mrs Stockton said *'Comment allez-vous?'* to the children. One of the boys had not managed to find a seat, and the only vacant chair was next to a girl. Mrs Stockton said: 'I'm afraid, young man, you'll have to risk life and limb and sit next to this young lady. If she attacks you just let me know.'

Next lesson the same boy was left standing and again was told he would 'have to risk life and limb and go and sit next to Lee Anne. If she attacks you, tell me.' Ball (1981, pp.27–8) reports a parallel incident where a girl called Dorothy is directed to a seat by Wally. She says, 'Ugh, I'm not sitting next to him', and moves the desk to create a gap between her and the boy.

Handling pupil reluctance to sit, or work, in co-educational groups is a problem for teachers, but ridicule does not seem to cure it. Pupils' own sexual prejudices cause educational problems, as the next sub-section shows, and little is done to counteract them.

Pupils' Sex Role Attitudes and Behaviours

Several authors have found hostility between male and female pupils (for example, Clarricoates, 1980; Shave, 1978). Karkau (1976) found 9-year-olds rigorously avoiding each other. Girls told him that if they went near boys, 'People will think you're "in love"'. Boys said 'if you touch a girl you get "cooties" or "girl-touch"', a form of pollution which had to be ritually cleansed.

Such avoidances have educational consequences. When pupils are forced to work in mixed groups they do not actually carry out the tasks. In science labs for example, the girls read out the work sheet while the boys do the manipulation of apparatus. Boys do the work, while the girls call them 'Magnus Pike' or its equivalent. Sarah Tann's (1981) research on primary school children's performance on small-group tasks reinforces earlier work. She found that no pupils chose to work in mixed groups, and girls were more likely to form groups of similar ability levels than boys were. The older the pupils involved, the more marked were sex differences. Girls were more consensus-oriented than boys, and also more hierarchical. Boys' groups had more arguments, and were more democratic. These findings reveal how important pupils' own prejudices can be for academic achievement, and how little is known about them.

In the US Leila Sussman (1977) has argued that pupils' own stereotypes become more extreme in 'progressive' classrooms and, therefore, supposedly 'democratic' or 'open' teachers paradoxically encourage sexist (and racist) pupil cultures in their schools. This is such a serious argument that it urgently needs investigation in Britain.

Across these five aspects of schooling, there is evidence of sexual segregations, sexist attitudes, and polarized stereotypes. Similar data are being gathered in the US and Canada (Lorimer and Long, 1979; Russell, 1979; Eichler, 1979; Pyke, 1977 and Stake *et al.*, 1978). Louis Smith (1978) has argued that sexism is 'institutionalized' (p. 48). Overall, schools are a conservative force where sex roles are concerned. The next section turns to the world beyond school.

Parents and Employers

This second part of the paper deals with parents and employers. The argument is that parents and employers are more tolerant of idiosyncratic behaviour from males and females than schools are. The evidence here is thoroughly shaky, and the argument must be seen as an hypothesis which urgently needs research. However, material of two different kinds is available. There are accounts by women who have taken unusual educational and career paths about the sources of their inspiration; and there is the research by John and Elizabeth Newson and their associates (1978). The Newsons have carried out the most thorough survey of childrearing we have in Britain, and have published an interesting paper on sex role stereotyping. They used two kinds of data, interviews with 700 mothers of 11-year-olds and with those children at 16. The Newsons argue that by seven 'the reported preoccupations and hobbies of the two sexes have drawn apart.' However, they also point out that interests and aptitudes are 'popularly conceptualized in a sex-loaded way'. For example, many girls were skilled with sewing machines, but this is not classified as a 'mechanical' interest. This means that the data we have are already sex-typed before they are presented to us.

The Newsons found that mothers were uncomfortable if their children were behaving in 'cissy' or 'tomboyish' ways. However,

> the mother does in fact defend the child's right as an individual to oppose cultural norms. She did teach him knitting or embroidery, encourage his music, buy the girl football boots. In this she is carrying out what we have … discussed as a distinctive aspect of the parental role: to protect the child's individuality from the indiscriminating urgency of cultural demands … the mother has to be aware of the power of the culture — sometimes … because the peer group is less protective of the child's individuality than she is.

When the Newsons enquired into what activities parents shared with children, they found that 43 per cent of mothers shared an interest with a son, and 46 per cent of fathers shared one with a daughter. Mothers and sons shared 'shopping, table games, cooking, tennis, reading football magazines, school subjects, making things, swimming and needlework.' Fathers shared with girls 'gardening, car-cleaning, model cars, swimming, serving in [father's] shop.' While no-one could deny that the *overall* impression gained from the Newsons' work is of strong cultural pressures on children to conform to traditional sex roles, there is also evidence of parental protection of 'unusual' interests and aptitudes. When we turn to the accounts provided by women in 'unusual' jobs, it is this protection which turns out to be crucial. Similarly, John and Elizabeth Newson (1977, pp. 177–8) found that whereas most parents regarded boys' educational success as more important than girls', there was a minority even in the working class who believed strongly in education for women:

> Now *I* don't see why a housewife should be illiterate. And that's the truth
> — because when they come home from school, the first person they ask if
> they want to know anything is their mother, isn't it?
>   He doesn't believe in this tale that education's wasted on a girl, he
> says that's ridiculous.

Parental encouragement for non-typical treatment of children is being supported by the mass media. Most recently *Woman* (27 June 1981) argued that sexually stereotyped childrearing was prehistoric, and gave an enthusiastic report on a non-sexist playgroup and plugged six unstereotyped books for young children.

My other source of data is autobiographies of people in 'unusual' jobs. In these parental support is *reported* as crucial. Of course the accounts cannot be taken as data in an unproblematic way, but we have few data of a reliable kind on high-achieving women in non-traditional jobs, or on males in 'feminine' occupations. These accounts rarely mention encouragement from schools or colleges but frequently mention familial or employer support and encouragement. John Curry and Robin Cousins in ice-skating, David Shilling in hat-designing, and several male hairdressers all report familial encouragement, but not educational.

In November 1978 *Cosmopolitan* ran an article on women engineers which included the following:

> Interest in making things begins with tinkering around in childhood.
> Maureen Smith, for example, assembled, aged $2\frac{1}{2}$, a knock-down tricycle
> her father had brought home to construct for her.... By eight or nine
> Maureen was souping up Triang toy buses and lorries with Triang toy
> sports car engines. A lot of girl engineers have engineering fathers.

Cosmopolitan contrasted this with the attitude of 50 headteachers invited to meet the Engineering Industry's Training Board. One head announced he would not encourage any girl pupil into engineering, and some schools refused to let the EITB in to talk to pupils. A similar picture emerges from Coote (1979), a book about 13 women in traditionally male jobs. The Production Engineer reports that her parents were tolerant and she had plenty of support from Marconi while training. The heavy lorry driver's father helped her to get her first job, and once employed she has kept jobs steadily for seven years. The forester was 'encouraged by her father' (p. 39) and got employment from the Forestry Commission. The plumber and the car mechanic were trained on TOPS courses, without much difficulty. One of the accountants featured had an accountant mother, and was steered to the occupation by a private vocational guidance service. The gardener learnt horticulture from her father and obtained a GLC apprenticeship. Of 13 women, only one (the car mechanic) reported hostility from workmates. Only one (the astronomer) reported being introduced to her subject by her school — in this case a physics master inspired her study of science. All the reports mention surprise from workmates at having a girl or woman alongside them, but the overall message is that workmates *can* learn to live alongside a woman in the workplace.

Even the highly traditional women's magazines have taken to presenting women in male jobs more enthusiastically than schools. For example *Woman's Realm* (28 April 1979) featured two women pilots and a naval officer, a station master and a Deputy Lord Mayor; and *Woman's Own* (24 June 1978) 12 women working as undertaker, lifeboatman, sports commentator, bus driver, film camera-man, carpenter, milkman, lorry driver, surgeon, pilot, gardener and plumber.

While these are not academic data, they do show that the schools have failed to accommodate to changing sex roles in the wider world. The next section offers an explanation for the way schools are today, in contrast to their role in the past.

The 'Double Conformity' Trap

The phrase 'double conformity' was originally used to describe a period in the history of St Luke's, the girls' public school where I collected data for my PhD (Delamont, 1973). It is fully explained and demonstrated elsewhere (Delamont, 1978). Briefly, the idea is that when the nineteenth-century pioneers of women's education were struggling to open up schools, higher education and high-status occupations, they faced a dilemma. They had to prove that females were intellectually equal to males (for example, in algebra) *and* demonstrate that achievement did not make females immoral, unmarriageable, and unladylike. The pioneers, therefore, insisted that staff and students in the early schools and colleges worked harder than men, *and* paid scrupulous attention to etiquette. These early educationalists kept girls away from boys and played down 'masculine' pursuits. No whisper of impropriety was allowed to sully the occupants of educational institutions, or the whole cause could be lost.

The history of the King Edward VI School for Girls in Birmingham (which was founded in 1883 sharing the boys' school building) tells us how 'the doors into the girls' part' were 'kept carefully locked' (Vardy, 1928, p. 24). Two small girls once followed a caretaker into the boys' building and were caught. This was 'a most dire offence, the true heinousness of which did not dawn on them till long afterwards'. Similarly, when Bedford got a girls' high school in 1882 it 'began at 9.15 so that boys and girls should not throng the streets at the same time' (Westaway, 1932, p. 23). The new school had a music room with glass partitions so 'a mistress sitting at a table in the space outside correcting her exercise books would be able to chaperone several masters at once' (p. 35). Schools had to be careful about introducing games, allowing acting, the advent of the bicycle, and the dress of their pupils. Public disapproval could be strongly expressed. In 1881 the Edgbaston Girls' High School (founded in 1876) staged a cricket match against another school. A local paper published a very hostile cartoon and wrote:

> We must confess to being in ignorance of the exact social standing of the pupils at the Edgbaston High School for Girls, but the name would seem to cover a good measure of gentility. It therefore strikes us as rather odd that the management should lately have allowed the schools' cricket match against the first eleven of a kindred establishment to be reported in the sporting columns of the local Press. The report describes the hitting as having been very spirited on both sides. We can only hope that when these muscular maidens come to be married no similar entry will have to be made in the chronicle of their connubial felicity. The report does not describe, unfortunately, the costume of the players, but we may assume that its feminine character must have been greatly modified. If the exhibition was in any sense public, we must confess to a preference for those less pretentious places of education where English lasses used to be taught modesty, if little science. (Whitcut, 1976, p. 43)

At a girls' school in Tunbridge Wells in 1911, 'an annual gym display was started for an audience of mothers only and fathers who were doctors' (GPDST, 1972, p. 32). This was sensible care against public censure. When in 1896 the ladies' bicycle reached Bedford the headmistress of the High School faced a dilemma:

> It was during these years that bicycling came into fashion for women; the first High School girl who was seen on a bicycle was considered to be bringing great disgrace on her school and the Head Mistress received a request from a number of parents to make a rule forbidding such behaviour ... very soon bicycling became most popular, but it was considered very important to have one's skirts of suitable length, and duly fastened down with elastic to keep one from showing too much of one's legs. (Westaway, 1932, pp. 50–1)

Dress outside school was also important, as we can see from the headmistress of the Oxford Girls' High School writing in 1872 that some girls had been seen without gloves: 'I have heard it objected to more than anything and it certainly gives our enemies reason to say that the High School makes girls rough and unfeminine'. (GPDST, 1972, p. 73). While these examples of fussiness seem laughable today, they were obviously necessary then. The middle and upper classes believed that men and women were very different, and that their education should be single-sex, based on different curricula, and organized on different lines. The pioneers had to accept some of the beliefs to obtain access for girls to the curricula normally offered to boys: to provide a worthwhile, academic education instead of frothy accomplishments. By worthwhile subjects, the pioneers meant, in effect, subjects which had previously only been taught to middle- and upper-class males, especially classics (Latin and Greek), mathematics (rather than simple arithmetic) and, later in the nineteenth century, science too. The desire for an academic education with typically male content, which would give women access to the high-status subjects which dominated the ancient universities, was eventually gratified.

In the nineteenth century double conformity was a conscious, deliberate strategy — packing the front rows of meetings with frail-looking ladies, for example — to achieve definite ends. Sara Burstall (1933, p. 65) summarized the *conscious* use of double conformity as a strategy. A Girton student from 1878 to 1881, she says: 'Two things mattered intensely; first that we should do well in our work...; second, that we should avoid giving offence or injuring the cause by any breach of conventional behaviour....' My argument here is that since 1945 double conformity has ceased to be a strategy of feminists to obtain feminist ends, and become an end in itself. This is how we can make sense of the draconian rules in the girls' grammar schools studied by Dale (1969). Many of the incidents we see in today's schools, such as Mandy Llewellyn's (1980) rich data from two girls' schools in the Midlands, show this clearly. In the secondary modern school there was relatively little attempt to teach the pupils outside the 'A' stream anything — the academic half of double conformity was absent — but the emphasis on ladylike behaviour was present. This is demonstrated by the school's reaction to Sandy, a violent misfit with girls and staff. The welfare officer was seen removing her from a corridor brawl saying: 'You're too old for fighting now. Look at the mess your hair and clothes are in. The least you could do is try and look nice.'

One of the senior women teachers told Mandy Llewellyn that she felt the school had failed with Sandy: 'She's got no decency. I can't see her ever settling down and making a loving home.... I don't mean she should only be a wife and mother ... but she won't get anywhere as she is....'

Llewellyn comments:

> The school had 'failed', not simply at the formal, but crucially subordin-ated, level of producing basic skills and qualifications, but also at the informal 'hidden' dominant level of transmitting ideologies of appropri-ate values and behaviour to the adolescent working-class girl.

What was once a strategy for middle-class, clever women, has become an end in itself for the non-academic, working-class girl. Double conformity has been transmuted.

There is a parallel here with another aspect of schooling — the gymslip — which illustrates the same point. At the turn of the century the gymslip was a highly charged symbol of liberation. It meant no corsets, and participation in sport — it was worn in private for athletic activities (Atkinson, 1978). In the inter-war period it was worn in schools for lessons, and symbolized the high-status grammar school education (for example, Holtby, 1936). By the 1950s it was old-fashioned and despised, and today it is chiefly notorious as a pornographic symbol like stocking tops. Other aspects of school life have changed their public meanings in the same way. Attempting to inculcate ladylike behaviour in females is now as anti-feminist as schoolgirl spanking movies. A similar argument can be made about boys' team games and their spurious association with character building (see Delamont, 1980).

Conclusion

Carol Dyhouse (1981, p. 175) has concluded that the nineteenth-century schools and colleges 'furnished space for self-development, affording some relief from the constrictions of family life'. The argument of this paper has been that today's schools are not providing this space — and the sooner they do so, the better they will be as academic and personal environments for teachers and taught.

Notes

1 Some of the data in this paper come from the ORACLE project, based at the University of Leicester, 1975–80. The full report of the research is forthcoming in Galton and Willcocks (1982). I am grateful to a wide range of colleagues for comments on this paper; the faults are entirely my own. Myrtle Robins typed this paper from my scruffy manuscript with her usual skill and care, and I am very much in her debt.

References

ATKINSON, P. (1978) 'Fitness, feminism and schooling', in DELAMONT, S. and DUFFIN, L. (1978).

BALL, S. (1981) *Beachside Comprehensive*, Cambridge, Cambridge University Press.

BURSTALL, S. (1933) *Retrospect and Prospect*, London, Longmans.

BUSWELL, C. (1981) 'Sexism in school routines and classroom practices', *Durham and Newcastle Research Review*, 9, 46, pp. 195–200.

CLARRICOATES, K. (1980) 'The importance of being Ernest ... Emma ... Tom ... Jane', in DEEM, R. (1980).

COOTE, A. (1979) *Equal at Work?* London, Collins.

DALE, R.R. (1969) *Mixed or Single Sex School?* London, Routledge.

DEEM, R. (Ed.) (1980) *Schooling for Women's Work*, London, Routledge.

DELAMONT, S. (1973) *Academic Conformity Observed*, unpublished PhD thesis, University of Edinburgh.

⸻ (1978) 'The contradictions in ladies' education', in DELAMONT, S. and DUFFIN, L. (1978).

⸻ (1980) *Sex Roles and the School*, London, Methuen.

DELAMONT, S. and DUFFIN, L. (Eds) (1978) *The Nineteenth Century Woman*, London, Croom Helm.

DYHOUSE, C. (1981) *Girls Growing Up*, London, Routledge.

EICHLER, M. (1979) 'Sex-role attitudes of male and female teachers in Toronto', *Interchange*, 10, 2, pp. 2–14.

GPDST (1972) *The Girls' Public Day School Trust, 1872–1972: A Century Review*, London, GPDST.

GALTON, M. and WILLCOCKS, J. (1982) *Leaving the Primary Classroom*, London Routledge & Kegan Paul.

HARDING, J. (1981) 'Sex differences in science examinations', in KELLY, A. (1981).

HARMAN, H. (1978) *Sex Discrimination in School*, London, NCCL.

HOLTBY, W. (1936) *South Riding* (reprinted 1974), Glasgow, Fontana.

KARKAU, K. (1976) 'A student teacher in 4th grade', in GUTTENTAG, M. and BRAY, H. (Eds) *Undoing Sex Stereotypes*, New York, McGraw Hill.

KELLY, A. (Ed.) (1981) *The Missing Half*, Manchester, Manchester University Press.

KING, R. (1978) *All Things Bright and Beautiful?*, Chichester, Wiley.

LLEWELLYN, M. (1980) 'Studying girls at school', in DEEM, R. (Ed.).

LORIMER, R. and LONG, M. (1979) Sex role stereotyping in elementary readers', *Interchange*, 10, 2, pp. 25–44.

NEWSON, J. and NEWSON, E. (1977) *Perspectives on School at Seven Years Old*, London, Allen and Unwin.

NEWSON, J. *et al.* (1978) 'Perspectives in sex-role stereotyping' in CHETWYND, J. and HARTNETT, O. (Eds) *The Sex Role System*, London, Routledge.

PYKE, S.W. (1977) 'Sex role socialization in the school system', in CARLTON, R. *et al.* (Eds) *Education, Change and Society* Toronto, Gage Educational.

RUSSELL, S. (1979) 'Learning sex roles in the high school', *Interchange*, 10, 2, pp. 57–66.

SAMUEL, J. (1981) 'The teachers' viewpoint', in KELLY, A. (Ed.).

SCRIBBINS, K. (1977) 'Women in education', *Journal of Further and Higher Education*, 1, 3, pp. 17–39.

SHAVE, S. (1978) 'Ten ways to counter sexism in a junior school', *Spare Rib*, 75, p. 42.

SMITH, L.M. (1978) 'Science education in the Alte schools', in STAKE, R. (Ed.).

SMITH, M.L. (1978) 'Teaching and science education in Fall River', in STAKE, R. (Ed.).

STAKE, R. *et al.* (Eds) (1978) *Case Studies in Science Education*, Champaign, Urbana, CIRCE, University of Illinois.

SUSSMAN, L. (1977) *Tales out of School*, Philadelphia, Temple University Press.

SUTHERLAND, M. (1981) *Sex Bias in Education*, Oxford, Basil Blackwell.

TANN, S. (1981) 'Grouping and group work', in SIMON, B. and WILLCOCKS, J. (Eds) *Research and Practice in the Primary Classroom*, London, Routledge.

VARDY, W.I. (1928) *King Edward VI High School for Girls, Birmingham, 1883–1925*, London, Ernest Benn.

WESTAWAY, K.M. (Ed.) (1932) *History of Bedford High School*, Bedford, privately printed.

WHITCUT, J. (1976) *Edgbaston High School 1876–1976*, Birmingham, privately printed.

WOLPE, A.-M. (1977) *Some Processes in Sexist Education*, London, WRRC.

7. Gender, Patriarchy and Class in the Popular Education of Women

Rosemary Deem, The Open University

Richard Johnson defines popular education as that which:[1]

> means starting from the problems, experiences and social position of excluded majorities, from the position of the working people, women and black people. It means recognizing the elements of realism in popular attitudes to schooling, including the rejection of schooling.... It means working up these lived experiences and insights until they fashion a real alternative. (p. 813)

This chapter examines a form of education for adults which starts precisely from the problems, experiences and social position of an excluded majority, women. This form, or rather forms, is not schooling, not compulsory, not organized primarily by the state, and is almost entirely conducted in single-sex groups. The education so provided can be considered 'popular' because women have organized it for themselves, albeit with some help from outside agencies, and because it recognizes, although not necessarily for the purposes of achieving radical change, that women share certain interests and hold a common position in society, particularly in the home, the family and community, hence building on women's 'lived experiences'. In order to achieve such education, women have had to struggle hard against dominant patriarchal power relations which try to confine women to the private sphere of the home and the family, away from the public sphere of production and formal political power. Just how hard this struggle has been is indicated by the following passage from Goodenough's book about the history of the Women's Institute (WI) in Britain. Talking of the early years of the WI after its formation in 1915, Goodenough notes:[2]

> When Branston WI started, one member recalls, 'Though people gave in their names, it was difficult to say straight off if you would join. You didn't know how the Husband would take it, if he would let his wife go out at night.' (p. 19)

The organizations with which this paper is concerned are influenced strongly by gender and by patriarchal relations and ideology. They are not unconnected with class relations, or hegemonic culture and ideology, although none of them transmits knowledge directly concerned with production. They open up a small public space for women outside the home[3] but are located outside, although not unregulated by, the state, in what Gramsci termed 'civil society'.[4] But the four women's organizations are not merely of importance because of the reasons outlined. They are also important in that they transmit knowledge and provide education largely outside the formal education system. Further, they provide an opportunity to examine not only the extent to which institutions in civil society are a means of exercising bourgeois hegemony, as Gramsci claimed,[5] but also whether they are subject to patriarchal hegemony (that is, the variety of material and ideological ways in which men dominate women) and help win consent to that domination of women by men. Much of the recent work by sociologists of education and by feminists tends to collapse the categories 'schooling' and 'education' into one, so that what happens to women (or men), after they leave full-time school or full-time higher/further education, has been little considered by educational theorists. Yet some of the same theories used to analyze schooling are equally relevant to adult education outside the formal system. For example, it has been argued by Shaw[6] and by Spender and Sarah[7] that single-sex schooling helps women to reject gender stereotypes and male dominance and make non-traditionally female curriculum choices. Yet, as we shall see in this study, single-sex educational groups of adult women are not necessarily oppositional or feminist. Further, if we look at adult women's education, that which is not organized primarily by the state does not necessarily differ much from that which is (this does not refer to course to private *schooling* which is a rather different matter), although there is in some quarters a belief that popular education outside the state is likely to be more radical.[8]

Women in Groups as an Educative Context

This chapter draws on a study conducted during 1980–81 in Milton Keynes, a new city in South-East England. The study involved, amongst other things, an examination of all clubs, organizations and other groups in the city which admitted women as members, and also of formal adult education evening and day classes. The research methods used included observation, questionnaires, structured and unstructured interviews and analysis of documents and pamphlets relating to the groups and organizations studied. Most of the evening and day classes and a few of the organizations were open to both sexes, although it was noticeable that where women were present they were either a tiny minority or formed over three-quarters of the group. The organizations, as opposed to the classes, in which women predominated had a number of striking features:

1   a high educational content in many activities;
2   use of traditional pedagogies;
3   passive learning styles;
4   exhibiting of deviance by some women from group activities, for instance, talking during the presence of a main speaker or demonstrator, about something unrelated. This has some similarities to certain forms of resistance by school pupils (Willis, 1977),[9] except that the women's attendance is voluntary whereas pupils are compelled to attend;
5   a strong concern with 'keeping order'.

Not *all* of these characteristics, of course, apply to *all* the groups.

Women's organizations and clubs have been examined by sociologists, for example, in Stacey's classic community studies of Banbury.[10] Research on leisure has noted their importance for women[11] and the 1973 Russell Report[12] on adult education recognized the relevance of voluntary groups in the provision of educational opportunities for adult women. Women's groups too are often connected with community and caring activities as observed by Gregory:[13]

> It is likely that women, during periods of having no paid employment have been particularly resourceful in their use of local communities to further ends that seem to them socially desirable. The work of the Women's Institute and voluntary caring organizations demonstrate an aspect of this.

It is also essential to consider why women are attracted to forming and joining such groups, and a number of possible reasons suggest themselves.

1   That men are more willing to allow women to attend educational or 'caring' or 'home-making' activities than alternative social activities such as dancing, mixed events or pubs.[14] This, of course, does not affect women who live apart from men, although as Stanley points out,[15] cultural expectations about what activities women should engage in affect all women, with 'policing' of many public and social meeting places by men, to ensure that women are either made to feel uncomfortable or keep away altogether. What men, collectively, 'allow' women to do has many connections with control over female sexuality, as well as the notion of women as male possessions in a marriage contract.

2   Largely because of the considerations outlined above, but also because of constraints like lack of childcare facilities, there *are* relatively few other places where women may meet socially with other women.

3   Women in public places in British society are expected to behave in circumscribed ways if in mixed company, for example, no gossiping or frivolous talk; lowering of eyes when talking to men who are not relatives; care about dress; not being alone after dark.[16] These constraints apply much less to educational contexts and women-only groups.

4   For women who are not engaged in paid employment, or only in part-time paid work, women's groups represent a chance to escape from the privacy and isolation of the household, even though the topics considered are often oriented towards 'home-making'.

5   Women actually enjoy and seek out the company of other women.

6   Women are interested in self-education.

Four Women's Groups: A Classification

The four groups referred to here can be classified according to Raymond Williams' categorization of types of cultural formation.[17]

1   Specializing formations which focus on a particular activity or interest, for example, Flower Arranging Club.

2   Alternative formations which develop where there is no existing

institutional provision; for example, Women's Institute Branch and Poundhill Women's Club.

3   Oppositional formations where there is active opposition to established Institutions and the conditions prevailing in these; for example, Women's Section of the Labour Party (not all such sections could be placed in this category; some would fit better into 2.)

Women's Organizations: State, Civil Society and Class Hegemony

The four groups outlined have a number of common features. They are all single-sex (the Flower Arranging Club does not debar men), they all hold meetings at regular times and in public halls or meeting places (which itself may impose formality on the knowledge transmission process), and all set out to transmit knowledges of various kinds to their members. All four have clear sets of objectives which affect their organization, social relations and pedagogy. As Dale says, 'The framing of objectives in *any* particular way has consequences for what can be taught and how it can be taught' (p. 75).[18]

In addition to these similarities, the four groups also operate in what Gramsci in his 'Notes on Italian History' called civil society;[19] 'hegemony of a social group over the entire national society exercised through the so-called private organizations like the Church, the Trades Unions, the schools etc.); it is precisely in civil society that intellectuals operate' (p. 56).

As Anderson recognizes, there are problems with the notion of civil society.[20] It is neither wise nor helpful to do as Althusser has done, which is to dismiss altogether the distinction between state and civil society, and to see all institutions like family, church and school as ideological state apparatuses which, 'form sectors of a single controlling state which is the precondition for any distinction between public and private' (pp. 136–7).[21]

For, as Anderson notes,[22]

Once the position is adopted that all ideological and political superstructures — including the family, reformist trade unions and parties, and private media — are by definition state apparatuses, in strict logic it becomes impossible and unnecessary to distinguish between bourgeois democracy and fascism. (p. 36).

Indeed, as Miliband points out, in bourgeois democracy ideological institutions retain a high degree of autonomy and are, therefore, more able to conceal the extent to which they do belong to the system of capitalist power.[23]

One of the most interesting characteristics of the four organizations under discussion is their almost total distance and removal from the production process. Further, although all four are regulated or influenced to some degree by state institutions, the extent of this and its effects are different in each case. The Flower Arranging Club and Poundhill Women's Club both meet in state or local authority funded premises, which impose certain restrictions on duration of meetings, which require formal officers for groups or some allocation of legal/administrative responsibility to individuals, and may restrict activities because of fire and safety regulations and local regulations about use of premises. The WI branches do not receive any grant from an LEA, as some branches do, but the WI National

Federation has received a grant from the DES since 1948 for the advancement of women's liberal education,[24] part of which goes towards the costs of its permanent educational establishment at Denman College. Past Presidents of the WI and other members have sat on government committees, and the WI (and its urban counterpart, the Townswomen's Guild) is often consulted by government, local authorities and quangos as well as by the civil service, on matters concerning women, home-making and rural life. In its early years the WI was taken for a while under the wing of the Board of Agriculture, and during both World Wars made a major contribution to food production at the invitation of the Ministry of Agriculture. Yet despite this apparent degree of incorporation, individual WI branches remain able to decide their own activities and have never been slow to criticize government and local authority policies especially those relating to women, family, marriage and children, as well as to many other issues of general interest.[25] The Labour Party Women's Section has a clear connection to the state through its parent organization's concern with parliamentary democracy as one means of achieving political objectives and its relation to a major political party, which operates both within the state and within civil society. However, this particular section is the closest to an oppositional feminist group of the four considered, and its activities owe little to state regulation. Indeed some of those activities are precisely directed against the policies of state institutions.

Despite the existence of some state regulation or connections to the state (the 'political society . . . or coercive apparatus to bring the mass of people into conformity with the specific type of production and the specific economy at a given moment'[26]) all the groups do have a private existence outside the state's sphere of influence. At the same time the groups offer women a toe-hold on the political world which Stacey and Price call the public sphere (which conflates state and civil society, since for these authors private refers to the domain of the family).[27] It is worth trying to separate state and civil society, however, even though, as Stacey and Price note:[28]

> the developments in capitalist formation and in the control exercised by the state, including paradoxically the legislation that has sought to liberate women . . . have had the effect of dissolving the hitherto existing distinction between the private and the public domains. (p. 11)

Although the theoretical boundaries of private and public spheres overlap with the theoretical boundaries of state and civil society, what Stacey and Price suggest is equally applicable to the state/civil society distinction; there is empirically no clear dividing line between state and civil society, but the two are not synonymous. Regulation by and contact with the state, for the WI for instance, does not mean that the WI is an ideological state apparatus, totally dominated by and determined through, agencies of the state.

Gramsci argues that the private organizations of civil society are means through which hegemony is exercised by fractions of the dominant classes.[29] So the next issue for consideration is the extent to which the groups discussed here actually exercise class hegemony and the extent to which some of these groups or members within them resist or refuse consent to that hegemony. The issue of how women may be assigned to a class position is a particularly difficult question to tackle, as Barrett recognizes when discussing the relation between gender and class structure.[30] Barrett suggests that there are four different theoretical positions on this relationship.

1 Gender is completely absorbed by class relations.
2 Gender divisions form a separate system of oppression from class relations.
3 The relation between gender and class can be discovered empirically.
4 It is possible to achieve a theoretical reconciliation between gender and class (Barrett's own position).

There is not the scope for a full-scale discussion of this issue here. However, Barrett's argument that whilst the wage relation of capitalism and the simultaneous separation of home and workplace have contributed to the present division of labour, sexual divisions also existed in various forms prior to capitalism, is a useful shorthand at this point.[31] Barrett proposes that women have a dual relationship to the class structure: one through their position in the labour force or their ownership of capital, and the other mediated for most women through their dependence on men and responsibility for domestic labour and childcare. Hence working-class women may be exploited directly by capital through their own wage labour and indirectly through dependence on a male breadwinner's earnings, whilst bourgeois women may own but lack control over capital.[32] Having previously established some gender similarities, we can now consider class position amongst members of the four organizations.

Flower Arranging Club

About half the members engaged in wage labour, some part-time. A considerable number of the remainder is retired from wage labour (that is, over 60 years); the rest are full-time housewives and mothers. Typical occupations of those in wage labour are clerical and secretarial, shopwork, with a few from the caring professions. This club does not consciously transmit hegemonic culture and ideology but certainly does not challenge the supremacy of fractions of the dominant class, even though few of its members are visibly present.

Women's Institute

The branches found in the research area vary in their class composition but typically fall into the following groups: local bourgeois women — owning business or involved in farming on a large scale (that is, not peasant farmers), or with husbands who own businesses or are managers; functional intellectuals — working in, or had previously worked in, professions; working class — mostly in clerical, secretarial, shop, cleaning and low-paid health/welfare work; full-time housewives. Bourgeois women were prominent, not numerically but intellectually, in most branches. The National Federation of Women's Institutes has been dominated since its inception by bourgeois women and by titled or untitled members of landed county families.[33]

Thus the organic intellectuals (Gramsci says 'every social group ... creates together with itself, organically, one or more strata of intellectuals which give it homogeneity and an awareness of its own function'[34]) of the WI are members of the dominant classes. And it is the WI, of all the four groups, which is the most overtly concerned with transmitting hegemonic values, ideology and culture, and the most regulated by the state.

Poundhill Women's Club

This club has the most restricted catchment area. Most members fall into two categories: wage labour in secretarial, clerical, shop, or technical/professional work; full-time housewives. All but a tiny number are married to men who are in professional, managerial or technical jobs rather than in manual work.

The less formal structure of this group and the diversity of its discussions, plus its lack of contact with or direct regulation by the state, mean that identification of organic intellectuals is difficult, although they are visited by organic intellectuals from other groups (for example, a local doctor, academics and experts) on occasions. The group does not often challenge class hegemonic values, ideologies or culture. One of its more striking characteristics is the concern of its members with upward social class mobility, through the purchase of previously rented Development Corporation housing, dress, values and other aspects of life-style; insofar as the group facilitates this concern, then it is subject to hegemony and acceptance of the rule of the dominant classes as well as the capitalist mode of production.

Women's Section of the Labour Party

This group is overwhelmingly composed of what Gramsci terms functional intellectuals: 'All ... are intellectuals ... but not all ... have in society the function of intellectuals ... in which their specific professional activity is weighted ... towards intellectual elaboration.'[35] Most members are in some way involved in education, principally as teachers. Of those few currently not engaged in paid labour teaching was a significant area of previous paid work. This group thus has an orientation to organic intellectuals opposed to class hegemony (socialist and Marxist writers, feminist writers) and, of the four groups is the only one actively working against the imposition of class hegemony, not only on its own members but on the working class as a whole, with a particular focus on women.

Cultural Production

The cultural role of all four groups is not to be found in cultural reproduction because such a concept is far too deterministic to accurately describe their activities, the lived experiences of their members, and the differences between those members' own lives and those experienced by their mothers. As Raymond Williams notes,[36] hegemony itself is not static or singular, has a highly complex set of internal structures and, does not just passively exist as a form of dominance.[37] It has continually to be renewed, recreated defended and modified. It is also continually resisted, limited, altered and challenged by pressures not all its own (p. 112).

If any of the groups were simply reproducing class hegemony or reproducing resistance to class hegemony, then their activities would be exactly the same as those of the members' own mothers and organizational predecessors. But even for the WI, the most class hegemonic of them all, there have been considerable developments since 1915,[38] and individual branches have some autonomy from county and national organization. Willis, discussing cultural reproduction and cultural production, says:[39]

> We should investigate the form of living collective cultural productions that occur on the determinate and contradictory grounds of what is inherited and what is currently suffered through imposition but in a way which is nevertheless creative and active. Such cultural productions are experienced as new by each generation, group and person (p. 49).

This seems to describe much more accurately what each group is doing than the notion of cultural reproduction, and could equally well be applied in analyses of formal schooling as in adult self-education, something which MacDonald, despite the title of her paper, actually moves towards in her discussion of the complex ways in which identity formation takes place in girls, in and out of school.[40]

The Process of Educational Transmission in the Four Women's Groups

The main focus here is on the ways in which educational knowledge is transmitted in each of the four groups. Bernstein suggests that educational knowledge is realized through three message systems, namely curriculum, pedagogy and evaluation, and that two main types of educational knowledge code or sets of educational principles underlie the shaping of these three message systems.[41] The two codes are the collection code, in which the organization of knowledge has a high degree of boundary maintenance (for example, between high- and low-status knowledge or between teacher and taught) and the integrated code where boundaries are blurred (for example, between areas of knowledge, or between teacher and taught). As with most theoretical work, this requires some modification when applied to empirical material but is nevertheless helpful in understanding the educational differences among the four groups.

Flower Arranging Club

The club has formal officers and a committee. It meets monthly in the evening, using a public hall. Members pay an annual subscription plus a fee for each meeting. Meetings usually consist of a demonstration or talk by a visitor plus some 'business' conducted by the committee and opportunities to purchase materials from a stall. Members sit in rows of chairs in the body of the hall. The visitor speaks and demonstrates from the platform, is formally introduced and thanked and usually provides an opportunity for questions after completion of the talk or demonstration. The Chair*man* (sic) or secretary tries to keep the members quiet if they become too noisy. The curriculum has a narrow range — arranging flowers, choosing and growing suitable flowers and care and display of household plants. Pedagogy is traditional; members are not encouraged to interrupt a speaker or demonstrator, do not take notes, and may only ask questions when specifically instructed to do so. Those sitting at the back of the hall may have difficulty in hearing or seeing what is going on at the front of the platform, and one consequence is that such members may engage in their own conversations, not necessarily about flower arranging. Such conversations are apt to grow louder in any quiet parts of the proceedings. There is some informal (not directed at the platform) discussion of the talk/demonstration after the speaker has finished. Demonstrators make use of the 'look and see how I do it' method rather than the 'this is how you might do it' method. Members have little chance to discuss their own efforts at flower arranging or their own ideas on the subject within the formal context of the meeting. The Club does however run some special classes separately for beginners. Those who get most from the club in terms of knowledge of flower arranging (as opposed to those who are more interested in sociability with other women) appear to be those with the most experience of the craft; absolute beginners might enjoy watching a demonstration but probably would not learn from that alone how to arrange flowers, which is actually quite a complex task.

Women's Institute

All branches have a president and a formal committee. There is also a complex county and national organization, which is mostly elected. Members pay an annual subscription, and for refreshments at each meeting. Meetings are held once a month; some branches meet in the afternoon and others in the evening. A public or church hall is normally used. Members sit in the body of the hall, with the president and speaker on a platform. Meetings usually take the following form: singing of Jerusalem; reading of minutes of the last meeting; the president stands on the platform and goes through any business — classes, arrangements for markets, visits to other branches, outings, county and national affairs, and fund-raising. Then there is usually a speaker or demonstration, followed by questions, a competition for members (for the best cake or soft toy or piece of embroidery, which members bring with them) followed by serving of tea. The curriculum is much wider than the flower arranging club, covering a wide range of rural and domestic crafts, from corn dollies to dressmaking and cookery, as well as discussion of topical issues related to the community, women's rights and citizenship; thus a variety of skills may be learnt and there is access to several different fields of knowledge. Classes are also run locally, by the county organization and at Denman College. Pedagogy is traditional; no questions are encouraged until the speaker has completed the talk or demonstration. Members do not write anything whilst listening and watching. Throughout the meeting the president keeps order with a bell. Nevertheless, like any classroom, and the Flower Arranging Club, the meeting has its deviants, who talk in whispers and from time to time burst into louder conversation, especially those in the back few rows. A 'buzz' of talk is almost always audible. Presidents of branches distinguish between 'good' and 'bad' branches according to the degree of ease or difficulty they experience in keeping the meeting to order. Members do have the opportunity to talk informally to the speaker and to each other when tea is served at the end of the meeting.

Poundhill Women's Club

The Club has a chairperson (very unusual terminology in a non-feminist women's group) and a formal committee. Membership is open to any women living on the estate the club is named after and there is a small membership fee. Meetings are held fortnightly in a community room attached to a middle school. There is no connection with any other group and it was started by a group of women new to the area who wanted to get out of their houses and meet other women socially, but at the same time learn something useful. The potential curriculum is very wide, and certainly not confined to domestic concerns; a variety of local people are approached to give talks about hobbies, the community, their job, a craft. Outings and meals out are also arranged, and the group does some fund-raising for good causes. There is no platform in the room used, members sit round in a circle and there is much less formality when a speaker attends than in either of the organizations discussed previously. Members may interrupt a speaker to ask a question and fairly lively discussions often ensue, without constantly referring back to the invited speaker after every contribution; the speaker is treated as an equal and in consequence pedagogy is much more informal, and the experience of members equally valid. There is relatively little concern with keeping order except at the very beginning of a meeting when business and minutes are dealt with. Partly for these reasons and partly because the meetings contain only about 15–25 women (as opposed to 60+ in the WI and Flower Arranging Club) there is no continual 'buzz' of conversation nor any deviant back row. Whereas the Flower Arranging Club and the WI may be seen to operate a form of collection code — classification of valid and non-valid knowledge, quite strong boundaries between teacher and taught, and a concern with keeping order — the Women's Club has moved towards a more integrated code, with weak boundaries between different areas of knowledge, little insulation of teacher from taught and little concern with maintenance of order.

Women's Section of the Labour Party

There is a formal committee because the relationship of the Section to the local Constituency Labour Party demands it. However, in reality the formal committee is operative only insofar as secretarial work goes, and even this is usually shared among several members. The Section is open to any woman who is a Party member or who intends to become one. Meetings are held once a month in the evenings. There is no separate membership subscription (party subscriptions are paid to a local branch, not the Section) and money is raised through a variety of activities when required. Meetings include an agenda and minutes and a discussion, which is usually led by a talk; a different chairperson is elected for each meeting. Members sit in a circle; proceedings are informal. The curriculum covers many political activities and interests, including feminist and socialist theories, direct action, positive action inside and outside the party, and consideration of members' own roles as women. Speakers are alternately group members or invited from outside, but are treated no differently from other members and may be interrupted and quizzed at any point. Sometimes a particular text is used as a basis for discussion, or a topical issue. Pedagogy is informal and sometimes almost invisible. Some collective work is presented. Members take notes if they wish, and most join in discussions at some length. This is the only group of the four which is both feminist and whose discussions relate to capitalist production, domestic life and childcare (the other three never mention childcare or capitalist production in any explicit way, although of course individuals may discuss these things informally) but in an oppositional way. There is no concern with order and when several people speak at once, their topics always relate to the main discussion. The existence of an integrated code is much more strongly indicated here than in the previous group, with very weak classification and framing of knowledge.[42] This is despite the fact that the group is part of a highly bureaucratic and hierarchical national political party not so far noted for highly democratized procedures.

It is useful to briefly compare the four groups with a conventional adult education evening class in 'O' level Sociology.

'O' Level Sociology Evening Class

This is a one-year course with an examination at the end, two-and-a-half terms of meeting for two hours once a week, plus homework. There are 20 students, paying a termly fee; most are women. The tutor is male. Students sit in rows of desks; the tutor talks from the table facing the class. Over half the time is taken up with a lecture, on which students take extensive notes. Discussion is at specified points except when someone has an urgent question or does not understand a point. The tutor spends much of the discussion period trying to wean people away from discussing their everyday experiences and to instead talk 'sociologically'. Most of the class seem uncertain what this is. The few male members dominate the discussion and the tutor's attention.[43] Some women rarely participate unless asked a direct question. Discussion does not flow freely but is referred back constantly to the tutor. The curriculum is determined by the relevant 'O' level syllabus and the interests of the tutor. Pedagogy is traditional and there are strong boundaries between teacher and taught as well as between 'commonsense' and 'sociology'. The formality and principles of transmission are similar to the Flower Arranging Club and the WI but the mixed group inhibits the women both from participating in the discussion and from discussion about other topics with their friends. This is congruent with the arguments and research presented by Spender in her analysis of the reasons why women prefer to talk to women.[44] It is also clear that the quality of the learning experience in the class is no better than in the Flower Arranging Club and the WI ; in all three the women are fairly passive although eager learners. Further, both the groups offer their members a say in what topics are discussed or demonstrated, whilst this option does not exist in the evening class. The comparison suggests that where women's own experiences, problems and social position have some influence on the educational context, (that is, the education is popular) although such education is not necessarily radical or oppositional, it does meet a real need amongst women and offer a positive if traditional learning and/or social experience, whether formally or informally.

Exercise of and Consent to Patriarchal Hegemony

The one question which remains to be asked about the four groups is the extent to which, as well as being subject to or resisting class hegemony, these groups also exercise or resist patriarchal hegemony. If we place the groups on a continuum from non-feminist to feminist, we find the following placings:

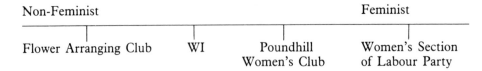

Non-Feminist   Feminist

Flower Arranging Club   WI   Poundhill   Women's Section
                                                  Women's Club   of Labour Party

As Stanley[45] and Barrett[46] both argue, what we need to do when examining the sources of women's oppression is to discover precisely what mechanisms operate to oppress women, who controls those mechanisms and to what extent they actually determine women's position and gender stereotypes as well as their power relationshiips to men. Whilst Stanley dislikes many of the deterministic aspects of theories about oppression by patriarchal structures, Barrett favours restricted use of the concept of patriarchy, utilizing it only[47]

> in contexts where male domination is expressed through the power of the father over men and over younger men [and] elements of what might properly be called patriarchal power in . . . for instance . . . the relations of the bourgeois family in the nineteenth century (p. 250).

but sees no role for the concept in explaining the whole of male domination over women. Beechey suggests that a satisfactory theory of patriarchy involves examining its forms and operation in historically specific situations and looking at the different forms of patriarchy which exist in present-day social institutions,[48]

> depending upon the role of the particular institution within the organization of the capitalist economy as a whole, the form of its material organization, and the form of ideology and power relations which prevail within it (p. 80)

and this formulation seems helpful here.

For the groups examined here, we have seen that they have no clear connection to the organization of the capitalist economy (although the WI operates regular produce markets), and that only one has any well-defined connections with, and regulation by, the state. It has also become clear that single-sex groups of women, whilst avoiding some of the problems of male language domination,[49] do not necessarily take on an oppositional character and do not always challenge the sexual division of labour, either through activities or through their existence as groups of women, even though to set up those groups may have represented a successful struggle over male dominance of certain women. Thus, the activities of the Flower Arranging Club and the WI rest heavily on a sexual division of labour in which women's main activities are domestically oriented just as those two organizations, overtly or covertly, are subject to class hegemony and give consent to that hegemony. As Stacey and Price, quoting Chamberlain's study of Fenland women, note, 'the Gislea women were clear that women have a special and separate contribution to make to parish affairs',[50] so the women in these two groups see their activities and their positions in semi-public life as legitimate because these can be linked to women's traditional roles. The other two groups, however, have started to move away from this position, perhaps because their members are younger and have had more contact with the modern women's movement. Their difference lies not only in their capacity to extend their discussions beyond domestic affairs or to a critique of women's position but also in their efforts to develop a more open and active mode of teaching and learning than is present in either the Flower Arranging Club or the Women's Institute branch. Also, in the case of the women's section, their organic intellectuals are either feminist or oppositional, or both. Yet the Flower Arranging Club and the WI offer much of value to women including informal as well as formal sociability and educational opportunities, even though some of the skills and knowledge they offer are either antiquated or socially devalued. In some cases the experience that holding positions of authority in organizations like the WI provides, has enabled women to enter public life at a more openly political level.[51] This suggests that like class hegemony, patriarchal hegemony is not static, has many complex structures, some of which are contradictory, and that the exercise of such hegemony is continually resisted, changed and modified. The Flower Arranging Club and the WI certainly do not reproduce patriarchal hegemony although they may culturally produce it. And whilst they may prop up some aspects of women's oppression, such as their position in the sexual division of labour, they challenge and take up others, such as the right of women to an independent social life and a place in civil society outside the home. Equally, neither the Poundhill Women's Club nor the Labour Party Women's Section successfully challenges all aspects of patriarchy in all social institutions; it is usually women themselves who have to arrange childcare whilst they attend meetings of those groups; it is often they who have to prepare a meal before going out, who have to re-organize their whole day or week in order to be an active member of their group. Despite the encouragement and confidence which the Labour Party Women's Section gives to its members, men still dominate the Constituency Party, hold many of the important offices in the party and form most of the successful candidates in local government elections. So each group is subject to, resists and adapts to different segments and aspects of patriarchy.

Women's Popular Education

Sociologists of education may have much to learn by looking sometimes at forms of education other than schooling. Women's adult education takes place in a variety of settings, transmits several different types of knowledge and offers different degrees of consent, resistance and adaptation to both class and patriarchal hegemony. Although the four groups which have been examined have many similarities, they display differences in modes of teaching and learning as well as in their curriculum, and not all of them are radical despite the undoubted popular character of their struggle for existence. Further, the analysis here emphasizes that the demand for single-sex forms of schooling for girls[52] may run into many difficulties and achieve less in terms of overcoming women's oppression than has been suggested by some writers, unless we begin to analyze in considerable detail the internal workings of a variety of all-female institutions and groups. Schooling, as Arnot points out when discussing the political economy perspective,[53] cannot be analyzed in isolation from other social institutions. It is only by examining an assortment of educational contexts that we can hope to fully understand the workings of class, gender and patriarchy both inside and outside education.

Notes

1 JOHNSON, R. (1981a) 'Socialism and popular education', *Socialism and Education*, 8, 1, p. 813.
2 GOODENOUGH, S. (1977) *Jam and Jerusalem. A Pictorial History of the Women's Institute*, Collins, p. 19.
3 STACEY, M. and PRICE, M. (1981) *Women*, Power and Politics, Tavistock.
4 GRAMSCI, A. (1971) (Trans. HOARE, Q. and NOWELL-SMITH, G.) 'Notes on Italian history', *Selections from Prison Notebooks*, Lawrence and Wishart, p. 56.
5 *Ibid.*
6 SHAW, J. (1980) 'Education and the individual: Schooling for girls, or mixed schooling — a mixed blessing', in DEEM, R. (Ed.) *Schooling for Women's Work*, Routledge and Kegan Paul.
7 SPENDER, D. and SARAH, E. (1980) *Learning to Lose*, The Women's Press.
8 See CENTRE FOR CONTEMPORARY CULTURAL STUDIES (1981) *Unpopular Education*, Hutchinson; JOHNSON, R. (1981a) *op. cit.*; JOHNSON, R. (1981b) 'Education and popular politics', *Society, Education and the State*, Open University, Unit 1, Course E353.
9 WILLIS, P. (1977) *Learning to Labour*, Saxon House.
10 STACEY, M. (1960) *Tradition and Change*, Oxford University Press; STACEY, M. *et al.* (1975) *Power, Persistence and Change*, Routledge and Kegan Paul.
11 PARRY, N. and JOHNSON, D. (1974) 'Sexual divisions in life style and leisure', unpublished paper given to British Sociological Association Conference, University of Aberdeen; ROBERTS, K. (1978) *Contemporary Society and the Growth of Leisure*, Longmans; DELAMONT, S. (1980) *The Sociology of Women*, Allen and Unwin.
12 DES, Committee of Enquiry (1973) *Adult Education: A Plan for Development*, HMSO.
13 GREGORY, S. (1982) 'Women among others — Another view', *Journal of Leisure Studies*, 1, 1.
14 DEEM, R. (1982) 'Women, leisure and inequality', *Journal of Leisure Studies*, 1, 1, pp. 29–46. See also DELAMONT, S. (1980) *op. cit.* and PARRY, N. and JOHNSON, D. (1974) *op. cit.*
15 STANLEY, L. (1980) 'The problem of women and leisure: An ideological construction and a radical feminist alternative', *Leisure in the 80s Forum*, Capital Radio, 26–28 September.
16 *Ibid.*
17 WILLIAMS, R. (1981) *Culture*, Fontana.
18 DALE, R. (1981) 'From expectations to outcomes in education systems', *Interchange*, 12, 2–3, p. 75.
19 GRAMSCI, A. (1971) *op. cit.*
20 ANDERSON, P. (1976/77) 'The antinomies of Antonio Gramsci', *New Left Review*, 100, November-January, pp. 5–78.
21 ALTHUSSER, L. (1971) 'Ideology and ideological state apparatuses', in *Lenin and Philosophy and Other Essays*, New Left Books, pp. 136–7.
22 ANDERSON, P. *op. cit.*, p. 36.
23 MILIBAND, R. (1970) 'The capitalist state: A reply to Nicos Poulantzas', *New Left Review*, 59, January-February.
24 GOODENOUGH, S. (1977) *op. cit.*
25 *Ibid.*
26 GRAMSCI, A. (1971) *op. cit.*
27 STACEY, M. and PRICE M. (1981) *op. cit.*
28 *Ibid.*, p. 11.
29 GRAMSCI, A. (1971) *op. cit.*
30 BARRETT, M. (1980) *Women's Oppression Today*, Verso/New Left Books.
31 *Ibid.*, p. 137.
32 *Ibid.*, p. 139.

33 GOODENOUGH, S. (1977) *op. cit.* gives an account of the holders of the office of National President.

34 GRAMSCI, A. (1971) *op. cit.*, 'The Intellectuals', p. 5.

35 *Ibid.*, p. 9.

36 WILLIAMS, R. (1977) *Marxism and Literature*, Oxford University Press.

37 *Ibid.*, p. 112.

38 GOODENOUGH, S. (1977) *op. cit.*

39 WILLIS, P. (1981) 'Cultural production is different from cultural reproduction is different from social reproduction is different from reproduction', *Interchange*, 12, 2–3, pp. 48–67.

40 MACDONALD, M. (1981) 'Schooling and the reproduction of class and gender relations', in DALE, R. *et al.* (Eds) *Education and the State: Politics, Patriarchy and Practice*, Falmer Press.

41 BERNSTEIN, B. (1975) 'On the classification and framing of educational knowledge', *Class Codes and Control*, Vol. 3, first edition, Routledge and Kegan Paul.

42 *Ibid.*

43 See SPENDER, D. (1981) *Man-Made Language*, Routledge and Kegan Paul, for a discussion of how men often dominate discussion in mixed-sex groups.

44 *Ibid.*

45 STANLEY, L. (1980) *op. cit.*

46 BARRETT, M. (1980) *op. cit.*

47 *Ibid.*, p. 250.

48 BEECHEY, V. (1979) 'On patriarchy', *Feminist Review*, 3, pp. 66–82.

49 SPENDER, D. (1981) *op. cit.*

50 STACEY, M. and PRICE, M. (1981) *op. cit.*, p. 165, quoting from CHAMBERLAIN, M. (1975) *Fenwomen*, Virago/Quartet Books, pp. 135–6.

51 STACEY, M. and PRICE, M. (1981) *op. cit.*, Chapter 7.

52 SPENDER, D. and SARAH, E. (1981) *op. cit.* and SHAW, J. (1980) *op. cit.*

53 ARNOT, M. (1981) 'Culture and political economy: Dual perspectives in the sociology of women's education', *Educational Analysis*, 3, 1.

8. Women and Teaching: A Semi-Detached Sociology of a Semi-Profession

Sandra Acker, University of Bristol

... no country should pride itself on its educational system if the teaching profession has become predominantly a world of women.[1]

... there can be little doubt that in the past much of the sense of a second-rate profession attached to teaching has been the fact that it was predominantly female in membership. A large number of well qualified and professionally minded men in teaching might not only give men a greater equality with women, but also improve the social status of teaching.[2]

Is the teaching profession a 'world of women'? In 1979, 59 per cent of 443,028 full-time teachers in maintained schools in England and Wales were women.[3] This figure conceals considerable variation by level: women are 77 per cent of primary school teachers but 44 per cent of secondary school teachers. In higher and further education, women are clearly a minority; they make up about 20 per cent of the further education teaching staff and 13 per cent of university academics.

Is schoolteaching female dominated? Not if we take domination to mean the exercise of authority. While nearly all teachers and heads of nursery and infant schools are female, women become increasingly underrepresented as we move up the age range. In junior-with-infant schools women are 74 per cent of the teachers, but 26 per cent of the heads; in junior-without-infant schools, they are 65 per cent of the teachers, but only 16 per cent of the heads. In the secondary sector, women hold 60 per cent of the Scale 1 posts but only 32 per cent of deputy headships and 16 per cent of the headships. Interestingly, women are overrepresented in the 'second master/mistress' category (62 per cent), one traditionally reserved for women in cases where the deputy is male. Most part-time teachers (of whom there were 33,017 in 1979) are women (94 per cent). A consequence of differential representation in promotion posts is differential salaries. The average salary for men in 1979 was £5479; for women £4762. While 30 per cent of men earned £6000 or more, the same was true for only 10 per cent of women.

If we consider the modal location of men and women teachers, we observe that men and women typically teach different subjects to different groups of children, hold responsibilities for different functions within schools, and generally have different chances for rewards within the system. Women are more likely to teach younger children, men older; women to teach girls, men boys; women to teach domestic subjects and humanities, men technological subjects and physical sciences; women to have pastoral responsibilities, men administrative and curricular ones.[4] As Strober and Tyack put it, women teach and men manage.[5] The divisions are not of caste-like rigidity, but the probabilities that the sexes will experience differential career lines and typical locations in school are striking enough to allow us to speak confidently of a sexual division of labour in teaching.

What have sociologists to tell us about the sexual division of labour in teaching? Such divisions appear to have been so taken for granted that the majority of books and articles on schools and teaching make hardly any reference to them, and many a school ethnographer has entirely missed the chance to tell us about the impact of gender on relationships among teachers, or between teachers and heads, or between teachers and pupils. When writers do consider women teachers, they frequently resort to commonsense and unsubstantiated assumptions about their deficiencies. Earlier works sketch a stereotype of the spinster teacher,[6] now largely replaced by an image of a married woman who shows a half-hearted interest in teaching while getting on with her 'family responsibilities'.[7] This is such a powerful image it seems to have prevented sociologists of education asking a range of other questions about the nature of the sexual division of labour in teaching. Why are women in a subordinate position in the education system? Can we say anything about gender relations and power relations in schools? What do we learn if we try to make these divisions problematic instead of part of the natural order?

This chapter gives an account of a journey through some of the sociological literature on teachers that I took in an attempt to answer the question of why a sexual division of labour occurs within teaching that appears to place women in a disadvantaged position. I concentrate on British and American studies of school-teaching as a profession and as a career.[8] Limitations of space mean leaving out interesting material on the role of the teacher, on teacher-pupil interaction, and on teacher unionism, as well as confining attention to the primary and secondary sectors. I examine not only the shortcomings of individual studies but also the deeper deficiencies of this literature, including the commonsense assumptions about women that (mis) inform much of it. The studies chosen for detailed review are frequently cited ones that should provide evidence for main themes that run through the literature. These studies all have in their favour recognition of gender as in some way important; there are others, not reviewed here, that make no reference, or only very minimal reference, to gender. In the conclusion, I briefly consider some theoretical approaches to the analysis of sexual divisions and what promise they hold for improving the sociology of teaching.

Sociological Work on Women and Teaching

Women teachers are most often specifically mentioned in discussions of commitment, careers, and claims of the occupation to professional status. What seems to run through such discussions is a conception of women teachers as damaging, deficient, distracted, and sometimes even dim. As the emphasis seems to change somewhat over the years, the literature can be considered in two parts, with the dividing line around 1970.

Semi-Professions and Sexist Stereotypes

In the 1950s and 1960s, a number of commentators expressed concern over the disastrous consequences they supposed must follow from the predominance of women in teaching. 'Most educational psychologists', Lieberman reported in 1956, believe that young boys who lack suitable masculine role models among their teachers will not only become reading failures or behaviour problems, but might end up in the nearest pool hall in search of a gang leader to emulate.[9] For the profession itself, discontinuities in women's employment are 'devastating'.[10] Unlike many subsequent writers, Lieberman does discuss discrimination against women teachers. By noting that the existence of a huge reserve supply of female labour allows school boards to resist teacher demands for better pay and conditions,[11] he manages to go beyond the charge that women themselves are to blame for low status and salaries in teaching.

By the late sixties the subtleties of that distinction appeared largely lost, as is apparent in *The Semi-Professions and their Organization*, edited by Amitai Etzioni.[12] Semi-professions are schoolteaching, social work, nursing, and librarianship. All are highly 'feminized'. The chapter in the collection that best represents the blame-the-woman approach is 'Women and bureaucracy in the semi-professions' by Richard and Ida Simpson. It is certainly a caricature and might almost be a parody. The Simpsons see bureaucratic control, that is, that found in workplaces with strong emphases on hierarchical authority and rules and low worker autonomy, as a *consequence* of the presence of women:

A woman's primary attachment is to the family role; women are therefore less intrinsically committed to work than men and less likely to maintain a high level of specialized knowledge. Because their work motives are more utilitarian and less intrinsically task-oriented than those of men, they may require more control. Women's stronger competing attachments to their family roles and ... to their clients make them less likely than men to develop colleague reference group orientations. For these reasons, and because they often share the general cultural norm that women should defer to men, women are more willing than men to accept the bureaucratic controls imposed upon them in semi-professional organizations, and less likely to seek a genuinely professional status.[13]

Many pages follow on the harm women do to the professional hopes of the occupations in question. Psychological inventories of college students and workers show that women attracted to the semi-professions possess such damning characteristics as altruistic motivations, desires for pleasant social relationships with colleagues, and preferences to work with people rather than things. It is only by twisting the meaning of some of the research findings, and adding unsupported statements, that the Simpsons come to their conclusions. For example, altruistic motivations toward work are dismissed by the argument that since women can satisfy their desire for service through family life without outside work, even strong humanitarian motives are insufficient to create vocational commitments. Statements like 'women seem less able than men to disagree impersonally, without emotional involvement'[14] are thrown in without evidence. Women are accused of a lack of drive toward intellectual mastery on the basis of Coleman's research on adolescents which found girls' marks in school concentrated in the 'B' category. The Simpsons also discuss career discontinuities and commitments: 'A woman's family situation makes it improbable that she will develop a strong professional commitment, or in the unlikely event that she had one to begin with, that she will be able to maintain it.'[15]

In 1970 Timothy Leggatt imported some of these ideas into Britain.[16] In his contribution to *Professions and Professionalization*, he dwells on the negative consequences for teaching of its high proportion of women, echoing many of the Simpsons' sentiments. He argues that the bureaucratic nature of the work context is compatible with women's traditional characteristics which include submissiveness, acceptance of authority, lack of ambition, and nurturance. Women are unconcerned with collegial affiliations because their family activities are less compatible than men's with extra-familial group loyalties (this on the strength of Lionel Tiger's *Men in Groups*). High rates of 'turnover' plus the large size of the occupation result in a loosely structured uncohesive occupation, reinforced by the 'tenuous loyalty of women members'.[17] Leggatt writes as if all women teachers are married (although he states only half are), and he gives very little evidence for most of his statements about women.

Teacher Careers and Double Standards

From the mid-seventies the accusatory tone in the works reviewed above lightens. Studies of this period are less preoccupied with 'profession' and more with 'career'. Many are explicitly or implicitly in the symbolic interactionist tradition within which the study of 'work and occupations' is usually traced back to Everett Hughes and Chicago sociology.

Lortie was a student of Hughes and the influence is apparent in his major book on the sociology of teaching, published in 1975.[18] He draws on survey and interview data, mostly from the 1960s, but goes considerably beyond simple reporting of figures to a sensitive and impressive analysis of teacher sentiments, meanings, rewards and interpretations. Lortie shows an awareness of sexual divisions in teaching at a number of points in his book, especially when he examines the interacting influences of sex, age and marital status on teacher satisfaction and involvement.[19] Few women teachers, he reports, become heavily involved in teaching during their twenties, as they are 'hedging their bets' to cover contingencies related to husband, children or husband's job changes. Older married women teachers are split between home and work commitments but are 'serious about their work'; older single women are deeply invested in their work but not as satisfied as the married women, perhaps because they are more isolated from the adult world. Among men, secondary school teachers under 40 who hope for promotion show very high involvement. My favourite finding is that the small number of male primary teachers in the sample had low commitment and low interest in their work. Nevertheless, they all hoped to be principals (heads) within five years.[20] Lortie does not discuss the influence of marital status on men. Unlike some of the other writers, he avoids the temptation to make simple equations between women and doomed professionalism, but he does observe that careers in teaching work out well for those with 'less than full commitment', from which they paradoxically gain a kind of autonomy.[21]

In British studies of the 1970s, we also see a move away from sexism and toward a concern with a concept of 'career'. In *The Socialization of Teachers*, Lacey starts promisingly by pointing to sex differentiated opportunities in teaching.[22] The career structure, he writes, favours men, and they dominate the higher posts. However, the remainder of the book, which explores ways in which teachers in training are socialized into orientations to teaching, fails even to question whether the process works differently for women and men.

The relative promotion chances of men and women do vary by type of school, we learn from Hilsum and Start's *Promotion and Careers in Teaching*.[23] Mostly their report (which is distinguished by its complete lack of theory of any kind) tells us that men do a lot better: they are promoted faster and further. Hilsum and Start are in little doubt that the reasons for the imbalances lie in women's lower aspirations.[24] In answers to questions about aspirations, men consistently wanted headships more than women did: 54 versus 16 per cent for primary; 17 versus 4 per cent for secondary.[25] The great majority of applications for vacant headships in 1972 was from men.[26] Although 17 per cent of women primary teachers and 20 per cent of women secondary teachers believed 'being a man' aided promotion,[27] the authors are not convinced. Despite lacking direct evidence, they blame sex differences in motivation, basing their conclusions on 'our general discussions with teachers, headteachers and LEAs and our own general acquaintance with the educational scene'.[28]

The most recent book on teacher careers is by Lyons, who interviewed 122 teachers in five comprehensive schools.[29] His theoretical framework is a symbolic interactionist one, and he is particularly concerned to develop the concept of 'career maps'. Lyons notes that more senior positions go to males, adding that females do not apply.[30] He is one of the very few writers to note that promotions for women are concentrated in stereotypically female subject areas, and he also remarks that many young women interviewed expressed dissatisfaction with the career structure offered them.[31] Lyons comments on those woman teachers who have moved geographically following husbands and how much effort it took them to obtain new jobs and how damaging to their promotion prospects these moves had been.[32]

Lyons is more sensitive to problems arising from gender relations than many, but his book still reflects the obsession with the married woman teacher characteristic of such writing. The result is that women are discussed almost entirely in relation to their family roles. They are left out entirely in the main chapter on strategies, 'good' career maps, how to get to the top, sponsorship. The strategies of males in top positions are discussed there; women in senior positions are discussed separately in a context full of speculation about marriage and husbands. So again we have a double standard — we learn nothing about men's family commitments and we learn nothing about school-based barriers or supports to women's careers.

Underlying Assumptions

Let us now go beyond charting the idiosyncratic inadequacies of representative studies and instead examine their underlying assumptions. I suggest that most conventional sociological writing on the influence of gender on teacher careers and on teaching as a profession suffers from the following shortcomings:

1   a 'deficit model' of women that leads to a blame-the-victim approach as well as conceptual confusion;
2   what appears to be a low regard for the intellectual capacities of teachers, perhaps especially women teachers;

3   a persistent tendency to see women exclusively in family role terms;
4   a poor sense of history coupled with an inability to anticipate social change;
5   an oversimplified view of causality;
6   a pervasive ideology of individual choice, deeply embedded in American writing about women's work and often uncritically applied in British literature.

Deficit Models and Conceptual Confusions

In a previous paper I wrote about a 'deficit model' of women, analogous to the much-criticized deficit model of the working-class child in some educational literature.[33] Components include a tendency to 'blame the victim' (and thus distract attention from structural obstacles) and to take male experience as the norm to which women are then (unfavourably) compared. These tendencies are apparent in the literature under consideration. Women teachers are frequently blamed for the low status of the profession and for their own low status within it. The male-as-norm-assumption is also evident. As there are so many women in teaching, it seems this can only be sustained either by taking 'the norm' to be the established professions (to which teaching is then unfavourably compared) or senior posts in teaching (ambition for which is then called 'commitment'). Writers get tangled up trying to equate 'commitment' with what men do. 'Lack of commitment' turns out to mean interruptions for childrearing; 'commitment' to mean furthering one's own career, especially by moving out of classroom teaching. A recent study by Nias suggests writers have only been investigating a narrow set of meanings for 'commitment'.[34] To the primary teachers (of both sexes) interviewed, commitment usually meant a vocation for caring, or a concern with competence (doing the job well, working hard). Only three of nearly 100 teachers used commitment as career-continuance. This did not mean the teachers did not want 'careers' — many did. Also, the NUT survey of women teachers reports that most respondents (82 per cent), married or otherwise, see themselves as 'consciously pursuing a career'; 77 per cent intended teaching until retirement.[35]

There are also problems with other concepts which frequently appear in the literature. Most writers say teachers are 'isolated' — but with little empirical evidence and various meanings (from one another? from the outside world?). Does this 'isolation' really prohibit 'collegiality' or 'solidarity'? In a study of a primary school, McPherson comments on the solidarity teachers have with each other against the principal and parents, only broken by loyalty to the class they teach, for example, when they fight for its rights on the playground.[36] The Simpsons dismissed women semi-professionals' concern with social relationships at work by assuming they talk about dress styles, not professional tasks.[37] King found infant teachers discussing husbands, children, and shopping in the staffroom — but also school affairs and incidents from the classroom.[38]

All these concepts (commitment, isolation, collegiality, careermindedness) need more refinement and differentiation: under what circumstances, in what kinds of schools, with what kinds of colleagues, with what sort of pupils, teaching what sort of subjects do we find commitment, collegiality, etc.? Simply distinguishing stereotypically between women and men is surely sociologically simplistic.

Not Too Bright?

Much of the literature on schoolteachers reflects a lack of respect, if not outright contempt, for their intellectual abilities. Traces of this orientation are evident in the literature reviewed here. Lortie and Leggatt both emphasize the lack of technical terminology in teachers' vocabularies. Lortie refers to an analysis of some of his interview tapes that showed teachers mostly used common English words rather than a professional argot.[39] As Hargreaves suggests in his critique of Sharp and Green's study, it may be that the interviewing context itself produces the particular type of response.[40] Leggatt also cites Philip Jackson's interviews with 50 outstanding primary school teachers (almost all women) as evidence for 'conceptual simplicity'. Jackson writes that teachers show

> 1) an uncomplicated view of causality; 2) an intuitive, rather than rational approach to classroom events; 3) an opinionated, as opposed to an open-minded, stance when confronted with alternative teaching practices; and 4) a narrowness in the working definitions assigned to abstract terms.[41]

If these are defects, many of the researchers on teachers show rather similar ones in their own work.

Jackson does, in fact, conclude that the 'intuitive' approach is more suitable to the task than a highly rational one would be. He also raises the question, wisely not fully answering it, of whether this intuition is merely due to women 'exercising their feminine birthright'.[42]

Women and Marriage

Another defect in this literature is that women teachers are almost inevitably discussed in terms of their marital status. Four associated problems arise. First, the impression given in study after study is that all women teachers are married (ironically in view of the history of marriage bars). Whenever reasons are advanced for lack of ambition and the like, marriage is always cited as one of these, even when not accompanied by any empirical evidence comparing single and married women.

Second, if all women teachers are married, apparently no men ever are. No published source to my knowledge discusses any conflicts arising from men's marriages. Interestingly, one unpublished study of a local NUT Association found most men reluctant to participate further at a regional or national level because of their 'family commitments'.[43] Nor do researchers remark on the assistance men's families might provide towards fulfilling career ambitions. The literature on academic and certain other professional workers (and countless book prefaces) suggests that men are often enabled to immerse themselves fully in their careers because they have a 70-hour-a-week housewife backing them up.[44] Is the same true for 'successful' male teachers?

Third, marriage and parenthood are never sufficiently distinguished from one another. Women are always said to leave 'on marriage'. Childcare may be more likely to be the problem. Only a few writers mention the provision of childcare or nurseries as relevant to teacher commitment or career continuity.[45]

Most seriously, it appears that to discuss women teachers means *only* to discuss family/work conflicts. When other aspects of being a teacher are discussed, women, or sex differences generally, are rarely singled out. Lacey does not tell us anything about sex differences in socialization into teaching; Lyons does not tell us anything about differential access to sponsorship. Perhaps there was none — but how can we know? What we have here is the notion that beyond personality characteristics, the only remotely sociological factor that affects women teachers' careers is 'marriage'. The consequence is that there is no serious investigation of in-school or other factors that influence women's experiences and outcomes. Richardson's study of Nailsea school[46] stands almost alone in the research literature in its sensitivity to double binds in which senior female staff found themselves. The way they were treated by male staff affected their ambitions as much as personality and family role characteristics. Buchan's and Whitbread's autobiographical accounts also suggest some of the negative pressures that male colleagues and superiors may bring to bear on women teachers.[47]

Suspension in the Present

It is easy, but incorrect, to assume that the sexual division of labour in teaching always has existed, and always will exist, in the form we see today.[48] The relative proportions of men and women; of single women and married women; of female heads and male heads have all varied over time in response to government policies, wars, population trends, social attitudes, economic circumstances. For example, the 'payment by results' system of the 1862 Revised Code led to reductions in education spending, teacher training, and teacher status, and was followed by an exodus of men from the occupation.[49] The expansion of state schooling after 1870 relied on large numbers of untrained women 'supplementary teachers' and further 'feminized' the teaching force.[50] At other times, the balance has shifted towards men, for example after World War II, when two-thirds of those trained by the Emergency Training Scheme were men. Tropp remarks that the profession 'shed its mass of cheap untrained female labour' as the proportion of women in the 'old elementary' sector (primary plus secondary modern) dropped from 75 per cent in 1900 to 65 per cent in 1954.[51]

Whether married women were allowed to teach also depended on demand and circumstance. In the first part of the twentieth century many authorities operated bars against married women teachers, though they were not required by any government edict. Exceptions were made, for example, in remote rural areas, or sometimes when 'hardship' might result from dismissal upon marriage.[52] London ended its marriage bar in 1935 when the Labour Party came to power locally and finally the 1944 Education Act ended the practice altogether.[53] During the World Wars and in the severe teacher shortages of the 1950s and 1960s married women were encouraged to teach.

Who heads schools has also been subject to change. The proportion of women heads in the primary sector was high in the 1920s but fell rapidly between the wars, with the closure of small village schools, amalgamations of infant with junior schools, fewer single-sex schools for 7 to 11-year-olds, and a campaign by the NAS to resist women being put in positions of authority over men teachers.[54] While women might still head small rural schools and infant schools, large mixed junior schools became the province of men. Similarly, where women have headed secondary schools, they have usually been girls' schools. The move towards co-education in state secondary schools has reduced the proportion of head teachers who are women.[55]

It would be unfair to expect the studies of teaching as a profession and as a career to predict the future. But it is not unreasonable to expect that some sense of history might prevent them adopting the framework that regards women's status in teaching as *unchanging* and based solely on personal preferences. When studies (for example, Simpson and Simpson) use figures on women's labour market participation or surveys on college student values to back up their assertions, there is no suggestion these might reflect anything but eternal verities. Writers happily cite results of surveys of teachers done ten or 20 years earlier without apparently recognizing that social change might have intervened.

Even if women teachers were much less career-oriented than men in the past, one cannot project such findings into an unchanging future. Women's labour market participation and sex-role attitudes have changed dramatically over 20 years.[56] In addition, many of the recent trends in education appear potentially harmful to the interests of women teachers. Closures and amalgamations of teacher training colleges as well as limits on places for trainee teachers and higher entry qualifications have lessened opportunities both for women students and staff.[57] Curtailment in openings for part-time teachers may mean that an entire generation of women teachers who had expected to return after childraising through the part-time route will now find it difficult or impossible to do so; this also implies schools will lack sufficient numbers of highly experienced female teachers to move into senior posts.[58] Areas of the curriculum now defined as 'shortage subjects' and given most protection are those traditionally taught by men (mathematics; physics; craft, design and technology). There is also the argument that masses of women classroom teachers are undergoing deskilling while a smaller number of teachers, more often male, experience reskilling.[59]

Such changes in ideological, demographic, and economic conditions, accompanied by shifts in government education policies, alter the context within which women teachers' commitments and career patterns are shaped. An example would be the way in which the decline in opportunities for part-time teaching and re-entry, plus changes in maternity leave provision, have apparently resulted in more women making the 'choice' to take maternity leave and to continue teaching even if their personal preferences might have been otherwise.[60] It is to be hoped that future studies on career patterns of women teachers will build in a sensitivity to social change that has heretofore been frequently absent.

Causality

An oversimplified view of causality also characterizes much of the literature under review. For example, some writers assume that the predominance of women in teaching is the cause of the low status of the occupation. As Kelsall and Kelsall pointed out in 1970,[61] if this is true it is a function of the status accorded to women in a given society, not simply of the presence of women. Another dubious argument is the Simpsons' charge that women's personality characteristics *require* bureaucratic organizational control. In contrast, Kanter has argued, more convincingly to my mind, that many so-called sex difference findings about behaviour in organizations can be more satisfactorily explained by differences in opportunities, numerical representation, access to power that often *coincide* with sex.[62]

Hilsum and Start, as we have seen, doubt that expectations of sex discrimination will lead to women not applying for promotion posts. They may be right, but they fail to note that there may be a whole sequence of experiences and events that put someone in a position to apply for such posts. Women may have had less access than men to some of these experiences; they may less often be 'groomed for seniority and responsibility by their mainly male heads'.[63] It is too simple merely to assume that lack of ambition plus family responsibilities produce low commitment or lack of interest in promotion among married women teachers. The sequence of events and decisions may be more complex than is usually appreciated. Nias reports that most of the 26 primary school teachers she interviewed who had left work to have children told her that their timing was precipitated by discontent with the particular school and its administration; they had children in order to leave work, so to speak, rather than the reverse.[64] Moreover, the strong numerical presence of women (including married women) in *certain* senior posts (primary school heads and deputies; secondary school senior mistresses) suggests modifications need to be made to any generalized thesis about women's reluctance to seek promotion. *Under what circumstances* do women seek promotion? And under what circumstances are women actively sought or encouraged to apply for promotion? Researchers should ask these questions rather than simply repeat commonsense views about women.

Choice and Constraint

As should be clear by now, much of the literature under discussion displays what might be called an ideology of individual choice, and a corresponding neglect of constraint at any but a familial level. Aspirations and motivations have crowded out everything else. The American literature on women and education (especially higher education), until very recently, was a long saga of social psychological studies of career aspirations, career orientations, career salience, career ambition. Most studies tried to distinguish between 'career-oriented' and 'marriage-oriented' women university students, not quite sure which option was the deviant one.[65] The roots of this approach may lie in what Bledstein calls the 'culture of professionalism' which he traces from its nineteenth-century origins and regards as a characteristic world-view held by the American middle class.[66] Diversity in standards of living is not seen as the result of class structures but as the product of 'individual attainment at a fleeting moment in a career'.[67] Even the virtual confinement of nineteenth-century married middle-class women to the home was seen as a consequence of individual *choice*: such women merely chose to develop their special gifts and sensitivities in the professionalization of domesticity.[68]

It is not only the American literature on women and education that has emphasized choice while neglecting constraint: British studies of the early seventies show the same tendencies.[69] And as I have shown, the British literature on women and teaching is as likely as the American to reflect this orientation. Lortie was perceptive enough to break free from this framework when he observed that choosing a career in teaching because of its compatibility with marriage and motherhood could be seen as a constraint as much as a choice.[70] It is to be hoped that future researchers on women and teaching will clarify the subtle balance between choice and constraint, as they typically endeavour to do within sociology of education generally.

Conclusion

I have tried to make problematic some issues related to the sexual division of labour in teaching and the careers of women teachers. I have reviewed some key sociological studies on teacher careers and the teaching profession and criticized these studies on various grounds, perhaps the most serious of which is their insistence that women's aspirations and family role responsibilities are sufficient explanations for their subordinate position in teaching. In the past few years a handful of textbooks on women and education and a few empirical studies have brought sexual divisions in teaching to our attention and have begun to expand our knowledge of how these operate.[71] What can we do now, then, to ensure that future research avoids the pitfalls of the past?

If we begin by seeking guidance from the literature, feminist and otherwise, on gender relations we speedily discover that it is a massive task, not yet accomplished to my knowledge, to review and synthesize the vast literature which attempts to answer the question of how women as a group have come to be subordinate to men as a group. One distinction that I have made is between what we could call *fundamental* and *implementary* theories (using 'theory' loosely to include any attempt to impose an explanatory framework). Fundamental theories are those that try to explain *why* the different social positions of men and women exist. They seek to uncover one or a set of basic principles which make sense of as many as possible diverse observations comparing the sexes. They fall into two sub-groups. The first includes those approaches which use a 'sex difference' framework and see social arrangements, especially gender relationships, as rooted in and limited by human nature, specifically biology. The other sub-group contains theories which postulate some ultimate feature of the social structure as the limiting influence (at least for the immediate future) on human possibilities, especially on the life chances of women. This group includes some of the functionalist theories (maintaining that the stability of society requires a sexual division of labour much like the present one) and those that look to capitalism or patriarchy to explain the oppression of women. Needless to say, theories which come under the heading 'fundamental' are not necessarily mutually compatible.

The other major group of 'theories', the implementary ones, are sometimes presented as 'why' theories, but I think they are better described as 'how' theories. Rather than seek first causes, they focus on how the subordination of women is perpetuated. Approaches which rely on processes such as socialization, sex discrimination, or role conflict for explanations of sex inequality are examples of those we can assign to the implementary category, because they lack the 'fundamental' character of the theories which trace everything back to human nature or social structure. The 'how' theories are important in that they fill in the gaps: how it is that nature's demands or social requisites 'work' in the everyday world. They are more often situation- and culture-specific.

It is clear that so far most work on women teachers within mainstream sociology of education has stayed at the implementary level except when it has made reference to supposedly fundamental 'sex differences' of a bio-psychological sort. Most attempts to conceptualize women's position in teaching have been very limited. Even in their more sociological forms they rely on an assumption that family responsibilities or marriage/career conflicts will produce attitudes and behaviours (low promotion orientation, willingness to submit to bureaucratic control) that have certain implications for the profession (lack of militancy, low status) and for individual women's careers (intermittent, uncommitted, 'flat'). Such approaches are extremely one-sided, placing the emphasis on the individual woman as 'actor' with little or no attempt to assess the structures within which action takes place. This is partly a side-effect of typical sociological techniques which are better suited to the analysis of individual attitudes than to capturing the subtleties of the school environment, let alone the impact of the wider society. There has been considerable interest in recent years in the effects of teacher expectations on pupil behaviour. Why not also ask what effect the expectations of colleagues and superiors have on the behaviour of (women) teachers? What kind of humour, what traditions, what beliefs about women teachers, married women, women in general surround the woman teacher daily? In my years teaching experienced teachers on advanced courses, I have heard many stories about incompetent men given scale posts within primary schools; women teachers who continue to work after maternity leave believing they are under constant scrutiny from disapproving heads to prove no loss of competence; unsuccessful women applicants for senior posts told in confidence that a man was preferred in order to discipline older children or satisfy village prejudices. I also hear complaints from men teachers about the lack of commitment and interest shown by the women in their schools. None of these stories has any but anecdotal weight; but where is the research that will show what gender relations are truly like in schools and how they influence women teachers' 'choices'? Such studies are likely to be on the 'implementary' level — they will not tell us 'why' sexual divisions occur, but they could do immense service in telling us how they are perpetuated.

What about the fundamental theories, especially those that invoke capitalism or the patriarchal order; how do we draw upon these to understand the sexual division of labour and career chances of women teachers? Some of the textbooks use this kind of framework. But how can we use these theories to inform our empirical research? A major theme to come out of feminist work at this level when applied to education is that the sexual division of labour among teachers contributes to the reproduction of patriarchal and/or capitalist social order, especially by providing models to students of male-female power relations and sex differentiated subject specialities and responsibilities that reinforce the connection of 'femininity' with caring, serving, conforming, mothering.[72] Some very interesting questions arise.

To take one example, why is it that teaching very young children is regarded as an occupation suitable only for women? Men who wish to teach such children run the risk of being branded as sexually deviant.[73] Once one stops assuming the answer is rooted solely in natural proclivities such as women's love for children or motherliness a series of interesting possibilities emerges. At one level answers may lie in tradition and the economic advantages to the state of a cheap mass female occupation.[74] The need for a mass teaching force that could be increased or decreased according to demographic change or political whim may have increased the preference for women teachers who would be 'dispensable'. Lortie tells us that schools in America developed on an 'egg crate' model where rooms and teachers in them could be added on or taken away without disturbing the functioning of the school.[75] There is also the possibility that once women had carved out this area of influence they held on to it as one of the few arenas in which they could exert any power, even at the expense of further reinforcing stereotypes about women's sphere. Another line of reasoning stresses more specifically the part schools play in social and cultural reproduction; some argue that the development of the 'male sex role' may depend on experiencing resistance against a 'feminine' environment in early school as well as at home.[76]

There is no doubt that the image of women teachers as 'substitute mothers' is replete with contradictions. Although the primary school teacher may appear motherly, it is a professional sort of motherliness, accompanied by the necessity to evaluate and assess impartially and to enforce what may be an authoritarian regime within the school.[77] Other contradictions, as David has shown,[78] are located in the expectations that women teachers transmit a sex-differentiated curriculum to prepare girls for domesticity. In the past such teachers were single (especially when marriage bars operated) and thus presumably had little direct experience of the life they were advocating; now they may be married, but are themselves choosing to work outside the home in preference to full-time domesticity.

There is a number of interesting questions that derive from fundamental theories about women and schooling. But how can we design research that confirms or disconfirms such theories? If we are simply looking for a 'good fit' between the phenomenon and the theory, some of the strange and uncongenial socio-biological theories currently popular in America seem to 'fit' just as well. Fundamental theories also have the disadvantage of leaving us terribly frustrated in any attempt to change things. It is certainly easier to imagine we can change socialization practices or role relationships in our schools and personal lives than it is to bring about the demise of capitalism or patriarchy.

While we cannot pursue, let alone resolve, all the methodological and epistemological questions that arise from an attempt to develop and apply fundamental and implementary theories, it should be clear that a rapprochement between certain feminist theories and the sociology of teaching could be promising and productive. Fundamental theories might lead us to investigate whether there is a correspondence between the sexual division of labour in teaching and the sexual division of labour in the family and the economy. Implementary approaches could result in empirical studies of schools, wherein we could consider, for example, gender relationships among teachers, sexual harassment, sponsorship, the relationship of deskilling to gender, the balance of resistance and accommodation in the lives of women teachers. I imagine there are other exciting possibilities, once we break away from the prison of the prevailing paradigm within which such work has proceeded to date. The result should be considerably enriched understanding of teachers and teaching.

Acknowledgement

I am grateful to Geoff Millerson and Gill Blunden for comments on drafts of this chapter, to Maureen Harvey for typing, to Angela Hope for helpful discussions, and to Dan Lortie for originally stimulating my interest in the study of teachers.

Notes

1 LANGEVELD, M.J. (1963) 'The psychology of teachers and the teaching profession', in BEREDAY, G.Z.F. and LAUWERYS, J.A. (Eds) *The Yearbook of Education 1963: The Education and Training of Teachers*, London, Evans Brothers, p. 404.
2 MORRISH, I. (1978) *The Sociology of Education*, London, Allen and Unwin, p. 234.

3 The figures which follow on primary, secondary and further education are from DEPARTMENT OF EDUCATION AND SCIENCE (1981) *Statistics of Education 1979 Vol. 4: Teachers*, London, HMSO, pp. 28–35, and refer to the maintained sector in England and Wales. The figure for university academics is from DES and UNIVERSITY GRANTS COMMITTEE (1981) *Statistics of Education 1978 Vol. 6: Universities*, London, HMSO, p. 67. Women are 88 per cent of primary school teachers and 43 per cent of secondary school teachers in Scotland. See MEGARRY, J. *et al.* (1981) *Sex, Gender and Education*, Glasgow, Jordanhill College of Education, p. 30, for more detail. Figures for the United States can be found in SCHMUCK, P. (1980) 'Differentiation by sex in educational professions', in STOCKARD, J. *et al. Sex Equity in Education*, New York, Academic Press. It is important to be aware that American statistics do not usually include 'administrators' (the equivalents of heads and deputy heads) with 'classroom teachers'.

4 See BYRNE, E. (1978) *Women and Education*, London, Tavistock, Chapter 7; HOPE, A. (1979) *Up the Down Staircase: Careers of Women Teachers*, unpublished MEd dissertation, University of Bristol; LACEY, C. (1977) *The Socialization of Teachers*, London, Methuen, pp. 32–3; NATIONAL UNION OF TEACHERS (1980) *Promotion and the Woman Teacher*, London, NUT. Historians have paid more attention to sexual divisions in teaching than have sociologists. Divisions of class, sex, and religion are deeply embedded in the history of teaching, and some writers argue these have facilitated state control and impeded the development of professionalism. See PARRY, N. and PARRY, J. (1974) 'The teachers and professionalism: The failure of an occupational strategy', in FLUDE, M. and AHIER, J. (Eds) *Educability, Schools and Ideology*, London, Croom Helm. The history of the campaign for equal pay for women with men (not fully implemented until *1961*) shows sexual divisions were often accompanied by considerable hostility. See GOSDEN, P.H.J.H. (1972) *The Evolution of a Profession*, Oxford, Blackwell, Chapter 5.

5 STROBER, M. and TYACK, D. (1980) 'Why do women teach and men manage? A report on research on schools', *Signs*, 5, 3, pp. 494–503.

6 See WALLER, W. (1932/65) *The Sociology of Teaching*, New York, Wiley, p. 409.

7 NUT, *op. cit.*, (Note 4) points to the married woman stereotype, p. 54.

8 For a general review of literature on teaching as a profession, see HOYLE, E. (1982) 'Sociological approaches to the teaching profession', in HARTNETT, A. (Ed.) *The Social Sciences in Educational Studies*, London, Heinemann; on careers, including teachers' careers, see DALE, R. (1976) *Work, Career and the Self*, Open University Press, Milton Keynes, Course DE 351, Unit 7. Although I refer to studies as 'British' it should be kept in mind that most are in fact specifically about teachers in England.

9 LIEBERMAN, M. (1956) *Education as a Profession*, Englewood Cliffs, New Jersey, Prentice-Hall, p. 245.

10 *Ibid.*, p. 249.

11 *Ibid.*, p. 253.

12 ETZIONI, A. (Ed.) (1969) *The Semi-Professions and Their Organization*, New York, The Free Press.

13 SIMPSON, R.L. and SIMPSON, I.H. (1969) 'Women and bureaucracy in the semi-professions', in ETZIONI (Ed.), *op. cit.*, pp. 199–200. Recent research findings contradict some of these assertions; see GRANDJEAN, B. and BERNAL, H. (1979) 'Sex and centralization in a semi-profession', *Sociology of Work and Occupations*, 6, 1, pp. 84–102.

14 SIMPSON, R.L. and SIMPSON, I.H. *op. cit.*, p. 241.

15 *Ibid.*, p. 219.

16 LEGGATT, T. (1970) 'Teaching as a profession', in JACKSON, J. (Ed.) *Professions and Professionalization*, Cambridge, Cambridge University Press.

17 *Ibid.*, p. 165.

18 LORTIE, D.C. (1975) *Schoolteachers: A Sociological Study*, Chicago, University of Chicago Press.

19 *Ibid.*, Chapter 4, especially pp. 89–95.

20 *Ibid.*, p. 95. This is reminiscent of Moeller's finding that male primary school teachers had a stronger sense of power *vis-à-vis* the school system than did any other teacher group.

See MOELLER, G. (1964) 'Bureaucracy and teachers' sense of power', *School Review*, 72, pp. 137–57.

21 LORTIE, D.C., *op. cit.*, pp. 99–100.

22 LACEY, C. *op. cit.* (Note 4).

23 HILSUM, S. and START, K.B. (1974) *Promotion and Careers in Teaching*, Windsor, NFER.

24 *Ibid.*, p. 270.

25 *Ibid.*, pp. 271–2.

26 *Ibid.*, p. 45.

27 *Ibid.*, pp. 110–11.

28 *Ibid.*, p. 72.

29 LYONS, G. (1980) *Teacher Careers and Career Perceptions*, Windsor, NFER Nelson. Some of Lyons' findings are also reported in LYONS, G. and MCCLEARY, L. (1980) 'Careers in teaching', in HOYLE, E. and MEGARRY, J. (Eds) *World Yearbook of Education 1980: Professional Development of Teachers*, London, Kogan Page.

30 LYONS, G. *op. cit.*, p. 114.

31 *Ibid.*, p. 115.

32 *Ibid.*, p. 119.

33 ACKER, S. (1980) 'Women, the other academics', *British Journal of Sociology of Education*, 1, 1, pp. 81–91.

34 NIAS, J. (1981) ' "Commitment" and motivation in primary school teachers', *Educational Review*, 33, 3, pp. 181–90.

35 NUT, *op. cit.* (Note 4), pp. 28–9. Various writers have suggested that the vertical model of 'career' needs supplementing if not replacing by alternative conceptualizations more appropriate to women's lives (and probably to men's). For example, Lewin and Olesen develop the concept of lateralness, a feature of the careers of certain of the nurses they studied. The nurses' careers were not characterized by advancement but by 'rewards of intensification', that is, greater personal satisfactions derived from increased competence. This pattern is in part structurally imposed and in part actively chosen. Lewin and Olesen argue, as I do in this chapter, against viewing such outcomes as simply deviations from a 'normal' male pattern. LEWIN, E. and OLESEN, V. (1981) 'Lateralness in women's work: New views on success', *Sex Roles*, 6, pp. 619–30.

36 MCPHERSON, G. (1972) *Small Town Teacher*, Cambridge, Mass., Harvard University Press.

37 SIMPSON, R.L. and SIMPSON, I.H. *op. cit.* (Note 13), p. 241.

38 KING, R. (1978) *All Things Bright and Beautiful?* Chichester, Wiley, p. 73.

39 LORTIE, D., *op. cit.* (Note 18), p. 73.

40 HARGREAVES, D. (1978) 'Whatever happened to symbolic interactionism?', in BARTON, L. and MEIGHAN, R. (Eds) *Sociological Interpretations of Schooling and Classrooms: A Re-Appraisal*, Driffield, Nafferton.

41 JACKSON, P. (1968) *Life in Classrooms*, New York, Holt, Rinehart and Winston, p. 144.

42 *Ibid.*, p. 146.

43 WALKER, B. (1981) *Women and the N.U.T.*, unpublished MEd dissertation, University of Bristol.

44 ACKER, S. *op. cit.* (Note 33).

45 OLLERENSHAW, K. and FLUDE, C. (1974) *Returning to Teaching*, Lancaster, University of Lancaster, showed that the vast majority of women teachers who left teaching left upon becoming mothers, not wives. Two writers who do mention lack of childcare or nursery provision as impediments to teacher-mothers are KELSALL, R.K. (1963) *Women and Teaching*, London, HMSO, p. 22 and PURVIS, J. (1973) 'Schoolteaching as a professional career', *British Journal of Sociology*, 24, pp. 43–57.

46 RICHARDSON, E. (1973) *The Teacher, the School and the Task of Management*, London, Heinemann.

47 BUCHAN, L. (1980) 'It's a good job for a girl (but an awful career for a woman)', in SPENDER, D. and SARAH, E. (Eds) *Learning to Lose: Sexism and Education*, London, The

Women's Press; WHITBREAD, A. (1980) 'Female teachers are women first: Sexual harassment at work', in SPENDER and SARAH, *op. cit.*

48 Most of the writers under consideration do not add an historical perspective. An exception is LORTIE, D.C. *op. cit.* (Note 18). For an account of changes over time in the sex composition of the teaching force in the United States, see LORTIE, D.C. *op. cit.*, or STROBER, M. and TYACK, D. *op. cit.* (Note 5).

49 DAVID, M.E. (1980) *The State, the Family and Education*, London, Routledge and Kegan Paul, p. 114.

50 *Ibid.*, p. 129; PURVIS, J. (1981) 'Women and teaching in the nineteenth century', in DALE, R. *et al.* (Eds) *Education and the State: Vol. II*, Barcombe, Falmer; TROPP, A. (1957) *The School Teachers*, London, Heinemann, p. 118.

51 TROPP, A. *op. cit.*, p. 262.

52 PARTINGTON, G. (1976) *Women Teachers in the Twentieth Century in England and Wales*, Windsor, NFER, pp. 30–2.

53 *Ibid.*, p. 51.

54 *Ibid.*, p. 36.

55 TROWN, E.A. and NEEDHAM, G. (1981) 'Headships for women: Long-term effects of the re-entry problem', *Educational Studies*, 7, 1, pp. 41–5; BYRNE, E., *op. cit.* (Note 4), p. 229.

56 DAVID, M.E. *op cit.* (Note 49), p. 237; FONDA, N. and MOSS, P. (Eds) (1976) *Mothers in Employment*, Uxbridge, Brunel University Management Programme and Thomas Coram Research Unit; FARLEY, J., BREWER, J.H. and FINE, S.W. (1977) 'Women's values: Changing faster than men's?', *Sociology of Education*, 50, p. 151.

57 BONE, A. (1980) *The Effect on Women's Opportunities of Teacher Training Cuts*, Manchester, Equal Opportunities Commission.

58 TROWN, A. and NEEDHAM, G. (1980) *Reduction in Part-Time Teaching: Implications for Schools and Women Teachers*, Manchester, Equal Opportunities Commission p. 48; OLLERENSHAW, K. and FLUDE, C. *op. cit.* (Note 45).

59 BUSWELL, C. (1980) 'Pedagogic change and social change', *British Journal of Sociology of Education*, 1, 3, pp. 293–306, and see APPLE, this volume.

60 TROWN, A. and NEEDHAM, G. *op. cit.* (Note 58), p. 126; THURSTON, G.J. (1981) *Women Teachers and Maternity Leave*, unpublished MEd dissertation. University College, Cardiff. Numbers of part-time teachers in England and Wales declined from 42,164 in 1975 to 33,017 in 1979, according to DES (1981) *op. cit.* (Note 3), p. 35.

61 KELSALL, R.K. and KELSALL, H.M. (1970) 'The status, role and future of teachers', in KING, E.J. (Ed.) *The Teacher and the Needs of Society in Evolution*, Oxford, Pergamon, p. 118.

62 KANTER, R.M. (1977) *Men and Women of the Corporation*, New York, Basic Books.

63 BYRNE, E. *op. cit.* (Note 4), p. 227.

64 NIAS, J. (1981) 'Teacher satisfaction and dissatisfaction: Herzberg's "two-factor" hypothesis revisited', *British Journal of Sociology of Education*, 2, 3, pp. 235–46.

65 ACKER, S. (1978) *Sex Differences in Graduate Student Ambition*, unpublished PhD dissertation, University of Chicago; ASTIN, H., SUNIEWICK, N. and DWECK, S. (Eds) (1971) *Women: A Bibliography on Their Education and Careers*, Washington, DC, Human Services Press.

66 BLEDSTEIN, B.J. (1976) *The Culture of Professionalism*, New York, Norton.

67 *Ibid.*, p. 21.

68 *Ibid.*, p. 118.

69 See ACKER, S. (1980) *op. cit.* (Note 33), p. 87, for further discussion.

70 LORTIE, D.C. *op. cit.* (Note 18), p. 50.

71 For example, see BYRNE, E. *op. cit.* (Note 4); DAVID, M.E. *op. cit.* (Note 49); DEEM, R. (1978) *Women and Schooling*, London, Routledge and Kegan Paul; DELAMONT, S. (1980) *Sex Roles and the School*, London, Methuen; SPENDER, D. and SARAH, E. *op. cit.*, (Note 47); NUT, *op. cit.* (Note 4); TROWN, A. and NEEDHAM, G. (1980) *op. cit.* (Note 58).

72 MACDONALD, M. (1980) 'Schooling in the reproduction of class and gender relations', in BARTON, L., MEIGHAN, R. and WALKER, S. (Eds) *Schooling, Ideology and the Curriculum*, Barcombe, Falmer.

73 LEE, P.C. (1973) 'Male and female teachers in elementary schools: An ecological analysis', *Teachers College Record*, 75, 1, pp. 79–98.

74 *Ibid.*

75 LORTIE, D.C. *op. cit.* (Note 18), pp. 14–15.

76 LEE, P.C. *op. cit.* (Note 73); on the impact of mothering on male and female gender roles, see CHODOROW, N. (1978) *The Reproduction of Mothering*, Berkeley, University of California Press.

77 See GRUMET, M. (1981) 'Pedagogy for patriarchy: The feminization of teaching', *Interchange*, 12, 2–3, pp. 165–84; KING, R. *op. cit.* (Note 38), pp. 71–2; PARSONS, T. (1961) 'The school class as a social system', in HALSEY, A.H., FLOUD, J. and ANDERSON, C.A. (Eds) *Education, Economy, and Society*, New York, The Free Press.

78 DAVID, M.E. *op. cit.*, (Note 49), Chapter 6.

9. Sex, Education and Social Policy: A New Moral Economy?

Miriam David, University of Bristol

Sex is now clearly an issue in public policy. It is no longer hidden and private. It is even raised as a topic for inclusion in school curricula. How it is to be covered in schools is very specific. It is part and parcel of the debate on the implementation of family policies. The dominant tendencies are essentially conservative. Sex education or family-life education is to be taught as part of a broader education in moral values, specifically to stem the decline in social order and family life. It is argued that preaching or teaching about traditional familial virtues and family privacy will halt, or perhaps reverse, new sexual patterns, such as teenage pregnancy or parenthood and sexual promiscuity.

This approach to sex in education contrasts markedly with the tendency over the last two decades to address the question of sex explicitly to change the social structure and break down the fact and ideology of the sexual division of labour in social and economic life. Yet it is not independent of it. I shall argue that it constitutes a reaction, or rather a backlash, to the albeit slender developments in dealing with sex discrimination. In the US, this has become known as anti-feminism where feminism is the attempt to promote sexual equality in public life.[1]

The shifts in approach to sex and the family, especially the public rhetoric about the privacy of the family and sexuality, are occurring in both Britain and the US. I shall draw attention here to the similarities in the way the issues are raised by the 'New Right' and compare how they relate to the breakdown of the prevailing political consensus about the principles governing educational provision. I would contend that the shift is two-fold — it is an attempt to rescind equal opportunities policies and legislation, and to replace them with specific policies which promote sex difference.

The main evidence I want to use is from the state's debates about education and its effect on the socio-economic system. In particular, I will focus on national politics, looking at what the British government, through its Department of Education and Science, has discussed and, in the US, the way this issue is on the agenda of the Federal Government both in Congress and in Presidential initiatives.

I will not look at the evidence in local communities or individual schools because of lack of space and time. I do not think, however, that this evidence would contradict my thesis that a shift is beginning to occur, however thinly veiled and contradictory some aspects of it are.[2] Indeed some may argue that the liberal/social democratic consensus was never applied at the school level, and hence there is no shift against it, but a continuance of past patriarchal practices.

The Breakdown in Political Consensus and the Rise of the New Right

The shifts in ideologies about education are occurring in both Britain and the US because of recent changes in national political complexions, towards more right-wing governments, bolstered up by particular, conservative political pressure groups. In this context, both the British Prime Minister, Mrs Thatcher, and the American President, Mr Reagan, hold broadly similar views on the role of the state in relation to the economy and especially on state policies in the area of domestic policy. I do not want to argue that Thatcher and Reagan hold the same political views, that they represent the same interests, that their economic policies are the same or, most importantly, that their policies when implemented would have the same impacts since the two socio-economic systems and demographic contexts are rather different. Nevertheless, there are certain crucial similarities that make comparison relevant. Both Britain and the US are advanced capitalist societies experiencing serious economic recessions. Reagan and Thatcher hold similar views as to how to manage recession, especially on how the state should respond. In particular, they raise explicitly the question of the relationship not only between the public and private, but also between the family and the economy, and the use of education in mediating these various relationships. These merit further examination.

It is now commonplace to argue that there has been a breakdown in the political consensus that has prevailed since at least World War II on the role of the state within the economy. Thatcherism for Britain and Reaganism for the United States are cited as the main evidence of these shifts, and arguments are presented about them both separately and together.

The evidence for Britain suggests that Thatcherism is a radical break not only with the social democratic, or Labour, political consensus but also with the post-war Tory position.[3] These last two have been nicknamed Butskellism. Not only is Thatcherism different from previous post-war political ideologies but it takes off from the failure of the social democratic consensus to deal with the economic recession. Its answer to the management of the economy is to repudiate all that has been tried. In particular, as Taylor-Gooby has cogently if convolutedly argued, it aims to reduce the scale and scope of the welfare state both at the material and ideological levels.[4] The welfare state has failed both to convince and to deliver. Its form has perpetuated an individualistic approach to social provision which, it is now claimed, is better met by private, familial means than by the state.

Comparisons between Thatcherism and Reaganism draw attention to the similarity between their approaches to the management of the economy as well as the attempts to dismantle the welfare state and return social services to the individual private sphere. Mouffe, for example, mentions that both orchestrate an attack on 'big government' and re-assert traditional values about the family, particularly women — what she calls 'social and moral issues'.[5] She is not alone in persuading us to look to the centrality of these ideas, or rather this ideology,[6] as the defining characteristic. Indeed, most commentators on America make it absolutely clear that the New Right represents a sharp break with the old Liberal political consensus on the grounds of its social and moral values about the family and especially women. They argue that the New Right arose out of the failure of Liberalism to deal with recession but that it only became successful when it began to address social rather than economic questions.[7] Nevertheless, although some have argued that these were 'single-issue movements' around a variety of topics such as 'law and order', 'bussing', anti-abortion, anti-gay rights, anti-the Equal Rights Amendment (ERA), they coalesced into 'the defence of the sanctity of white suburban family life'.[8] Not only, as Piven and Cloward have so eloquently presented it,[9] do they attack 'the new moral economy' whereby a political acceptance had developed over the last 30 years of the legitimacy of state intervention to provide for social and economic well-being, but also, as Petchesky has chillingly shown us,[10] they attack quite deliberately women and what has been won through feminist politics. Both Petchesky and Eisenstein document the development of the New Right's strategy around the question of women in general, and the issues of abortion and feminism in particular.[11] However, none of those writing about New Right politics is convinced of its lasting political acceptability.[12] All point us to what Taylor-Gooby has called its 'fragility' and claim that the alliances within the New Right may be unstable.[13] Notwithstanding this cautious optimism, what is clearly now a central theme in the rise of the New Right in both the US and Britain is not only the attack on the state in the economy but the exploitation of ideas about sex and the family. What is less commonly referred to in the theme I want to address is the breakdown of the political consensus about the uses of education for both the economy and the family *and* the rise of the New Right's approach here. I would argue that the breakdown of the political consensus has affected arguments about education and, in particular, the New Right has begun to promulgate a new notion about education which is profoundly moral. Not only is it developing an overall new approach to schooling and its relation to the family but it is also advocating new subjects in attempts to transform education. The new subject is moral education to include variously sex education, or rather family life education, education for parenthood, health education, religious education, social and life skills and personal values or what, in the US, is known as values clarification.

Although there is no necessary unanimity in the aims and content of these subjects, what is significant is the way in which they have been put together as a new curricular package and are being promoted together. Indeed, it could be argued that any one of these subjects alone is both radical and progressive. Certainly, in the past, the main proponents of sex education have been progressives. In this instance, however, the New Right has colonized sex education as an important component of family life education with the professed aim of using it to promote strict values about family behaviour and responsibility: hence also its links with moral education rather than with biology, its usual associate.

The Equality of Educational Opportunity Consensus

It is now well-established that in the post-war period in both Britain and the US, a broad political consensus has obtained on using education as an economic and social investment to serve economic growth, by means of the principle, at least, of equality of educational opportunity. I do not want to argue that the political pursuit of this principle did not, in fact, serve in the reproduction of the socio-economic system, but rather to acknowledge the strength of the political arguments, strategies and educational policies linked to achieving equality of educational opportunity in government circles. Indeed, it has been argued that the academic study of education, in the 1950s was begun by attempts to help politicians with this objective.[14] More recently sociologists of education have attacked that paradigm and tried to analyze the underlying, conservative nature of such a set of strategies.[15]

The way the principle has been enunciated and applied has varied in time and place between Britain and the US. But in both countries the position and claims of three social categories have been addressed in implementing the principle: social class, ethnicity and, most recently, sex (or rather gender).

I think it would be fair to argue that in America the main concern has been with breaking down the linkages between ethnicity and poverty, through education, rather than with social class *per se*. The landmark decisions and policies that demonstrate the way the principle has been applied and old relationships challenged are the 1954 Supreme Court decision on Brown versus the School Board of Topeka, Kansas and The Great Society Legislation of 1964–65, including the War on Poverty.[16] The Supreme Court decision was the first of several to establish that the principle of separate but equal, or rather racially segregated, schools was unconstitutional. It started the process of desegregation in the Southern States and later affected the attempts to achieve racially integrated schools in the North[17] (where de jure segregation had never been a problem but de facto segregation on the basis of residence had). The strategy to achieve racial balance eventually became that of bussing, ratified by a Supreme Court decision in 1971.[18] It still remains politically contentious, although established as a legal principle to achieve equality of educational opportunity among ethnic groups.

The Great Society legislation was a further political effort to develop a strategy of achieving equality of educational opportunity. Various efforts were tried: dealing with ethnicity in schools through the Civil Rights Act of 1964; relying on educational strategies for the poor through the Economic Opportunity Act of 1964, variously developing early opportunities for pre-school children and later opportunities for youth, and incorporating schooling into the Community Action Programmes (CAPs); providing new Federal funds to state and local agencies through the Elementary and Secondary Education Act, 1965, to achieve more equality in spending on schools. Significantly the Civil Rights Act mandated a social science survey on *Equality of Educational Opportunity* which was conducted and directed by Professor James Coleman and resulted in a mammoth report, two years later, on which further policies were based.[19] The Federal Government began its involvement with financing and directing educational policies.

British strategies to achieve equality of educational opportunity were developed with less public fanfare but were equally dramatic and seen as a change of direction. More attention was given to equality of access in terms of social class rather than race.[20] In particular, in the 1960s, the Labour Government's efforts to move from tripartite secondary education to comprehensive schools were based upon the view that they would widen educational opportunities. Labour also started the process of considering the role of the public schools in the education system although it failed finally to take action. The other strategy that the Labour Government pursued was borrowed from the United States: the creation, as a result of the Plowden Committee's report in 1967, of educational priority areas (EPAs) based on identification of community poverty. The EPAs, however, were less numerous and less clearly a strategy to deal with racial problems than the CAPs.[21]

In sum, the broad political consensus has been similar but the actual strategies to achieve the goal focussed upon different types of inequality. On the whole, the American approach (in a more litigious society) has resulted in more litigation to resolve policy issues than Britain, although the re-organization of comprehensive schools has not been immune from this.[22]

The process of applying the principle to social class and poor, ethnic minorities has continued in both Britain and America throughout the 1970s albeit with growing acrimony and resistance. In Britain, although the majority of secondary schools are now comprehensive, the present Tory Government has reneged on commitment to the principle. In the US, commitment to bussing as the method of achieving racial integration has waned and counter-strategies developed by vociferous local groups, all with anti-bussing in their titles. At present Congress is considering a law against bussing.[23]

The application of the principle of equality of educational opportunity to other social categories has, instead, developed out of these measures. As a result of major socio-economic changes, economic growth and some feminist political action both the US and Britain have tried to reduce sex differences in access to, and treatment within, the education system.[24] Again, I would argue that the US has developed a greater legal framework than Britain, with a longer history, and one that has resulted in more legal and political action to acquire the entitlements created through the legislation.

Recent US initiatives to reduce sex discrimination in public and economic life specifically started with the Civil Rights Act of 1964, although there is now much academic controversy about the origins of this. The major object of the legislation was to reduce discrimination against certain ethnic minorities, especially the blacks. Jo Freeman, amongst others, has argued that the inclusion of women as a category in one of the 'titles' or clauses of the Act was an 'accident'.[25] However, prior to 1965, recognition in the polity of women's exclusion was noted and a Committee on the Status of Women had been established in 1961 by President Kennedy. For whatever reason, progress in implementing the Act's provisions for women was limited. Between 1965 and 1967, shifts occurred in policy implementation for ethnic minorities, especially over whether individuals or groups should be covered. By 1965, the President, through an Executive Order, initiated a strategy of what quickly became known as Affirmative Action, similar to what is also known as positive discrimination — taking steps to ensure that categories of people, rather than individuals alone, were not discriminated against. As affirmative action was pursued the techniques developed for achieving equal treatment in jobs, housing and education were the setting of quotas for ethnic minorities in relation to their presence in the population. Glazer has called this the method of 'statistical parity'.[26] It has also been referred to as reverse discrimination.[27]

Gradually, this technique has been applied to sex discrimination in education. It was applied to all institutions with federal contracts, and this policy was strengthened through the Educational Amendments of 1972. Title IX specifically prohibits discrimination on the basis of sex in elementary and secondary schools, colleges and universities. It states:

> No person in the USA shall, on the basis of sex be excluded from participation in, be denied the benefits of, or be subjected to discrimination under any education program or activity receiving federal financial assistance ....[28]

At the same time, the body set up to monitor and enforce the Civil Rights legislation — the Equal Employment Opportunities Commission (EEOC) — was given stronger and tighter powers. Two years later Congress enacted the Women's Educational Equity Act (1974) specifically to achieve more equality of opportunity in the education profession. It dealt with discrimination in teachers' pay, maternity leave for teachers and finances to schools for particular subjects, courses, testing procedures, and also guidance and counselling.

By 1975 a complex legal framework had been created to deal with what Davidson, Ginsburg and Kay call 'sex-based discrimination', and many cases were brought to test the limits of this legislation, including a wide range on education.[29]

British strategies to provide equal educational opportunities for men and women, boys and girls have a much shorter pedigree. Essentially, the only provision is through the Sex Discrimination Act of 1975. Although HMIs had taken the initiative to study 'curricular differences between boys and girls' in the two years prior to the passing of the Act, their findings did not weigh heavily in the development of a legislative framework for education.[30] Education, too, was treated differently from other policy areas, such as housing and employment, with responsibility for implementation being placed with the DES or individual acts of litigation, rather than the EOC. It should be noted, however, that, unlike the situation in the US, teachers' conditions in Britain were more equitable. Women teachers, after a 50-year campaign, achieved equal pay by 1961.[31] Moreover, maternity leave and benefit established only in 1978 as an entitlement for teachers in the US, through the Pregnancy Disability Law,[32] had been granted in Britain after World War II. Moreover, some LEAs had developed their own maternity allowances, as a strategy to employ women teachers, in the early decades of the twentieth century. It cannot be argued that the US has been more committed to achieving equal educational opportunities for men and women. The question depends upon whether it is the treatment of students and pupils alone or the organization, structure of and access to education that is addressed. Both Britain and the US have, in different ways, developed a complex legal apparatus for tackling the thorny issue of sex discrimination in schooling and in the related area of the organization of employment. It is important to note the application of the principle of equality of opportunity — it is to those areas of economic and social life that are traditionally seen as public. The wider question of the division between public and private life was not addressed. The sexual division of labour in the family, as it affects both the structure of schooling and the economy, was not on the political agenda. In other words, the political consensus about equality of opportunity was very specific: it was about the structure or rather the *form* (to use Bowles and Gintis' terms) of schooling, in terms of access to and type of educational institution.[33] The content of schooling and more specifically the general *curriculum* was not really at issue. At the national or Federal political level non-intervention in the curriculum was a very deliberate policy.

In Britain, although central government has, since World War II, had strong powers over the organization of education, through the Ministry and later the Department of Education, it has quite consciously aeschewed involvement in the curriculum, maintaining a strong separation of powers. LEAs were given the duty, in the 1944 Education Act, to 'contribute towards the spiritual, moral, mental and physical development of the community', although these were not detailed. The only subject that was specified for the curriculum in law was religious instruction, allied to the statutory requirement to hold a religious assembly regularly. This was written into educational legislation as a concession to the religious authorities who agreed to more state control as an exchange, although the settlement between church and local authorities was reached in a way in which the LEAs did not win wide powers over the religious voluntary organizations running schools. The partnership remained relatively unequal. Equality of opportunity among religious affiliations has not been a subject for educational legislation in Britain.

In the US, equality of opportunity among religious groups has been achieved through constitutional means — the separation of church and state. Hence religious instruction is declared unconstitutional in schools which are publicly supported. Religious schools have been denied public support or funding. A Supreme Court ruling of 1922 legitimized the dual nature of public and denominational schools. Although all schools receiving public funds are to be completely secular, the state does not lay down the subjects or courses to be taught in schools. It outlaws courses which are deemed to be religious rather than scientific.

The Breakdown of the Educational Consensus

This political consensus that the object of education is to achieve equality of opportunity among social groups (on the basis of class, race, ethnicity or sex) is beginning to break down. The shift away from this principle is not fully or well articulated and vestiges of the commitment to it remain. Nevertheless, I think that the shifts are highly significant and may, eventually, affect the whole nature of schooling. The shifts are profoundly *moral*: they are about entitlements to schooling and about what schooling itself gives, or should give, in adult life. The shift towards a concern with the content of schooling — the school curriculum — rather than the social organization of schools reflects a new or a revived concern with social order and social values. In other words, attempts are being made to ensure that schooling confirms the legitimacy of the present inegalitarian socioeconomic system. Children are to be taught to accept a future in which employment may not be guaranteed. It is also, I believe, the first time in the history of compulsory schooling that such an explicit effort has been made to use the school curriculum to teach the virtues of patriarchal social organization, family patterns and especially relationships between men and women. I do not want to argue that such ideas have not permeated the school curriculum before. Indeed, they have been fundamental to school organization and to the relations between schooling and the family since modern education was established.[34] But hitherto the patriarchal order was the essence of the hidden curriculum.

The shifts are partly new and partly a reversal. The methods of achieving old ends are new. It seems to me this is the first time a concerted effort has been made to teach such subjects as moral education or family-life education. Such issues were seen before as private, taboo and not an area in which the state should intervene. If at all an issue, they were a subject for the family, to be taught by parents to their children. So what is new is the state's desire to take over parental responsibility to ensure that these ideas are taught. The curious contradiction is that what is to be taught are old, apparently traditional values of family privacy and duty and personal liberty.

These shifts towards moral education and away from sex equality in education are not only about ideas or ideology but also about material circumstances. They are about the legitimacy of the present inegalitarian social and sexual order, its work ethic and ethic of familialism. But they are also, equally importantly, about how best to prepare children for their real roles in the social and sexual division of labour. They may also be analyzed as reactions to the failure of social democracy in Britain and liberalism in the US to deal with economic recession. Education is part of the political armoury for coping with recession as well as growth. Indeed, it has been argued, for Britain at least, that 'education has been scapegoated for our economic ills'.[35] The New Right wants to find new goals for education. Liberal or Social Democratic schooling has failed to deliver the goods: equality of educational opportunity did not exploit talents which would ensure the participation of the most able in the jobs for which they were best suited. A meritocracy in social terms would not work. Education could, happily, be returned to its initial elite system of selection and social control since neither the strong nor the weak definitions of equality of educational opportunity had achieved what was hoped.[36]

A more important reaction of the New Right, however, is to the failure of Social Democracy of Liberalism to contain the breakdown of family life. On the one hand, they want, themselves, to reverse this demographic tidal wave and, on the other, they accuse, by implication, particular radical tendencies for creating and/or condoning this breakdown. The demographic trends which are a cause of major concern are the increase in divorce; the growth of what we in Britain refer to rather oddly, I always feel, as one-parent families and what the Americans call much more appropriately, if pompously, female-headed households, and within this category perhaps most politically significant, especially in the US, teenage pregnancy, particularly out-of-wedlock, schoolgirl mothers. Finally, the pheno-menon of 'working mothers' causes a good deal of political conflict.

There is little doubt or disagreement about these demographic trends in either country.[37] The conflict is over whether the trends should be reversed, consolidated or stabilized. The New Right wants to stem this tide and believes that its main enemy is women or feminism. Feminists are blamed for creating the demographic trends and applying political pressure to obtain social policies that reinforce these tendencies. The policies that are now under attack are equal rights legislation especially for women and mothers in the labour market, and, in the US, the attempt to add an amendment to the US constitution — the Equal Rights Amendment (ERA) — plus social benefits to mothers alone with children, child care policies and abortion policy. Indeed, in the US what arouses the most ire from elements of the New Right — it is what Jerry Falwell, leader of the Moral Majority described as 'America's biological holocaust' — is abortion policy. All the popular weekly magazines such as *Time*, *Newsweek* and *US News and World Report* have claimed that the two key domestic issues on the political agenda are 'abortion and school-prayer'.

Not only are certain domestic policies already enacted under attack but also ther is an attempt to replace them with new, more right-wing policies. Whether these attempts at replacement will be successful must remain, for the moment, a matter for conjecture. In the US, it has been claimed that the political alliances creating the New Right are inherently unstable.[38] In Britain, these attempts to rescind supposedly feminist social policies are much more veiled, nonetheless they remain potent.[39]

In general, the arguments of the New Right, especially about social policy, are politically appealing because of the psychological and social threats posed by the rapid social, familial and demographic changes that Britain and the US have witnessed in the last couple of decades. Although it is unlikely that the New Right's domestic policies will reverse demographic patterns, such as female or rather maternal employment or the rate of divorce, they will not confirm or consolidate such developments and they will feed people's (both men's and women's) anxieties about changing patterns of sexuality and the social, familial roles attendant upon them.[40] In other words, women will be forced to shoulder the double burden of employment and motherhood without respite, help or condolence from the state.

What evidence is there then of the New Right's new moralism and positive, rather than negative, policies to change family policies in education?

The New Politics of the School Curriculum

In Britain, the breakdown of the political consensus about equality of educational opportunity began under the Labour Government in the 1970s. That government committed itself to transforming the education system, to tie it more clearly to the needs of the economy. Several policies were developed to that end, including setting in train a review of school curricula. This approach, however, remained within the political consensus however much it diverged from previous Labour policies. Hall has argued that 'the Tories gained territory without having to take power', and most of his evidence is drawn from the changes in strategies on education.[41] Further concrete examples of this shift towards vocationalism and training have also been presented.[42] The Tories, on taking power, have, however, further shifted the terrain of educational debate, whilst drawing on Labour initiatives such as in *Education in Schools: A Consultative Document*.[43]

Their discussion about future schools policy has centred upon the question of the school curriculum with three major policy statements having been produced on this issue in the last two years. The fact that they have produced three major pieces of educational legislation must not be ignored. These three Education Acts, however, bolster up my contention that there has been a shift in political orientation. All three reinforce parental rights in education, in which individual parental choice weights more heavily than ensuring that equality of opportunity among children of different parental, social backgrounds is enforced. Although the past legislation on educational opportunities is not technically rescinded, the Education Acts go a long way to reversing them in practice. The 1979 Education Act, for instance, reneges on the commitment to comprehensive secondary schooling. This is confirmed by the current Secretary of State for Education's policy on sixth forms in schools — retaining those of 'proven worth' — rather than pursuing a policy of equal opportunities for children above the minimum school leaving age. It is also reinforced by the policy on assisted places, reviving the direct grant scheme in an individualistic form. The 1980 Education Act, drawing on a bill drafted by the Labour administration, also legislated for parental choice, both by requiring LEAs to provide school prospectuses on which parents could make 'informed' decisions about their own children's schooling, and by allowing for the representation of a parent on a school's governing body. This form of parental representation, as I have argued elsewhere, will not make for more parental participation and does not, in essence, transform school governance.[44] The change is symbolic rather than real — towards the rhetoric rather than the fact of parental control. Governing bodies are not afforded greater powers over the running of schools than hitherto. The shift in the treatment of 'special educational needs', through the Education Act of 1981, is also likely to be away from creating educational opportunities. The emphasis is on educational integration and the treatment of special needs within so-called normal schools, rather than in special educational institutions. Parents, again, are afforded, individually, more rights over type of school and are given the right of appeal or redress over LEA decisions.

Given the individualistic nature of these rights, differences among children are extolled, rather than similarity of treatment.

Most significant, however, of the shifts in educational policy are the official pronouncements on the school curriculum, set out in three documents — *A Framework for the School Curriculum*; *The School Curriculum*; and Circular 6/81.[45] This is the first time since World War II that official, government statements have been made on the *content* rather than the form of schooling, although some attempts have been made to alter the system of school examinations. Perhaps it is the case that the Government itself was not fully aware of the important step it was taking:[46]

> The legal responsibility for the curriculum is laid down in broad terms in the Education Acts. The Secretaries of State believe that these statutory provisions are sound and do not intend to change them. But there is an accumulation of evidence . . . that there is a need to review the way these responsibilities are exercised.

In fact, the recommendations went further than judging responsibilities. The DES finally made pronouncements on the subjects to be taught in schools and argued the case for the introduction of *new* academic areas:

> There are frequently demands, for which a good case can be made, for new subjects to be taught in schools and for new areas to be covered within the rubric of traditional subjects. New claims are always being made — for example, for the development of economic understanding, environmental education, *preparation for parenthood*, education for international understanding, *political and social education* and consumer affairs.[47] (my emphases)

So, even in the Government's own terms, the review of the school curriculum was to ensure not only its adequate teaching but also its adequacy in terms of coverage and subject-matter. Although the concern, in the reviews, was with the key, traditional subjects in the curriculum such as mathematics and English, and the development of a core, or a common curriculum, consisting of, at least, these two subjects, a major focus of the review was to ensure the emphasis on moral values and their specific inclusion in the curriculum. In other words, the Government was less concerned to ensure that, through schools, children were imbued with the correct skills (especially vocational) to participate in employment than that they developed, to use Benton's phraseology, the right dispositions to the socio-economic structure.[48] This balance of emphasis becomes more evident through the three documents. The initial document spelled out the supposed general aims of schooling, a common core curriculum of English, mathematics, some appreciation of science, modern languages and physical education, and added that: 'The Secretaries of State consider it is right, as is commonly the case, for religious education to be linked with the wider consideration of personal and social values.'[49] It goes on to argue that, contrary to the previous Labour Government's focus, from which it takes its general starting point, schools should prepare not only for working life but also for adult life.[50] This kind of preparation is much broader than hitherto and the term *adult* is added advisedly. The paragraph continues:

This requires many additions to the core subjects discussed above, in areas such as craft, design and technology; the arts, including music and drama; history and geography (either as separate subjects or as components in a programme of environmental and social education); *moral education, health education, preparation for parenthood and an adult role in family life*; careers education and vocational guidance; and preparation for a participatory role in adult society ... at one stage or another all *should* find a place in the education of every pupil.[51] (my emphases)

From this it is clearly evident that the Government is set on using schools to prepare children not only for work life but also for differential roles in adulthood. Here familial roles weigh heavily. It seems no accident that preparation for family responsibilities is linked with both moral and health education. The Government clearly holds a particular view of sexual relationships and sexual responsibilities within the family and, inevitably, outside it. Equal responsibilities are not articulated. Indeed, earlier in the document a commitment to reducing sexual inequalities in work life had been expressed but the commitment was very muted. The statement ran:

Special consideration should be given by both authorities and schools to the curricular needs of ethnic minorities, the handicapped, the less able and gifted, and *to the avoidance of discrimination between the sexes*. This last point is not met simply by making particular subjects and options formally open to boys and girls on equal terms; it is important that the educational and career implications of particular choices should be made clear, and *efforts made to prevent traditional differences in the education of boys and girls exercising too strong an influence.*[52] (my emphases)

No definition was given of what efforts should be made to prevent tradition holding sway. Although lip-service is now paid to the statutory framework concerning sex discrimination (The Sex Discrimination Act, 1975), the strategies and tactics to be used to overcome this discrimination, albeit very vague in the Act for education, are not even articulated here.[53] Moreover, discrimination against girls is linked to treatment of minorities — ethnicity, handicap, disability — rather than seen as central and a majority concern. The commitment, moreover, is not even to equality but rather that inequality should not appear to be too strong! In this respect, a commitment to family responsibilities, and the hidden agenda of the sexual division of labour within the family, would not conflict with that to reduce sexual inequalities in work life. On the other hand, the goal of equal opportunities in work life could not be achieved without a reduction of sexual inequalities in family life. But this is clearly not a part of this agenda.

In the firm policy document, from the DES — *The School Curriculum* — and the circular detailing how the policy is to be properly implemented even more explicit views of the role of sex in family and work life are articulated. Although the two documents do not (and cannot, within the present terms of the Education Acts) have the force of law, the DES fully and seriously *intends* there to be a change of practice on this score, and suggests how the new responsibilities of teachers, headteachers, governing bodies and LEAs should be exercised.

The School Curriculum spells out in great detail the aims and *content* of education in all schools supported financially by central and local government together. Although initially a broad ideological frame is given for the aims of schooling (which, in fact, closely conforms to those spelled out in the Labour Government's discussion document), most of the document is framed with a concern for *subjects* to be taught in order to acquire skills or areas of experience. It is argued, though, that:

> What is taught in schools, and the way it is taught, must appropriately reflect *fundamental values* in our society .... Three ... issues deserve special mention. First, our society has become multi-cultural ....
> Second, the effect of technology on employment patterns sets a new premium on *adaptability, self-reliance* and other *personal qualities*. Third, the equal treatment of men and women embodied in our law needs to be supported in the curriculum. It is essential to ensure that *equal curricular opportunity* is genuinely available to both boys and girls.[54] (my emphases)

Despite this apparent commitment to equality of opportunity between the sexes, the DES's preference is clearly for the reinforcement of sexual differentiation, especially in the family. It now claims that certain new subjects are *necessary* to the curriculum:

> There are also some *essential constituents* of the school curriculum which are often identified as subjects but which are as likely to feature in a variety of courses and programmes and may be more effectively covered if they are distributed *across* the curriculum. These concern personal and social development, and can conveniently be grouped under the headings of *moral education, health education* (including *sex education*) and *preparation for parenthood and family life*[55] (my emphases)

In defining what constitutes these various topics, it is stated that 'preparation for parenthood and family life should help pupils to recognise the importance of those human relationships which sustain, and are sustained by, family life, and the demands and duties that all impose on parents.'[56] The DES now clearly acknowledges that family life is not entirely a private matter but is circumscribed by public laws and state policies. It accepts its own duty to clarify to children what the state believes is entailed in being a parent. Nevertheless, the extent to which parenthood (and its corollary, sexuality) is legitimately a matter for state intervention, especially for schools, is hedged. It is not yet treated as synonymous with other school subjects or topics. The DES continues to regard it as a partly private, personal issue, and elevates it to a special status in the curriculum:

> Sex education is one of the most sensitive parts of broad programmes of health education, and the fullest consultation and cooperation with parents are necessary before it is embarked upon.[57]

Moreover, to that end, regulations have been given legal status, through the 1980 Education Act, which 'require LEAs to inform parents of the ways and contexts in which sex education is provided.[58] Sex education is clearly viewed as a grey area of public and private concern and, to the extent that it is still treated as private and hidden, it is not available for public policy change. Hence, the social roles that are predicated upon supposed biological sex roles being partly hidden within the family are not the subject of policies to achieve equality of opportunity. In other words, the social roles of motherhood and fatherhood (which stem from the biological fact of being a woman or a man) are not available for social policy change. Moves to modify the sexual division of labour in the economy can only be of limited relevance if no parallel moves are taken to modify family roles and they remain hidden and private. Thus, the commitment in the rest of the document to sexual equality of opportunity is limited. It is clearly only about public opportunities, although the DES veils this by referring only to *adult life*, rather than to its original broader concept of adult and work life. Nevertheless, adulthood is now apparently a synonym for economic life since the whole emphasis is on the links between education and the economy, especially industry and the development of careers. Lip-service is therefore paid to using schools to promote sexual equality in job opportunities:

> It is essential that career opportunities should be kept equally open to boys and to girls. The obstacles to equal employment opportunities for women are deeply rooted in attitudes in the home and in society. Schools can do much to diminish these obstacles through the content of the curriculum ....[59]

The commitment is quite evidently towards equality between men and women who have no maternal responsibilities. Otherwise, this pious wish to eradicate sex differences in curricular offerings would run directly counter to its efforts to ensure the teaching of a broad spectrum of moral education, emphasizing parental responsibilities in society. The root notion of the family to be used in these latter subjects is patriarchal or of unequal sexual relations in which fathers rule in the family and women are subordinate. Woman's main roles, through marriage, are as economically dependent on her husband and as housewife, caring for both husband and children. In this family model, women are, by virtue of their work within the family as both wives and mothers, effectively excluded from equal participation in the labour force.

This patriarchal notion of the family is not on the political agenda to be changed. Rather it is to be reinforced not only through changes in the school curriculum towards the teaching of parenthood but also through other moves to dismantle aspects of the Welfare State and return mothering to its proper place in the family. For instance, another feature of the 1980 Education Act which bears heavily on this issue is the removal of the legal responsibility on LEAs to provide nursery education for children aged three to five. In a recent clarificatory circular it is clear that there is no obligation on LEAs to provide nursery school sessions that bear any relation to compulsory schooling.[60] Indeed, it is recommended that nursery teachers effectively work a 'double-shift', teaching in two schools each week. The net effect of these policy changes will be to increase the burden on mothers of early childcare. This becomes even more obvious when it is seen that the other traditional governmental partner in childcare provision — the DHSS — has stated categorically that childcare arrangements for both pre-school children and school-age children after the schoolday or in the holidays are not a state responsibility but one entirely for parents.[61] No attempts are being made by this Government to support working mothers by improving their conditions of service to provide statutory parental rights to leave for sick children, let alone benefits. Indeed, maternal rights in employment have been severely curtailed.[62]

The Thatcher Government has an absolutely clear notion of the family and parental responsibility. The state has to enforce the notion that mothers should not shirk, and will not be assisted by state policies in shirking their childcare obligations. To this end, the government is dismantling those parts of the Welfare State which allow the family to abrogate responsibility for childcare and childrearing. More importantly, it is beginning to use schools explicitly to reinforce notions of family, especially maternal, responsibility.

Although it can be argued that sex education is not necessarily conservative and, indeed, there is much evidence to suggest that previous attempts to get it included in school curricula were very progressive, at this juncture it seems that it is to be used to bolster up the patriarchal family. For instance, the Festival of Light, a very reactionary pressure group welcomed the DES's initiatives on sex education but demanded that more thorough guidelines be sent to LEAs.[63] It wanted the guidelines to state that sex education should be on the basis of 'chastity before marriage and fidelity within it.... We suggest that in reviewing sex education schemes, the DES should emphasize the crucial importance of the married partnership as the only adequate basis for family life.' Indeed, its call for a sex education review is because, in the last decade, there has been a dramatic rise in teenage pregnancy and one-parent families, which they attribute to the growth of secular sex education programmes. Interestingly, and significantly, they do not demand an end to such programmes but their transformation to a religious commitment to the family. Sex education can be both an incentive to and a prevention against promiscuity. It clearly depends upon context.

The Politics of Family Protection through Schools

In the US, the shifts away from the principle of equality of opportunity in education began under the ostensibly liberal Carter Administration, although, as for Britain, it could be argued, prompted by New Right political pressure.[64] For instance, Carter tried to convert the well-established decennial White House Conference on Children into one on the family. But he failed to achieve any policy outcomes because he vacillated over definitions of the family. In so doing, he initiated what has been called 'the war over the family'.[65] Under the Reagan Administration, the New Right pressure has been accepted unquestioningly and forms the basis for changes in educational policy. It is a simple and uncomplicated moral stance, aiming to return responsibility to the family, the model being the white, suburban, middle-class, heterosexual, nuclear family.[66] In this, the 100-year-old tradition, or ideal, of community, public, secular education is to be destroyed, and replaced by parental and religious control of schools. The key way in which this is to be enacted is through the Family Protection Act, currently going through Congress.[67] Its main provisions are educational, although it also deals with tax laws and other principles affecting the family. It aims both to rescind much of the recent equal opportunities legislation for race and sex and to replace it with traditional moral and familial education. Thus, Federal aid, which is now considerable, will be withheld from schools which prohibit either voluntary school prayer or sex segregation in 'sports or school-related activities' on affirmative action grounds; or which provide 'any program which produces or promotes courses of instruction or curriculum seeking to inculcate values or modes of behaviour which contradict the demonstrated beliefs and values of the community', or any program which supports 'educational materials or studies . . . [which] would tend to denigra diminish or deny role differences between the sexes as it [sic] has been historica..y understood in the United States.'[68] Moreover, parents are to be entitled to preview or rather *censor* textbooks prior to their use. In other words, the whole focus of the school curriculum is to be transformed to one in which traditional moral and especially religious values play a greater part. Here sex differentiation is to be applauded. Moreover, the belief that the religious family is the repository of all that is good underpins other dramatic policy changes, namely tax concessions for parents whose children attend private or parochial schools and also the removal of Federal control over discrimination in private schools. Racial, sexual and religious segregation is promoted by endorsing parental or 'Christian' schools, and tax penalties removed. The Act, in sum, 'protects' the traditional family and especially women by endorsing moral and religious notions and reversing policies seeking to promote racial and sexual equality. The abolition of the Federal Department of Education — part of the policy of 'New Federalism' — confirms the idea that the family should be responsible rather than the state, for education and the inculcation of values. The values to be upheld are religious; confirmed, at another level, by the various efforts in state supreme courts to allow the teaching of 'creationism' as a 'scientific' rather than religious theory.[69]

The shift in political ideologies about education is even more explicit in the US than in Britain. Not only are all educational attempts at equal opportunities to be reversed, but also the religious patriarchal family is to suffuse both the curriculum and educational organization if the Moral Majority (the Chairman of whom introduced the Family Protection Act) is to have its way. Reagan, although supporting reductions in 'big government' and hence Federal interference in cases of school discrimination, has not yet endorsed the Family Protection Act. The Act does present a curious contradiction: Federal and local enforcement of preaching and teaching private, familial values.

The New Moral Economy

In conclusion, I suggest that in the last few years in both Britain and the US political ideologies about education have shifted towards a concern with 'fundamental values' about social organization. These ideologies are, in fact, a reversal of the post-war political consensus on equality of educational opportunity. They are all part of an attempt to return social and economic organization to the status quo ante World War II. In particular, the focus is upon family life in its myriad forms: five changes in sexual patterns prompt concern. They are the rise in teenage, out-of-wedlock pregnancy and parenthood; the growth of one-parent families; the increase in divorce; the phenomenon of 'working mothers', especially with very young children; and the development of abortion policy. All are essentially about women's place in society and women's rights. The present desire is to stem these changes and, if possible, reverse them and bring back the family form of a nuclear, two-parent family with a male breadwinner and dependent housewife, caring, at home, for the children.

The method of achieving these traditional ends is what is new and significant. It is by means of moral exhortation and special teaching of moral or religious education. What cannot be achieved privately by social constraints and fiscal and financial policies alone which give support to the patriarchal family is to be produced publicly in the education system. This overt shift to the public domain to preach family privacy and responsibility is a curious contradiction. Although the subject-matter of education remains in harmony with the New Right's initiatives to reduce 'big government' and to dismantle the Welfare State, by returning responsibility to the family itself and its womenfolk in particular the method adopted of using education to instil these private, familial values is at odds with this strategy. For instance, Pelham has claimed that 'there is no firm estimate yet of what the Family Protection Act would cost the Treasury in terms of lost revenues, but the figure would be in the billions.'[70] Neither has the implementation of England's *School Curriculum* been publicly costed but, clearly, it could not be achieved without considerable, additional public expenditure. Perhaps we should not fear this new rationale for schooling but rather take it at its face value. It is moral exhortation from right-wing pressure groups who, in all likelihood, fear feminism more realistically than we should fear them.[71] Their stand is, in respect of education, obviously defensive and, in all probability, impossible to implement fully. Nevertheless, it is significant that they have captured the political terrain to espouse their position and so forcefully re-assert the virtues, particularly of 'patriarchal motherhood'.[72] Even if the curricular package of moral and sex education is not incorporated into most schools, the other elements of the agenda undoubtedly will be achieved in the short run — the reversal of anti-discrimination policies and returning welfare responsibilities to the family — for these are already set in train.

What can be done to counter such tendencies? Is it possible to take back the political terrain and recover sex and moral education for a more progressive stance? Zillah Eisenstein has persuasively argued that although liberalism alone is not essentially radical there are still radical possibilities in liberal feminism.[73] Can we, as feminists and socialists, regain the arena of state education and transform it to popular, radical ideology? Given the contradictions in the New Right's scenarios and the claims made by other academic commentators of the instability of this 'authoritarian populism', the outlook is probably not as bleak as I have indicated.[74] Neither sex education nor the family are in and of themselves entirely reactionary forces. They can be used to develop a more radical strategy to counter the state's now vigorous policy initiatives to keep women in their homely place.

Notes

1 EISENSTEIN, Z. (1981) 'Antifeminism in the politics and election of 1980', *Feminist Studies* 7, 2, pp. 187–206; and PETCHESKY, R.P. (1981) 'Antiabortion, antifeminism and the rise of the New Right', *Feminist Studies* 7, 2, pp. 206–47.

2 PUGH, G. (1981) 'Progress on the parenting project', *Concern*, 41, Autumn, pp. 27–30.

3 See, for example, ROWTHORN, B. (1982) 'The past strikes back', *Marxism Today*, 26, 1, pp. 6–14.

4 TAYLOR-GOOBY, P. (1981) The New Right and social policy', *Critical Social Policy*, 1, 1, pp. 18–32.

5 MOUFFE, C. (1981) 'Democracy and the New Right', *Politics and Power 4*, Routledge and Kegan Paul, pp. 221–37, p. 231.

6 DAVIS, M. (1981) 'The New Right's road to power', *New Left Review 128*, July–August, pp. 28–49.

7 WOLFE, A. (1981) 'Sociology, liberalism and the radical right', *New Left Review 128*, July–August, pp. 3–27.

8 DAVIS, M. *op. cit.*, p. 38.

9 PIVEN, F.F. and COWARD, R. (1981) 'Moral economy and the Welfare State', plenary paper presented at the Annual Conference of the British Sociological Association, Aberystwyth, Wales, 9 April.

10 PETCHESKY, R.P. *op. cit.* (Note 1).

11 PETCHESKY, R.P. *ibid* and EISENSTEIN, Z. *op. cit.* See also, for a more thorough account, EISENSTEIN, Z. (1981) *The Radical Future of Liberal Feminism*, London, Longmans, especially Chapter 7.

12 MILLER, S.M. (1981) 'Reagan, Reaganism and the real world', *New Society*, 55, 950, pp. 91–3. PLOTKE, D. (1981) 'Reagan: Is it as bad as it sounds?', *Marxism Today*, 25, 2, pp. 6–13.

13 TAYLOR-GOOBY, P. *op. cit.*, p. 30.

14 FINN, D., GRANT, N. and JOHNSON, R. (1977) 'Social democracy, education and the crisis', in *On Ideology, Cultural Studies 10*, Birmingham Centre for Contemporary Cultural Studies and Hutchinson.

15 See, for example, YOUNG, M. and WHITTY, G. (1977) (Eds) *Society, State and Schooling*, Barcombe, Falmer Press.

16 See, for example, JENCKS, C. *et al.* (1973) *Inequality: A Reassessment of Family and Schooling in America*, Harmondsworth, Penguin; and BOWLES, S. and GINTIS, H. (1976) *Schooling in Capitalist America*, London, Routledge and Kegan Paul.

17 CRAIN, R. (1968) *The Politics of School Desegregation*, CHICAGO, ALDINE and ORFIELD, G. (1978) *Must We Bus? Segregated Schools and National Policy*, Washington, D.C., The Brookings Institution.

18 ORFIELD, G., *ibid.* and GLAZER, N. (1976) *Affirmative Discrimination*, New York, Basic Books.

19 MOSTELLER, F. and MOYNIHAN, D.P. (1972) On *Equality of Educational Opportunity*, New York, Random House.

20 WESTERGAARD, J. and RESLER, H. (1976) *Capital and Class*, Harmondsworth, Penguin.

21 HIGGINS, J. (1978) *The Poverty Business*, Oxford, Martin Robertson.

22 For a comparison of the litigious nature of Britain and the US, see Chapter 1 of HOROWITZ, D. (1980) *The Courts and Social Policy*, Washington, D.C., The Brookings Institution. For details of British litigation, see either FOWLER, G. *et al.* (1976) *Decision-Making in British Education*, London, Allen and Unwin, or GRIFFITH, J.A.G. (1980) *The Politics of the Judiciary*, London, Fontana, second edition.

23 For details, see *The Congressional Quarterly* (1981) 39, 47, 21 November, p. 2288.

24 For the US, see especially FISHEL, J. and POTTKER, A. (1978) *National Politics and Sex Discrimination in Education*, Boston, Lexington Books, or GUTTENTAG, M. and BRAY, H. (Eds) (1976) *Undoing Sex Stereotypes : Research and Resources for Educators*, New York, McGraw Hill. For Britain, see my own study, Part 3, DAVID, M.E. (1980) *The State, the Family and Education*, London, Routledge and Kegan Paul, or BYRNE, E. (1978) *Women and Education*, London, Tavistock.

25 FREEMAN, J. (1975) *The Politics of Women's Liberation*, London, Longmans.

26 GLAZER, N. *op. cit.*

27 DWORKIN, R. (1977) *Taking Rights Seriously*, London, Duckworths.

28 The Editors, *Harvard Educational Review* (1979) 49, 4, p. 504.

29 DAVIDSON, K.M., GINSBURG, R.B. and KAY, H. (1978) *Sex-Based Discrimination: Texts, Cases and Materials*, St Paul's, Minn., West Publishing Company.

30 DES (1975) *Curricular Differences for Boys and Girls*, Educational Survey No. 21, London, HMSO.

31 DAVID, M.E. *op. cit.*, Chapter 6.

32 ADAMS, C.T. and WINSTON, K.T. (1980) *Mothers at Work*, London, Longmans, p. 33.

33 BOWLES, S. and GINTIS, H. *op. cit.*

34 In my book (DAVID, M.E. *op. cit.*) I have tried to demonstrate the extent to which notions of the family underpin the social organization of schooling as well as define the ways in which the education system is organized. I have drawn on documentary evidence from English educational policy from the nineteenth century to the present.

35 SILVER, H. (1978) 'Education and social policy', *New Society*, 46, 843.

36 DES (1972) *Educational Priority*, Vol. 1, *Problems and Policies*, London, HMSO. See the introduction by Professor A.H. Halsey.

37 For Britain, the most recent evidence for these trends has been presented in *Population Trends 1981*, London, HMSO. For the US, a detailed review of ten books on the family presents the demographic evidence, citing how uncontroversial that in itself is, but referring to the political conflicts surrounding how to deal with it. HACKER, A. (1982) 'Farewell to the family?' *New York Review of Books*, 29, 4, pp. 37–44. See also SMITH, R. (Ed.) (1980) *The Subtle Revolution*, Washington, D.C., The Urban Institute.

38 DAVIS, M. *op. cit.*: WOLFE, A. *op. cit.*

39 COOTE, A. and COUSSINS, J. (1981) 'The family in the firing line', *Child Poverty Action Group*, pamphlet.

40 PETCHESKY, R.P. *op. cit.* makes a similar point in conclusion to her article on the politics of anti-feminism.

41 HALL, S. (1979) 'The great moving right show', *Marxism Today*, 23, 1, pp. 14–21.

42 CENTRE FOR CONTEMPORARY CULTURAL STUDIES (1981) *Unpopular Education*, London, Hutchinson.

43 DES (1977) *Education in Schools: A Consultative Document*, Cmnd 6869, London, HMSO.

44 DAVID, M.E. *op. cit.* See also DAVID, M.E. (1978) 'Parents and educational politics in 1977' in BROWN, M. and BALDWIN, S. (Eds) *The Yearbook of Social Policy 1977*, London, Routledge and Kegan Paul.

45 DES and WELSH OFFICE (1980) *A Framework for the School Curriculum*, London, DES, January; DES and WELSH OFFICE (1981) *The School Curriculum*, London, HMSO, 25 March; DES and WELSH OFFICE (1981) *The School Curriculum*, circular 6/81 DES, 1 October.

46 *A Framework...*, *op. cit.*, p. 1, para. 1.

47 *The School Curriculum*, *op. cit.*, p. 4, para. 13.

48 BENTON, T. (1974) 'Education and politics', in HOLLY, D. (Ed.) *Education or Domination*, London, Arrow.

49 *A Framework,... op. cit.*, p. 7, para. 28.

50 DES (1977), *op. cit.*

51 *A Framework,... op. cit.*, p. 8, para. 32.

52 *Ibid*, p. 4, para. 13.

53 For a basic description of the Act, see HARMAN, H. (1978) *Sex Discrimination in Schools: How to Fight it*, London, National Council for Civil Liberties.

54 *The School Curriculum*, *op. cit.*, pp. 6 and 7, para. 22.

55 *Ibid*, p. 7, para. 23.

56 *Ibid*, p. 8, para. 25.

57 *Ibid*, p. 8, para. 26.

58 *Ibid*.

59 *Ibid*, p. 19, para. 54.

60 DES and WELSH OFFICE (1981) *Nursery Education*, circular 7/81, October.

61 This has been articulated in several speeches by the Under-Secretary of State for Social Services, but most notably in Parliament. See *Hansard*, 4 November 1981.

62 COOTE, A., and COUSSINS, J., *op. cit.*

63 LODGE, B. (1981) 'Call for sex education review', *The Times Educational Supplement*, 30 December.

64 For a detailed critique of this period, see STEINER, G. (1980) *The Futility of Family Policy*, Washington, D.C., The Brookings Institution.

65 BERGER, B. (1981) 'The war over the family', *The Public Interest*, 65, Autumn, pp. 113–14.

66 PETCHESKY, R.P., *op. cit.*

67   For full details, see *The Congressional Quarterly* (1981) weekly report, 39, 40, 3 October, p. 1916.
68   *Ibid.*
69   For a thorough discussion, see DICKSON, D. (1981) 'Adam and Eve and Darwin', *New Society*, 55, 954.
70   PELHAM, A. (1981) 'Family Protection Act: Dear to the New Right, but unlikely to get out of committees', *The Congressional Quarterly*, 39, 40, 3 October, p. 1916.
71   Linda Gordon and Allen Hunter in a seminal article written in 1977 drew attention to this. GORDON, L. and HUNTER, A. (1977–78) 'Sex, family and the New Right', *Radical America*, 11, 6, pp. 9–25.
72   This is a term coined by Zillah Eisenstein. See EISENSTEIN, Z. (1981) *op. cit.*
73   *Ibid*, p. 248.
74   This term was used by HALL, S. *op. cit.*

10.   Social Theory, Social Relations and Education

Lorraine Culley, Leicester Polytechnic
Jack Demaine, Loughborough University

Introduction

The predominant trend in recent sociology of education has been the attempt to develop 'general theory' of social relations and their educational contexts. Attempts have been made to analyze class divisions and sexual divisions and indeed to combine concepts of 'class' and 'gender' in a theory of capitalist and patriarchal education. The problem usually addressed in such discourses is how educational institutions (or apparatuses), policies and practices relate to a general theory of the functioning of capitalist society or capitalist social relations.[1] Educational practices are commonly discussed in terms of a relation between education or 'schooling' and the 'needs' and 'interests' of capitalism and/or patriarchy. Political arguments, struggles and outcomes are conceived as the clash of different pre-given 'interests' or 'needs'.[2]

Such analyses are usually conducted in relation to discussions of an entity which is variously referred to as 'social democracy', 'liberal democracy' or the 'corporate state'.[3] The development of education and the forms of its development are conceived as determined by, or as a response to, the interests of 'capital', 'capitalism' or the 'capitalist mode of production' and secured by the action of an aggregate agency — the state in its capitalist or corporatist form. Such analyses were initially concerned with an explanation and critique of class inequalities in education and the reproduction of the social relations of production but subsequently there have been attempts to 'graft on' or in some way incorporate a series of other inequalities, social relations and divisions — predominantly 'racial' and sexual divisions.[4] That is to say, the argument has been that education is conditioned by the pre-given interests not only of 'capital' but also, in some way, of 'men' as a group or white people as a group.[5]

Recent literature is critical of earlier attempts to relate the education system to the needs of capital in a simple and crude manner.[6] However, it is a critique which only goes so far in rejecting a Marxist functionalism, and in effect constitutes a very limited form of problematizing earlier conceptions. *Unpopular Education*, for example, asks the reader to recognize that capitalism's needs are more complex than was first thought,

> In any specific historical situation industry's needs for labour power are themselves extremely complex: these are not so much a question of the 'requirements of capital' as the needs of different, co-existing capitals.[7]

We are told that the aim should be

> for a complex Marxism, modified by what can be learned from other

traditions and from the theorization of *further* contingencies. This means, among other things, that it is useful to think about determinations on or within 'education' aside from capital's requirements for self-reproduction.[8]

This does not entail a rejection of the discourse of 'needs' or 'interests'. The authors of *Unpopular Education* insist on a concept of the state, not as a tool of the ruling class, but as a site of struggle. Nevertheless, it is a struggle between interests which pre-exist it. *Unpopular Education* sets up the category of the 'popular' (in its most general sense) as those diverse groups who have interests which are not directly related to the needs of capital.[9] The complexity of determinations on educational policy arises as an effect of the complexity of 'needs' it attempts to fulfil, and pre-given interests it attempts to represent.

Similarly in the field of sexual differences in education, the inadequacy of a conception which reduces the education of women to a determination by the needs of capital is indicated, yet there is again a refusal to abandon the notion of pre-given needs. Deem, for example, following Scase, O'Connor and Gough, argues that

> the state in any capitalist country must try to meet the needs of capital and to provide conditions which are not inimical to the process of capital accumulation. But this does not necessarily mean that there is a close 'fit between the functions of capital and those of the state, since capital is also heterogenous, and what appeases one fraction will not do so for another. So we cannot see either state policies or ideologies about women as directly or only fulfilling the needs of capital, although there is a strong indirect connection ... the state in capitalist society, must assist in the reproduction of the labour force.[10]

Whilst in a sense these arguments are an advance over more vulgar functionalist Marxist positions, they remain within the discourse of a particular conception of interests. That is, a conception of interests as things inherent in a particular set of social relations *independent of any agency calculating those interests*. Due to their position in social relations certain classes/groups are seen to have a *common essential interest* which exists as long as those social relations exist and, as Tomlinson argues,[11] prior to and separate from any calculation (by the interests concerned) as to what those interests might be. It is this *ontological* conception of interests which must be displaced.

We are concerned then to establish some conceptual difficulties inherent in the posing of issues of class and sexual differences in education in terms of a concept of pre-given needs or interests. Our primary concern, however, is to demonstrate the *politically limiting* effects of those discourses which view politics, and educational politics in particular, as the play of sets of ontological interests or needs.

One effect of an insistence on the failure of politics in social democracy or liberal democracy to secure the '*real* interests' of classes, etc. is to minimize the possible forms of change within capitalist relations. The political effects of such positions are often debilitating and the specificity of contemporary struggles can be neglected in the vision of a coming general crisis of capitalism. Politically, such analyses are also an obstacle to innovations in political practice on the Left which are badly needed.[12] In addition, the political effects as far as the success of *feminist* objectives are concerned can be particularly obstructive.[13]

This chapter is not intended as a comprehensive critique of Marxist theories of education, but has the more limited objective of indicating some of the challenges which already exist to the kinds of argument which have a strong hold on educational discourses at the present time.

Politics and 'Ontological' Interests

The conception of definite institutional spheres, policies, etc. as registering the effects or reflecting the interests of something outside of those spheres is not confined to the field of education. A similar argument can be found in many contemporary Left analyses. Two areas where this conception and its effects have been criticized recently are to be found in analyses of arguments concerning the 'corporatist' nature of the state and trade union activity, and, in relation to sexual divisions, in analyses of the capitalist/sexist nature of the law.

In his article, 'Corporatism: A further sociologization of Marxism',[14] Jim Tomlinson has discussed the work of writers such as Hyman and Panitch, in which successive British governments are conceived as attempting to incorporate trade unions as effective agencies of the state, as a means of integrating the working class into capitalist society. In a review of Sachs and Hoff's *Sexism and the Law*,[15] Elizabeth Kingdom has criticized the explanation of the patterns of behaviour and activities of judges and other legal agents by reference to the material or economic interests of judges as upper-class males. Kingdom shows how in such an analysis judgements are conceived as representing something else — they represent pre-given interests, of which particular legal cases are exemplars. Both Tomlinson and Kingdom are concerned with the political consequences of these forms of argument. We will briefly outline Tomlinson's argument and indicate how such a critique of the concept of interests can be extended to the area of educational discourse.

As Tomlinson argues, one of the theoretical foundations of the corporatist argument is a notion of interests, conceived not as constructed in political argument, but as inherent in a particular set of social relations. They are interests which exist *independently* of any agency calculating them. Because of their position in social relations, certain groups or classes have a common essential interest which exists as long as those social relations exist, and prior to and separate from any calculation as to what those interests might.be. Capitalist social formations are conceived of as constructing two major sets of interests — those of labour and capital. These interests are necessarily in a contradictory relation to one another and although they may be temporarily reconciled, the contradiction is constantly re-asserting itself in a variety of forms. This is so because the contradiction is an ontological one. The working class has an interest as a consequence of its existence in the exploitative social relations of capitalism — an interest which is the suppression of those social relations. It is, as Tomlinson points out, an interest not necessarily calculated by the working class — it would still exist even if every single member of the working class were violently hostile to socialism.

This form of argument implies that ultimately current policies are necessarily in the interests of capital and against those of labour and that the consequences of these policies, if successfully pursued, are given in advance because they merely reflect the play of these pre-given interests. (This is a position which we can readily identify as one with a definite currency in educational debates.) However, as Tomlinson points out,

This latter is clearly problematic because it assumes that somewhere there is in effect being made a calculation as to the best interests of capital, and that this calculation is necessarily correct — this agency always perfectly knows where the interests of capital lie.[16]

The conception of pre-given interests has allied to it a particular conception of the nature of the state in capitalist society. The state acts in the interests of capital. This conception of the state is surrounded by all sorts of qualifications and equivocations, but its basic function is clear.

Tomlinson is concerned with the political consequences of the conception of ontological interests, which we have very briefly outlined. One effect is that it creates a form of political argument which always 'slides off' into a general discourse on capitalism/socialism. It makes impossible any calculation of socialist/ working class interests which fall outside a scale running from capitalism to socialism, because it is at that level that interests are operative. Thus the calculation of any possible gains under capitalism is undercut. One further consequence of conceiving of society as constituted by sets of inherent interests is that texts based on such notions become texts of *exemplification*. Particular policies, events, etc. are used, not as a means of raising problems, but as examples of what is already known. If interests are given, political argument becomes a question of allocating any particular policy to one of two categories. A policy can be 'good' or 'bad' according to whose interests it serves. The form of conceptualization then, as Tomlinson argues, makes it difficult or impossible to analyze particular political questions *in their own right* and not simply as emanations of interests constituted in another sphere.[17]

This kind of position, although discussed by Tomlinson in relation to discussions of corporatism and trade union activity, clearly has a resonance in the field of education.[18] Discourses concerning educational statutes, policies and practices frequently consist of the 'reading-off' of the intervention of pre-given interests. Education is seen as yet another field in which inherently opposed interests are compromised, be they the interests of capital versus labour, capital versus the popular or men versus women. Although it is conceded that there are struggles between interests, whilst capitalism remains the interests of capitalism/ patriarchy are by definition predominant, and the interests of labour/women are subordinate to them. The state is not usually conceived as a monolith (except in the cruder forms of the argument). It is conceived as the site of struggles and may even sometimes be seen to grant concessions to labour or women. Ultimately, however, its function is sustained. Workers may win the Welfare State, but this provides healthy workers — women or workers may win access to education but this provides a trained and ideologically complicit workforce. Despite various qualifications of the role of the state, this position represents

a fairly commonplace piece of Marxist functionalism.... It is known in advance that all state agencies *really* aid the bourgeoisie, and all the equivocations of 'relative autonomy' etc. ... cannot escape this initial functionalist premise.[19]

Particular educational policies or objectives can themselves be categorized according to whose interests they serve. The core curriculum, for example, can be categorized as 'bad' because it furthers the alignment of the school curriculum to the needs of capitalist industry. Such a position, evades the possibility that the core curriculum may be a good thing from a feminist viewpoint.[20] The construction of political objectives, the linking of them to particular levels of organization and the possibility of incompatibility between objectives, cannot be discussed in the simple dichotomies of pre-given interests.

The conception of pre-given interests and their representation in the state is a major source of political limitation. It excludes certain political practices which may enable socialists and feminists to make advances in certain countries. Struggle within the state apparatuses and against them is seen as possible, but as such the state is confined within necessarily capitalist limits. Such positions sharpen the reform/revolution couple.[21] If the state and educational apparatuses serve to reproduce capitalist interests they can only be opposed by revolutionary class struggle. One possible effect of these kinds of argument is a refusal to seriously engage with current political parties, policies, politics, etc. It leads to the idea that direct engagement with state policy, and so on, is to engage in dastardly liberal reformism. We will return to this issue later, but would add here that there is little point in arguing for generalized alternatives without also a calculation and specification of the political conditions of their realizability. If one argues that we have capitalist schooling because the capitalist mode of production requires it, then there seems little point in continually registering the capitalist nature of schooling as if it were some kind of effective criticism. We would argue that this quite simply has no purchase whatever in current political struggles around education.

We will return to discuss how an alternative conception of education and politics would require the abandonment of concepts of essential interests. Here we would like to make brief reference to two further conceptual difficulties involved in the notion of politics conceived as the representation of pre-given interests.

The first comment is that this argument is an example of the classical theory of representation, within which the represented is always prior to the representation which is its mark. Problems with this conception are discussed in Paul Hirst's *On Law and Ideology*. Mark Cousins has demonstrated the difficulty with this concept of representation in relation to the concept of patriarchy.[22]

A second and more fundamental though related problem is that analyses of education and educational politics as representing inherent interests clearly rely on a conception of social totality (capitalism) which is inevitably essentialist. The conception of capitalism as a social totality is criticized in Cutler *et al.*[23] An excellent summary of these criticisms of Marxist theories is given by Rosalind Coward.[24] Whilst not entirely uncritical of this 'rethinking of Marxism', Coward draws out the implications of it for feminism in particular. She demonstrates how dominant conceptions in Marxism, such as the primacy of the economic, have inevitably marginalized feminist concerns and how the arguments in Cutler *et al.*, in dismissing such essentialist concepts, are potentially very exciting for socialist feminists. It is to the issue of conceptions of sexual differences in education that we now turn.

Education and Patriarchy

We shall indicate here some broad criticisms of the concepts of 'patriarchy' and 'capitalist patriarchy' and their implications for those discussions of educational institutions, practices and agencies which utilize such concepts. Our comments are necessarily brief. We would simply like to point out some of the difficulties with, and objections to, ways of conceiving patriarchy and capitalist patriarchy made by writers sympathetic to socialist feminism. We will argue that the effects for political argument of the attempt to utilize concepts of patriarchy in the analysis of sexual differences (in general and in education) are similar to the effects of the essentialism of arguments concerning the needs or interests of capitalism discussed above. We will also give an outline of existing arguments which demonstrate the difficulties with, and politically limiting effects of, combining 'patriarchy' and 'capitalism' in some generalized structure.

The theoretical literature on 'patriarchy' and 'capitalist patriarchy' is extensive and cannot be reviewed in full here.[25] In radical feminist conceptions, patriarchy is discussed in terms of the domination of 'women' by 'men' — a relation which has always been ultimately determined by a biological distinction. As Parveen Adams has pointed out, 'What is set up is an antagonism between the sexes, grounded in a biological reality which is taken to pre-exist and to determine social relations.'[26] In addition, there are many who would reject an explanation in biological terms but who nonetheless retain the notion of patriarchy — the domination of women by men — as a general problem to be addressed. Other feminists invoke patriarchy as a set of systematic social relations, as the origin and mechanism of women's oppression. Michèle Barrett and other Marxist feminists have criticized such notions of patriarchy as being 'redolent of a universal and trans-historical oppression' and unable to specify historical limits, changes or differences.[27] Other forms of criticism, however, are of a more fundamental nature. Mark Cousins, for example, has seen the major problem with the concept of patriarchy as its inescapable circularity.

> In order to function as a cause, the concept of [patriarchy] has to assume the very thing it is supposed to demonstrate. Since the moment of the installation of patriarchy initiates an epoch and its realm of necessary effects, the 'moment' cannot be considered as an accident, but rather must be the realisation of an immanence already given in the relations of sexual difference. The concept of patriarchy purports to explain the relations of sexual difference, but has to assume that they always already exist in a form in which patriarchy can be installed.... In general, patriarchy is advanced as the 'material basis' of women's oppression, taking as its referent the 'universality' of that oppression. But because of the inescapable circularity of the concept, it stands as little more than an assertion of that universality.[28]

The notion of patriarchy as a set of social relations does not then overcome the difficulties of other concepts of patriarchy because 'since the field of effects of those social relations is the already constituted group of women and group of men, the social division which was to be explained has already been assumed as part of the explanation.'[29] The concept of patriarchy entails a definite essentialism.

> The essentialism is revealed in treating the category women as unprob-lematic in feminist analyses. It is merely a variant of the tradition in which humanity is composed of 'subjects' as individuals and upon which society acts. It thus necessitates a concept of a human essence which exists independently of and prior to the category of the social.[30]

The political effects of this essentialism are similar to the effects of Marxist essentialism. As Adams and Minson point out, once the entities 'men' and 'women' are introduced, together with their 'interests', the form of evaluation of politics that is frequently adopted tends to fall into a form of measurement of the realization or non-realization of the desires, capacities or 'interests' of women. The obstacle to this is 'men' and their interests — an antagonism which appears always present. Diana Adlam similarly argues that using such a concept, it is known *in advance* that all forms of social differentiation in terms of sex are precisely forms, different manifestations of a single and determining structure. It is not necessary to demonstrate that such a general structure exists for it is 'obvious' and armed with this obviousness we can find it everywhere.[31]

What these contributors argue for is the displacement of the concepts of 'men' and 'women' as *pre-given unities* (with pre-given interests) and the examination of the diversity of ways in which different discourses (legal, medical, political, etc.) construct different definitions of women. This is not to deny that sexual differences are central to existing social relations and forms of power, but that sexual difference is always a *constructed* one.

Capitalist Patriarchy

There have been many attempts to combine concepts of patriarchy and concepts of capitalism. Many feminists have rightly pointed out the problems with the priority given to class divisions in Marxist theory. Certainly, if politics is conceived of as the representation of class interests determined in economic relations, then the problem of sexual divisions is always secondary to the problem of the class organization of society.[32] Various attempts to make capitalism and patriarchy march together are reviewed by Barrett.[33] (The two most common forms of combining them are criticized by Adlam, in *m/f* No. 3.) The most prevalent way in which capitalist patriarchy is conceptualized is precisely to make capitalism a modification of patriarchy. Capitalism provides one set of conditions for the realization of patriarchy. Patriarchy, then, is an essential structure whose forms of appearance vary according to the mode of production; capitalism conditions those forms *according to its needs*. Functionalism is inherent and indeed necessary to the argument.[34]

In other attempts to combine patriarchy and capitalism in a general theory, the order of causality is reversed — capitalist relations operate as essence conditioned by the needs of patriarchy, a position which clearly does not overcome any of the difficulties of the former position. As Adlam says,

> It is difficult to avoid the impression that in juggling with patriarchy and capitalism as two determinant and determining structures, a great deal of writing is being devoted to the task of warding off the threat that at any moment one will collapse into the other.[35]

Moreover, as Mark Cousins has demonstrated, it is an effort which cannot succeed. Cousins has demonstrated the impossibility of combining two essential structures; the two 'materialisms' of patriarchy and capitalism as a social totality (determined in the last instance by the economic). 'In so far as they locate a different "material basis" and do so through a different concept of determination, they cannot be coherently sustained as being complementary.'[36]

Not only is such a general theory impossible, it is also unnecessary. As Adlam argues, socialist feminism can be a coherent political force without assuming that all the questions it addresses and theoretical issues it raises are directed towards two intertwining structures. It is only necessary to embark on the search for an underlying principle of unity if it is assumed in the first place that there is a pre-given unity, 'women's oppression.'[37]

As argued earlier, none of this is to deny sexual differences in social relations, and differences in power between men and women as they are constituted in contemporary social relations. It is quite clear that in the field of education different power, statuses and so on are distributed in terms of sexual categories. It is not to deny differences, but to contest that 'women' and 'men' are pre-given unitary categories, who can always be conceptualized into a single opposition, where men's interests are served and women's denied.[38]

Conclusions

We conclude with a necessarily limited account of a mode of reconceptualization of educational policy politics[39] which avoids the problems discussed above. A rejection of functionalist theories and ontological conceptions of needs and interests also displaces what Hindess has called the instrumentalist conception of the state as a unity. As he argues,

> Both liberal-democratic theory and classical Marxism treat the state apparatuses as instruments, of the assembly (and therefore of the people) or of the ruling class respectively. It is this conception that leads to the treatment of the state as a unity: the apparatuses are united by the hand that wields them.[40]

But, as Hindess correctly argues, 'this instrumentalist conception of the state is a grotesque misconception. It is necessary to treat the various state apparatuses as arenas of struggle in their own right.'[41] Just as there are significant internal struggles within, say, the Treasury or the military it is very clear that there are significant and complex struggles within the educational apparatus.

In taking the educational apparatus as an entity to be investigated in its own right we make no suggestion that education operates without conditions. Clearly, the effects of economic decline and decisions of parliament or cabinet as to how resources are to be distributed among the different state apparatuses are part of the complex process whereby external forces and internal struggles interact. To say that there are 'external' forces and that the effects of economic decline have been, and will most likely continue to be, of significance to education is not to say that education is determined by the economy. Economic conditions are important but the operations, processes and effects of education cannot be reduced to the effects of the economy or 'interests' said to represent the pre-given 'needs' of particular social relations. The educational apparatus is not determined by the economy, the cabinet, parliament or by the local education authority (LEA). On the contrary those loci of decision-making constitute important conditions.

Whilst 'external' forces and decisions are significant conditions in which the educational apparatus operates, it is clear that there are significant struggles *within* education which are not determined by 'external' forces or decisions. For example, as Rutter and his colleagues have shown,[42] there are significant differences among schools which are not necessarily dependent on external forces and differences. Schools themselves matter. With reference to expenditure policy, Hough has found widespread and significant differences in educational expenditure both among otherwise equivalent schools within local authorities and among schools in different local authorities.[43]

Once the politics of educational policy is disaggregated from the supposed unity of 'interests' or 'needs' it is imagined to represent, a whole range of significant arenas of decision-making and policy struggle is opened for investigation. For example, what is it about individual school policy that can make significant differences to children's educational opportunity? What are the politics of expenditure policy which produce such significant differences in school costs? These kinds of questions can only be ignored in the conception of the state as a unity acting in terms of pre-given interests or needs.

If we take the case of an individual school we find that in addition to these external conditions there is an array of internal conditions. Leaving aside the 'personal capacities' of individual teachers (which are nonetheless important) these internal conditions include the practices/ideologies of the headteacher and individual teachers, which are themselves the effects of the conditions of their training (both academic and professional) and their opportunities for retraining. This point could not be more clear with respect to sexist and racist practice within schools.[44]

The internal conditions of schools are themselves not reducible to the ideologies/practices of teachers (although their significance is becoming increasingly to be recognized).[45] Other significant conditions include specific teacher union policy/ideology, which may or may not have effects through the actions of individual teachers or groups of teachers acting together; local pressure groups acting either in their own right or as local representations of national groups such as ACE, CASE STOPP, etc.; the school governors; local political parties acting through effective school governors or through the local authority or local pressure groups; individual parents acting through the Parent-Teacher Association, the governors or through some other agency mentioned above. The local authority acts as a significant condition of the individual school and the politics of the LEA present another level and range of political arenas. Socialist and feminist politics, like any other politics, has to operate within these conditions and arenas of struggle if it is to have any chance of having effects in the educational apparatus.

One further point should be made here concerning the arenas of struggle in education policy politics. Not only are these arenas significant in themselves, as are relations between arenas, but the arenas and their relations can become the objects of political change. For example, the argument for the implementation of the Taylor Report[46] is a political argument concerned with the changing of relations between governors, teachers and parents in particular. First, this argument is not simply a *party* political argument but a political struggle in a much broader sense. Second, such change as the implementation of Taylor would bring would involve the restructuring of school governing bodies and their reconstitution into significant arenas of debate of the curriculum. The politics of education, like the politics of some other areas of social life, is concerned with struggle within arenas of policy decision-making that already exist, and with the redrawing and restructuring of certain of those arenas and their relations with others.

To conclude, then, we are arguing that it is important for feminists and for socialists to conceive of the forms of political organization and practice/ideology that develop in contemporary society, not as the field of play of pre-given and essential interests or needs, but as the outcomes of specific conditions and struggles. These struggles in education, as in other areas, will occur within specific conditions and within specific arenas which cannot be ignored by serious feminists and socialists. Many of the struggles will be of a highly specific character, involving issues which do not fall into simple pre-given categories. Education should be seen as the site of struggles around specific objectives and not as the site of the playing out of pre-given interests or needs.

Notes

1 A major reference point for such discourses is ALTHUSSER, L. (1971) 'Ideology and ideological state apparatuses' in *Lenin and Philosophy and Other Essays*, London, New Left Books. The best criticism of Althusser's theory of ideology is HIRST, P. (1979) *On Law and Ideology*, London, Macmillan. See also HIRST, P. and WOOLLEY, P. (1982) *Social Relations and Human Attributes*, London, Tavistock.
2 See, for example, BOWLES, S. and GINTIS, H. (1976) *Schooling in Capitalist America*, London, Routledge and Kegan Paul. For critical discussion, see DEMAINE, J. (1981) *Contemporary Theories in the Sociology of Education*, London, Macmillan.
3 It is not suggested that these concepts are the same in all respects.
4 An early attempt to relate sexual inequalities in education with the needs of capitalism is DEEM, R. (1978) *Women and Schooling*, London, Routledge and Kegan Paul.
5 We do not deal here with ethnic divisions. We discuss some attempts to combine concepts of capitalism and patriarchy later in the chapter.
6 See, for example, CENTRE FOR CONTEMPORARY CULTURAL STUDIES (1981) *Unpopular Education: Schooling and Social Democracy in England since 1944*, London, Hutchinson. The concepts of 'interests' and 'needs' criticized in this chapter are not confined to the above; nor do they appear in a 'pure form' in contemporary educational discourses. Rather, they are found in various forms and often hedged with qualifications and equivocations.
7 *Ibid.*, p. 21.
8 *Ibid.*
9 *Ibid.*
10 DEEM, R. (1981) 'State policy and ideology in the education of women, 1944–80', *British Journal of Sociology of Education*, 2, 2, p. 132.
11 TOMLINSON, J. (1982) 'Corporatism: A further sociologization of Marxism', *Politics and Power 4*, London, Routledge and Kegan Paul.
12 See HIRST, P. (1981) 'On struggle in the enterprise' in PRIOR, M. *The Popular and the Political: Essays on Socialism in the 1980s*, London, Routledge and Kegan Paul.
13 A concept of feminist *objectives* is radically different from an argument concerning the pre-given interests of women. Objectives, in this sense, are conceived of as the *product of political calculation and argument*.
14 TOMLINSON, J. (1982) *op. cit.*
15 KINGDOM, E.F. (1980) 'Women in law' *m/f*, 4, pp. 71–88.
16 TOMLINSON, J. (1982) *op. cit.*, p. 240.
17 As Tomlinson maintains, political argument based on the notion of inherent interests will always tend towards 'consciousness-raising' politics, the task of socialists being to make people aware of their *real* interests.
18 See Note 6.
19 TOMLINSON, J. (1982) *op. cit.*, p. 244.
20 We could add, here, 'and from a socialist viewpoint too'. For further discussion, see DEMAINE, J. (1981) *op. cit.*, pp. 130–51.
21 As PAUL HIRST argues, the reform/revolution dilemma is one produced by essentialist

theories of social relations, and has served to disarm the Left in Britain. For a discussion of the essentialism in Althusser's theory of social relations and ideology see HIRST, P. (1979) *op. cit.*

22   COUSINS, M. (1978) 'Material arguments and feminism' *m/f*, 2, pp. 62–70.

23   CUTLER, A.J., HINDESS, B., HIRST, P.Q. and HUSSAIN, A. (1977 and 1978) *Marx's Capital and Capitalism Today*, Vols. 1 and 2, London, Routledge and Kegan Paul. This criticism of the concept of social totality has been much misunderstood. The argument against a concept of social formation as a totality of 'levels' determined in the last instance by the economy, and against the notion of 'relative autonomy', is not an argument for an 'absolute autonomy' of the political, etc. As Hirst points out, the notion of 'autonomy' assumes the retention of the 'instances' or 'levels' as entities, promoting each to the status of an autonomous entity. 'How then is it possible to retain the concept of totality and how can those autonomous entities exist. The absurdity is not of our making, it results from the persistence of reading in terms of a certain social topography.' HIRST, P.Q. (1979) *op. cit.*, p. 18.

MCCT is not arguing that political forces, apparatuses and issues are without conditions, but that those conditions cannot be specified in a general concept as stemming from, say, the effects of the capitalist mode of production.

Hirst also discusses the charge that MCCT is positing a relativist epistemology. MCCT is arguing against epistemological discourses *per se* and 'relativism' is only possible *within* epistemology, as a general doctrine about a knowledge-being relation. See HIRST, P.Q. (1979) *op. cit.*, p. 21.

24   COWARD, R. (1978) 'Rethinking Marxism' *m/f*, 2, pp. 85–96.

25   Two recent collections of contributions are to be found in EISENSTEIN, Z.R. (Ed.) (1979) *Capitalist Patriarchy and the Case for Socialist Feminism*, New York, Monthly Review Press, and KUHN, A. and WOLPE, A.M. (Eds) (1978) *Feminism and Materialism*, London, Routledge and Kegan Paul. Both are reviewed in ADLAM, D. (1979) 'The case against capitalist patriarchy' *m/f*, 3. For a full bibliography, see BARRETT, M. (1980) *Women's Oppression Today*, London, Verso.

26   ADAMS, P. (1979) 'A note on the distinction between sexual division and sexual differences' *m/f*, 3, p. 52.

27   BARRETT, M. (1860) *op. cit.*, p. 14.

28   COUSINS, M. (1978) *op. cit.*, p. 65.

29   ADAMS, P. (1979) *op. cit.*, p. 52.

30   ADAMS, P. and MINSON, J. (1978) 'The "subject" of feminism' *m/f*, 2, p. 44.

31   ADLAM, D. (1979) *op. cit.*, p. 98.

32   The editorial in *m/f*, 1, 1978, discusses various attempts to insert the politics of women into Marxist analysis and the difficulties with them.

33   BARRETT, M. (1980) *op. cit.*

34   At several points in her discussion Michèle Barrett (*ibid.*) points out the difficulties of functionalist arguments and criticizes other writers for employing them, whilst simultaneously acknowledging that functionalism is necessarily involved in her own position on women's oppression and capitalism.

35   ADLAM, D. (1979) *op. cit.*, p. 89.

36   COUSINS, M. (1978) *op. cit.*, p. 65.

37   Barrett attacks the *m/f* discussions as being 'cast in an inpenetrable language' and, more importantly, as not providing any alternative basis for a feminist politics. The absence of the touchstone of general theory is certainly disconcerting for many feminists and socialists but there is nothing to be gained from clinging to redundant concepts. The question, 'what is the relationship between women's oppression and the general features of a mode of production', to which Barrett continues to seek, but not find, a satisfactory answer, *is* an obsolete question. The politics of socialists feminism is discussed in ADLAM, D. (1980) 'Socialist feminism and contemporary politics' *Politics and Power 1*, London, Routledge and Kegan Paul.

38   ADLAM, D. (1979) *op. cit.*, p. 99.

39 For further discussion, see DEMAINE, J. (1980) 'Compensatory education and social policy' in CRAFT, M., RAYNOR, J. and COHEN, L. (Eds) *Linking Home and School*, London, Harper and Row.

40 HINDESS, B. (1981) 'Parliamentary democracy and socialist politics' in PRIOR, M. *op. cit.*, p. 36.

41 *Ibid.*

42 RUTTER, M., MAUGHAN, B., MORTIMORE, P. and OUSTON, J. (1979) *Fifteen Thousand Hours: Secondary Schools and Their Effects on Children*, Shepton Mallet, Open Books.

43 HOUGH, J.R. (1981) *A Study of School Costs*, Windsor, NFER Nelson.

44 See, for example, Command Paper 8273 *West Indian Children in Our Schools* (The Rampton Report), London, HMSO.

45 *Ibid.*

46 TAYLOR, T. *et al.* (1977) *A New Partnership For Our Schools* (DES and Welsh Office), London, HMSO. For a discussion of the Taylor Report in the context of socialist policy, see DEMAINE, J. (1981) *op. cit.*

11. Gender, Class and Education: A Teaching Bibliography of European Studies

Maggie Coats, Loughborough University

Bibliography

In compiling this bibliography, I have selected books, papers and journal articles with an emphasis on *gender*. Very few sources relate to *both* gender *and* class and I have omitted those on class alone, since comprehensive bibliographies are available elsewhere.

Most of the material orginates in Great Britain but references from other European countries are included where the material is available in English.

Where books consist of collected papers, I have listed all the relevant papers individually, with a reference to the collected edition, so that readers should be able to trace all the material without difficulty.

Whilst *sociology*, *education* and *gender* were the major descriptors, I have also included references from other disciplines, notably history and psychology, where these seemed important.

All the material dates from 1970 onwards.

Journals

The list of journals includes those specifically concerned with gender and education as well as other feminist publications which regularly carry articles of relevance to education.

Groups

A list of groups concerned with various issues relating to gender and education is included, with their contact addresses.

Resource Centres and Libraries

Those centres and libraries listed provide additional information on gender and education. Addresses, telephone numbers and opening hours are correct at the time of publication; in some cases a small charge is made for the use of their facilities.

Bibliography

ACKER, S. (1980) 'Women, the other academics', *British Journal of Sociology of Education*, 1, 1, pp. 81–91.

ALLEN, S., SANDERS, L. and WALLIS, J. (Eds) (1974) *Conditions of Illusion — Papers from the Women's Movement*, Leeds, Feminist Books.

ARDENER, S. (Ed.) (1978) *Defining Females*, London, Croom Helm.

ASHTON, D. and MAGUIRE, M. (1980) 'Young women in the labour market: Stability and change', in DEEM, R. (Ed.), *op. cit.*

ATKINSON, P. (1978) 'Fitness, feminism and schooling', in DELAMONT, S. and DUFFIN, L. (Eds), *op. cit.*

BADGER, M.E. (1981) 'Why aren't girls better at Maths? — a review of research', *Educational Research*, 24, 1, pp. 11–13.

BAKER, B.K. (1975) 'How to succeed in a journeymen's world', *Manpower* (special issue *Womanpower*), 7, 11, pp. 38–42.

BARKER, D.L. and ALLEN, S. (Eds) (1976) *Sexual Divisions and Society: Process and Changes*, London, Tavistock.

BARKER LUNN, J.C. (1972) 'The influence of sex, achievement and social class on junior school children's attitudes', *British Journal of Educational Psychology*, 42, 1, pp. 70–4.

BARRETT, M. (1980) *Women's Oppression Today: Problems in Marxist Feminist Analysis.* London, Verso.

BARRY, C. (1980) 'Action plan to stamp our male privilege', *The Times Higher Educational Supplement*, No. 404, 25 July, p. 6.

_____ (1980) 'When the kitchen knife can be a utensil of liberation', *The Times Higher Educational Supplement*, No. 411, 19 September, p. 8.

BARTON, L., MEIGHAN, R. and WALKER, S. (Eds) (1981) *Schooling, Ideology and the Curriculum*, Barcombe, Falmer Press.

BELOTTI, E.G. (1975) *Little Girls — Social Conditioning and Its Effect on the Stereotyped Role of Women during Infancy*, London, Writers and Readers Publishing Co-operative.

BLACKSTONE, T. (1976) 'The education of girls today', in MITCHELL, J. and OAKLEY, A. (Eds), *op. cit.*

BLACKSTONE, T. and FULTON, O. (1975) 'Sex discrimination among university teachers: A British–American comparison', *British Journal of Sociology*, 26, 3, pp. 261–75.

BLACKSTONE, T. and WEINREICH–HASTE, H. (1980) 'Why are there so few women scientists and engineers?', *New Society*, 51, 907, pp. 383–5.

BONE, A. (1979) 'Women's demand and the supply of higher education', *Higher Education Review*, 11, 3, pp. 65–70.

_____ (1980) 'Education and manpower: The visibility of girls in education statistics', *EOC Research Bulletin*, 1, 4, pp. 86–98.

BRADLEY, J. and SILVERLEAF, J. (1979) 'Women teachers in further education', *Educational Research*, 12, 1, pp. 15–21.

BRIDGES, D. (1974) 'Feminism and education', *The New Era*, 55, 6, pp. 134–7.

BRIERLEY, J. (1975) 'Sex differences in education', *Trends in Education*, 75, 1, pp. 17–24.

BRISTOL WOMEN'S STUDIES GROUP (1979) *Half the Sky: And Introduction to Women's Studies*, London, Virago.

BUCHAN, L. (1980) 'It's a good job for a girl (but an awful career for a woman)', in SPENDER, D. and SARAH, E. (Eds), *op. cit.*

BURSTYN, J.N. (1980) *Victorian Education and the Ideal of Womanhood*, London, Croom Helm.

BUSWELL, C. (1981) 'Sexism in school routine and classroom practices', *Durham and Newcastle Review*, 9, 46, pp. 195–200.

BYRNE, E. (1975) 'Inequality in education — discriminatory resource allocation in schools?' *Educational Review*, 27, 3, pp. 179–91.

_____ (1978) *Women and Education*, London, Tavistock.

_____ (1979) *Equality of Education and Training for Girls. (10 to 18 years)*, Brussels, Commission of European Communities.

CENTERWALL, A. and STROMDAHL, B. (1974) *Boy, Girl, Does It Matter?*, Stockholm, Swedish National Board of Education.

CENTRAL COUNCIL OF EDUCATION (1978) *U90: Danish Educational Planning and Policy in a*

Social Context at the End of the Twentieth Century, Copenhagen, Ministry of Education.

CHABAUD, J. (1970) *The Education and Advancement of Women*, Paris, UNESCO.

CHANDLER, E.M. (1980) *Educating Adolescent Girls*, London, Allen and Unwin.

CHETWYND, J. and HARTNETT, O. (1978) *The Sex-Role System: Psychological and Sociological Perspectives*, London, Routledge and Kegan Paul.

CHILDREN'S RIGHTS WORKSHOP (1976) *Sexism in Children's Books: Facts, Figures and Guidelines*, London, Writers and Readers Publishing Co-operative.

CHISHOLM, L.A. (1978) 'The comparative career development of graduate women and men', *Women's Studies International Quarterly*, 1, 4, pp. 327–40.

CHISHOLM, L.A. and WOODWARD, D. (1980) 'The experience of women graduates in the labour market', in DEEM, R. (Ed.), *op. cit.*

CLARKE, M.J. (1979) 'Men, women and the post-primary principalships in Northern Ireland', *CORE*, 3, 1, (Microfiche 13 of 20).

CLARRICOATES, K. (1978) 'Dinosaurs in the classroom — a re-examination of some aspects of the hidden curriculum in primary schools', *Women's Studies International Quarterly*, 1, 4, pp. 353–64.

——————— (1980) 'All in a day's work', in SPENDER, D. and SARAH, E. (Eds), *op. cit.*

——————— (1980) 'The importance of being Earnest ... Emma ... Tom ... Jane: The perception and categorization of gender conformity and gender deviation in primary schools', in DEEM, R. *op. cit.*

CLEMENTS, M.A. (1979) 'Sex differences in mathematical performance: An historical perspective', *Educational Studies in Mathematics*, 10, 3, pp. 305–22.

COUNCIL FOR CULTURAL CO-OPERATION (1981) *'Action Femmes'* project (Chambery, France), Strasbourg, European Network of Instruction Projects in Adult Education.

COWELL, B. (1981) 'Mixed and single-sex grouping in secondary schools', *Oxford Review of Education*, 7, 2, pp. 165–72.

COWIE, C. and LEES, S. (1981) 'Slags or drags', *Feminist Review*, 9, pp. 17–31.

DALE, R., ESLAND, G., FERGUSSON, R. and MACDONALD, M. (1981) *Education and the State (Vol. II): Politics, Patriarchy and Practice*, Barcombe, Falmer Press, in association with The Open University Press.

DALE, R.R. (1969) *Mixed or Single-Sex School? Vol. 1: A Research Study about Pupil-Teacher Relationships*, London, Routledge and Kegan Paul.

——————— (1971) *Mixed or Single-Sex School? Vol. 2: Some Social Aspects*, London, Routledge and Kegan Paul.

——————— (1974) *Mixed or Single-Sex School? Vol. 3: Attainment, Attitudes and Overview*, London, Routledge and Kegan Paul.

DANISH COMMISSION ON THE POSITION OF WOMEN (1974) *The Position of Women in Society*, Copenhagen.

DAVID, M. (1980) *The State, the Family and Education*, London, Routledge and Kegan Paul.

DAVIES, L. and MEIGHAN, R. (1975) 'A review of schooling and sex-roles with particular reference to the experiences of girls in secondary schools', *Educational Review*, 27, 3, pp. 165–78.

DEEM, R. (1978) *Women and Schooling*. London; Routledge and Kegan Paul.

——————— (Ed.) (1980) *Schooling for Women's Work*, London, Routledge and Kegan Paul.

——————— (1981) 'State policy and ideology in the education of women', *British Journal of Sociology of Education*, 2, 2, pp. 131–43.

DELAMONT, S. (1978) 'The contradictions in ladies education', in DELAMONT, S. and DUFFIN, L. (Eds), *op. cit.*

——————— (1978) 'The domestic ideology and women's education', in DELAMONT, S. and DUFFIN, L. (Eds), *op. cit.*

——————— (1980) *Sex-Roles and the School*, London, Methuen.

——————— (1980) *The Sociology of Women*, London, Allen and Unwin.

DELAMONT, S. and DUFFIN, L. (Eds) (1978) *The Nineteenth Century Woman: Her Cultural and Physical World*, London, Croom Helm.

DEPARTMENT OF EDUCATION AND SCIENCE (1975) *Curricula Differences for Boys and Girls*, London, HMSO.

DE WOLFE, P. (1980) 'Women's studies: The contradictions for students', in SPENDER, D. and SARAH, E. (Eds), *op. cit.*

DIXON, B. (1977) *Catching Them Young — Race, Sex and Class in Children's Fiction*, London, Pluto Press.

DRIVER, G. (1980) 'How West Indians do better at school (especially the girls), *New Society*, 59, 902, pp. 111–14.

DYHOUSE, C. (1976) 'Social Darwinistic ideas and the development of women's education in England, 1800–1920', *History of Education*, 5, 1, pp. 41–58.

_____ (1977) 'Good wives and little mothers: Social anxieties and the schoolgirls curriculum, 1980–1920', *Oxford Review of Education*, 3, 1, pp. 21–35.

_____ (1978) 'Towards a "feminine" curriculum for English schoolgirls: The demands of ideology, 1870–1963', *Women's Studies International Quarterly*, 1, 4, pp. 297–311.

EAVES, A. (1978) 'Equal opportunities for men and women', *Trends in Education*, 4, pp. 7–10.

ELLIOTT, J. (1974) 'Sex role constraints on freedom of discussion: A neglected reality in the classroom', *The New Era*, 55, 6, pp. 147–55.

EQUAL OPPORTUNITIES COMMISSION (1979) *Equality in Education: Scotland*, Scottish Conference on Women, Education and Training, EOC.

_____ (1979) *Sex Discrimination and Equality of Opportunity in Primary and Secondary Schools*, EOC.

_____ (1980) *Do You Provide Equal Educational Opportunities?* EOC.

_____ (1980) *Equal Opportunities in Post-School Eduction*, EOC.

_____ (1980) *Equal Opportunities in Higher Education*, EOCSRHE Conference, Manchester, EOC.

_____ (1981) *Education for Girls — A Statistical Analysis*, EOC (1979, revised 1981).

EVANS, M. and MORGAN, D. (1979) *Work on Women*, London, Tavistock.

FENNEMA, E. (1979) 'Women and girls in mathematics: Equity in mathematics teaching', *Educational Studies in Mathematics*, 10, 4, pp. 389–401.

FLETCHER, S. (1980) *Feminists and Bureaucrats: A Study of the Development of Girls' Education in the Nineteenth Century*, Cambridge, Cambridge University Press.

FLUDE, M. and AHIER, J. (Eds) (1976) *Educability, Schools and Society*, London, Croom Helm.

FOREMAN, A. (1977) *Femininity as Alienation: Women and the Family in Marxism and Psychoanalysis*, London, Pluto Press.

FRANSELLA, F. and FROST, K. (1977) *On Being a Woman*, London, Tavistock.

FULLER, M. (1978) 'Sex-role stereotyping and social science', in CHETWYND, J. and HARTNETT, O. (Eds), *op. cit.*

_____ (1980) 'Black girls in a London comprehensive school', in DEEM, R. (Ed.), *op. cit.*

GERVER, E. (1980) 'Women in higher education in Scotland', *Scottish Journal of Adult Education*, 5, 1, pp. 22–6.

GRANT, N.D.C. (1974) 'Sexual equality in the communist world', *Compare*, 4, 1.

GRAY, R. and HUGHES, M. (1980) 'Half our future?', *Adult Education*, 52, 5, pp. 301–6.

GRIFFITHS, D. and SARAGA, E. (1979) 'Sex differences in cognitive abilities: A sterile field of enquiry?', in HARTNETT, O., BODEN, S. and FULLER, M. (Eds), *op. cit.*

GRIFFITHS, M. (1980) 'Women in higher education: A case study of The Open University', in DEEM, R. (Ed.), *op. cit.*

HANNON, V. (1979) 'Education for sex equality: What's the problem?', in RUBENSTEIN, D.

(Ed.), *op. cit.*

_____ (1981) *Ending Sex-Stereotyping in Schools: A Source Book for School-Based Teacher Workshops*, Equal Opportunities Commission.

HARDING, J. (1980) 'Sex differentiation and schooling', *Education in Science*, No. 89, p. 27.

_____ (1980) 'Sex difference in performance in science examinations', in DEEM, R. (Ed.), *op. cit.*

HARGREAVES, D. (1979) 'Sex roles and creativity', in HARTNETT, O., BODEN, S. and FULLER, M. (Eds), *op. cit.*

HARTLEY, D. (1978) 'Sex and social class: A case study of an infant school', *British Educational Research Journal*, 4, 2, pp. 75–81.

_____ (1978) 'Teachers' definitions of boys and girls: Some consequences', *Research in Education*, No. 20, pp. 23–35.

_____ (1980) 'Sex differences in the infant school', *British Journal of Sociology of Education*, 1, 1, pp. 93–105.

HARTNETT, O., RENDEL, M. and FAIRBAIRNS, Z. (Eds) (1975) *Women's Studies in the United Kingdom*, London, London Seminars.

HARTNETT, O., BODEN, S. and FULLER, M. (Eds) (1979) *Sex-Role Stereotyping*, London, Tavistock.

HOLTER, H. (1970) *Sex Roles and Social Structure*, Oslo, Universitetsforlaget.

HOOTSMANS, H.M. (1980) 'Educational and employment opportunities for women: Main issues in adult education in Europe', *Convergence*, 13, 1–2, pp. 79–90.

HUNT, A. and RAUTA, I. (1975) *Fifth Form Girls: Their Hopes for the Future*, London, HMSO.

HUNT, P. (1980) *Gender and Class Consciousness*, London, Macmillan.

ISAACSON, Z. and FREEMAN, N. (1980) 'Girls and mathematics: A response', *Mathematics Teaching*, No. 90, pp. 24–6.

JACKSON, S. (1980) 'Girls and sexual knowledge', in SPENDER, D. and SARAH, E. (Eds), *op. cit.*

JARDINE, T. (1976) 'Fair chances for boys and girls in school courses', *Scottish Educational Journal*, 59, 11, pp. 17–18.

_____ (1976) 'Girls don't figure in mathematics', *Scottish Educational Journal*, 59, 35, p. 7.

JONES, K. (1973) 'Women's education', in *Education, Economy and Politics*, Block 5, Part 4, E352, Milton Keynes, The Open University.

KAMM, J. (1976) *Hope Deferred: Girls Education in English History*, London, Methuen.

KEIL, T. and NEWTON, P. (1980) 'Into work: Continuity and change', in DEEM, R. (Ed.), *op. cit.*

KELLY, A. (1978) 'Why girls don't do science', *Newsletter 4*, Centre for Educational Sociology, University of Edinburgh.

_____ (1981) *The Missing Half: Girls and Science Education*, Manchester, Manchester University Press.

KING, J. (1971) ''Unequal access in education: Sex and social class', *Social and Economic Administration*, 5, pp. 167–75.

KOHNSTAMN INSTITUTE. (1979) *Educational Equality of Opportunity for Girls and Women*, The Hague, University of Amsterdam: data report for the Standing Conference of European Ministers of Education.

KUHN, A. (1978) 'Structures of patriarchy and capital in the family', in KUHN, A. and WOLPE, A.-M. (Eds), *op. cit.*

KUHN, A. and WOLPE, A.-M. (Eds) (1978) *Feminism and Materialism*, London, Routledge and Kegan Paul.

LAMB, F. and PICKTHORN, H. (1968) *Locked-up Daughters*, London, Hodder and Stoughton.

LAMBART, A. (1976) 'The Sisterhood', in WOODS, P. and HAMMERSLEY, M. (Eds) *The Process of Schooling: A Sociological Reader*, London, Routledge and Kegan Paul and The Open University Press.

LAVIGUER, J. (1980) 'Co-education and the tradition of separate needs', in SPENDER, D. and SARAH, E. (Eds), *op. cit.*

LEDER, G. (1980) 'Bright girls, mathematics and fear of success', *Educational Studies in Mathematics*, 11, 4, pp. 411–22.

LEE, A. (1980) 'Together we learn to read and write: Sexism and literacy', in SPENDER, D. and SARAH, E. (Eds), *op. cit.*

LEWIN, H.M. (1976) 'Educational opportunity and social inequality in Western Europe', *Social Problems*, 24, 2, pp. 148–72.

LLEWELLYN, A. (1980) 'Studying girls at school: The implications of confusion', in DEEM, R. (Ed.), *op. cit.*

LLOYDS, D. and ARCHER, J. (Eds) (1976) *Exploring Sex Differences*, London, Academic Press.

LOBBAN, G. (1974) 'The presentation of sex-roles in British reading schemes', *Forum*, 16, 2, pp. 57–60.

_____(1975) 'Sex-roles in reading schemes', *Educational Review*, 27, 3, pp. 202–10.

_____(1978) 'The influence of the school on sex-role stereotyping', in CHETWYND, J. and HARTNETT, O. (Eds), *op. cit.*

LOFTUS, M. (1974) 'Learning sexism and feminity', in ALLEN, S., SAUNDERS, L. and WALLIS, J. (Eds), *op. cit.*

LOMAX, P. (1977) 'The self-concept of girls in the context of a disadvantaging environment', *Educational Review*, 29, 2, pp. 107–19.

LOVELL, A. (1980) 'Fresh horizonts: Mature students', *Feminist Review*, No. 6, pp. 93–104.

LUETHI-PETERSON, N. (1974) 'Patriarchal attitudes — an experimental course at L'Ecole d'Humanité', *The New Era*, 55, 6, pp. 160–1.

MACAULAY, R.K.S. (1978) 'The myth of female superiority in language', *Journal of Child Language*, 5, 2, pp. 353–63.

MACDONALD, E. (1977) 'Woman at work: Opportunity knocks', *Training Officer*, 13, 5, pp. 118–21.

MACDONALD, M. (1980) 'Socio-cultural reproduction and women's education', in DEEM, R. (Ed.), *op. cit.*

_____(1981) 'Schooling and the reproduction of class and gender relations', in BARTON, L., MEIGHAN, R. and WALKER, S. (Eds), *op. cit.*

MACK, J. (1974) 'Women's studies in Cambridge', *The New Era*, 55, 6, pp. 162–4.

MARKS, P. (1976) 'Feminity in the classroom: An account of changing attitudes', in MITCHELL, J. and OAKLEY, A. (Eds), *op. cit.*

MCROBBIE, A. (1978) 'Working class girls and the culture of feminity', in WOMEN'S STUDENTS GROUP, CCCS, Birmingham (Eds), *op. cit.*

MCROBBIE, A. and GARBER, J. (1976) 'Girls and subcultures: An exploration', in HALL, S. and JEFFERSON, T. (Eds) *Resistance through Rituals: Youth Subcultures in Post-War Britain*, London, Hutchinson.

MCWILLIAMS-TULLBERG, R. (1971) *Women at Cambridge*, London, Gollancz.

MEYENN, R.G. (1980) 'School girls peer groups', in WOODS, P. (Ed.) *Pupil Strategies: Explorations in the Sociology of the School*, London, Croom Helm.

MITCHELL, J. and OAKLEY, A. (Eds) (1976) *The Rights and Wrongs of Women*, Harmondsworth, Penguin.

MONTEITH, M. (1979) 'Boys, girls and language', *English in Education*, 13, 2, pp. 3–6.

MOORE, J. (1976) 'Is there a minority sex?', *Compare*, 5, 3 (also 6, 1), pp. 15–19.

MORGAN, V. and DUNN, S. (1981) 'Late but in earnest: Mature women at university', *CORE*, 5, 2 (Microfiche 6 and 7 of 10).

MURPHY, M.W. (1975) 'Measured steps towards equality for women in Ireland: Education and legislation', *Convergence*, 8, 1, pp. 91–8.

MURPHY, R.J.L. (1979) 'Sex differences in examination performance: Do these reflect differences in ability or sex-role stereotypes?', in HARTNETT, O., BODEN, S. and FULLER, M. (Eds), *op. cit.*

———————— (1980) 'Sex differences in GCE examinations — entry statistics and success rates', *Educational Studies*, 6, 2, pp. 169–78.

NATIONAL UNION OF TEACHERS (1976) *Equal Opportunities for Women*, London, NUT.

NATIONAL UNION OF TEACHERS (and EQUAL OPPORTUNITIES COMMISSION) (1980) *Promotion and the Woman Teacher*, London, NUT.

NAVA, M. (1980) 'Gender and education', (review of BYRNE, E. and DEEM, R.) *Feminist Review*, No. 5, pp. 69–78.

NEWSON, J. and NEWSON, E. (1977) *Perspectives on School at Seven Years Old*, London, Allen and Unwin.

NORTHERN WOMEN'S GROUPS (1972) 'Sex role learning: A study of infant readers', in WANDOR, M. (Ed.), *op. cit.*

OAKLEY, A. (1981) *Subject Women*, Oxford, Martin Robertson.

————————(1981) 'This division of labour by gender', in *Contemporary Issues in Education*, Milton Keynes, The Open University Press, Unit 25, E200.

———————— (1972) *Sex, Gender and Society*, London, Temple Smith.

O'CONNOR, M. (1977) 'Who is liberated now?', *The Times Educational Supplement*, No. 3226 1 April, p. 17.

OKELEY, J. (1978) 'Privileged, schooled and finished: Boarding education for girls', in ARDENER, S. (Ed.), *op. cit.*

PARTINGTON, G. (1977) *Women Teachers in the Twentieth Century*, Windsor, NFER.

PAYNE, I. (1980) 'Sexist ideology and education', in SPENDER, D. and SARAH, E. (Eds), *op. cit.*

PREECE, M. (1979) 'Mathematics: The unpredictability of girls', *Mathematics Teaching*, No. 87, pp. 27–9.

PURVIS, J. (1981) 'Women and teaching in the nineteenth century', in DALE, R., ESLAND, G., FERGUSSON, R. and MACDONALD, M. (Eds), *op. cit.*

———————— (1981) 'Women's life is essentially domestic, public life being confined to men' (Comte): Separate spheres and inequality in the education of working-class women, 1854–1900', *History of Education*, 10, 4, pp. 227–43.

RAPOPORT, R. (1974) 'Sex differences in career development at three stages in the life cycles', *SSRC Newsletter*, No. 24, pp. 7–10.

RAVEN, M. and ROBB, B. (1981) 'Maternal employment and children's sex-role perception', *Educational Research*, 23, 3, pp. 223–5.

RENDEL, M. (1974) 'Equal opportunities for women in higher education in the US, Britain and France', *The New era*, 55, 6, pp. 145–6.

———————— (1975) 'Women and men in higher education', *Educational Review*, No. 17, pp. 192–201.

———————— (1978) 'The death of leadership or educating people to lead themselves', *Women's Studies International Quarterly*, 1, 4, pp. 313–25.

———————— (1980) 'How many women academics?', in DEEM, R. *op. cit.*

REYERSBACH, A. (1974) 'Ladies don't play football: Notes on sexism in primary school', *The New Era*, 55, 6, pp. 138–40.

ROBERTS, A. (1978) 'Boys and girls come out to play', *New Society*, 44, 817, pp. 482–4.

ROBERTS, H. (1981) 'Some of the boys won't play any more: The impact of feminism on sociology', in SPENDER, D. (Ed.), *op. cit.*

RUBENSTEIN, D. (Ed.) (1979) *Education and Equality*, Harmondsworth, Penguin.

SANDBERG, E. (1975) *Equality is the Goal*, Report of the Advisory Council to the Prime Minister of Sweden Stockholm, Swedish Institute.

SANYAL, B.C. and JOZEFOWICZ, A. (Eds) (1976) *Graduate Employment and Planning of Higher Education in Poland*, Paris, International Institute for Educational Planning.

SARAH, E. (1980) 'Teachers and students in the classroom', in SPENDER, D. and SARAH, E. (Eds), *op. cit.*

SARAH, E., SCOTT, M. and SPENDER, D. (1980) 'The education of feminists: The case for single-sex schools', in SPENDER, D. and SARAH, E. (Eds), *op. cit.*

SCOTT, M. (1980) 'Teach her a lesson: Sexist curriculum in patriarchal education', in

SPENDER, D. and SARAH, E. (Eds), *op. cit.*

SCOTTISH EDUCATION DEPARTMENT (1975) *Differences of Provision for Boys and Girls in Scottish Secondary Schools*, Edinburgh.

SCRIBBINS, K. (1977) 'Women in education : Some points for discussion', *Journal of Further and Higher Education*, 1, 3, pp. 17–39.

SECRETARIAT FOR NORDIC CULTURAL CO-OPERATION (1979) *Sex Roles and Education*, The Hague, Standing Conference of Ministers of Education.

SHAFER, S. (1976) 'The socialization of girls in the secondary schools of England and the two Germanies', *International Review of Education*, 22, 1, pp. 5–24.

SHARMA, S. and MEIGHAN, R. (1980) 'Schooling and sex roles: The case of GCE O level maths', *British Journal of Sociology of Education*, 1, 2, pp. 193–205.

SHARPE, S. (1976) *Just Like a Girl: How Girls Learn to be Women*, Harmondsworth, Penguin.

SHAW, J. (1976) 'Finishing school: Some implications of sex segregated education', in BARKER, D.L. and ALLEN, S. (Eds), *op. cit.*

————(1980) 'Education and the individual: Schooling for girls or mixed schooling — a mixed blessing?', in DEEM. R. (Ed.), *op. cit.*

SHEPHERD, A. (1971) 'Married women teachers — role perceptions and career patterns', *Educational Research*, 13, pp. 191–7.

SMART, C. and SMART, B. (Eds) (1978) *Women, Sexuality and Social Control*, London, Routledge and Kegan Paul.

SMITH, A. (1977) 'Sex typing begins before girls start typing', *Education*, 150, 19, p. 302.

SMITH, D.E. (1978) 'A peculiar eclipsing: Women's exclusion from men's culture', *Women's Studies International Quarterly*, 1, 4, pp. 281–95.

SMITH, G. (1974) 'The education of women in secondary schools', *The New Era*, 55, 6, pp. 140–4.

SPENDER, D. (1980) *Man-Made Language*, London, Routledge and Kegan Paul.

———————— (1980) 'Disappearing tricks'; 'Education or indoctrination'; 'Educational institutions: Where co-operation is called cheating'; 'Talking in class', in SPENDER, D. and SARAH, E. (Eds), *op. cit.*

————————(Ed.) (1981) *Men's Studies Modified: The Impact of Feminism on the Academic Disciplines*, Oxford, Pergamon Press.

————————(1981) 'The patriarchal paradigm and the response to feminism', in SPENDER, D. (Ed.), *op. cit.*

SPENDER, D. and SARAH, E. (Eds) (1980) *Learning to Lose: Sexism and Education*, London, The Women's Press.

STAMP, P. (1979) 'Girls and mathematics: Parental variables', *British Journal of Educational Psychology*, 49, 1, pp. 39–50.

STANWORTH, M. (1980) *Gender and Schooling: A Study of Sexual Divisions in the Classroom*, London, Women's Research and Resources Centre Publications Collective.

SUTHERLAND, M. (1981) *Sex Bias in Education*, Oxford, Basil Blackwell.

SVENSSON, A. (1980) 'On equality and university education in Sweden', *Scandinavian Journal of Educational Research*, 24, 1, pp. 79–92.

SWEDISH NATIONAL BOARD OF EDUCATION (1976) *Sex-Role Questions and Programmes for Equality*, Stockholm.

TREVOR, J. (1974) 'Moslem schoolgirls: Did our school help or hinder them?', *The New Era*, 55, 6, pp. 156–60.

TROWN, A. and NEEDHAM, G. (1980) *Reduction in Part-time Teaching: Implications for Schools and Women Teachers*, Equal Opportunities Commission.

TURNER, B. (1974) *Equality for Some: The Study of Girl's Education*, London, Ward Lock.

UNESCO (1975) *Women, Education and Equality — A Decade of Experiment*, Paris, UNESCO Press.

VER HEYDEN-HILLIARD, M.E. (1975) 'Cinderella doesn't live here anymore', *Manpower* (special issue *Womanpower*), 7, 11, pp. 34–7.

WANDOR, M. (1972) *The Body Politic; Writings from the Women's Liberation Movement in*

Britain: 1969–1972, London, Stage One.
WARD, J.P. (1975) 'Adolescent girls and modes of knowledge', *Educational Review*, 27, 3, pp. 221–8.
WARDLE, D. (1978) 'Sixty years on: The progress of women's education 1918–1978', *Trends in Education*, No. 4, pp. 3–7.
WEINER, G. (1978) 'Education and the Sex Discrimination Act', *Educational Research*, 20, 3, pp. 163–73.
——————(1980) 'Sex differences in mathematical performance: A review of research and possible action', in DEEM, R. (Ed.), *op. cit.*
WEINREICH-HASTE, H. (1979) 'What sex is science?', in HARTNETT, O., BODEN, S. and FULLER, M. (Eds), *op. cit.*
WEST, J. (1978) 'Woman, sex and class', in KUHN, A. and WOLPE, A.-M. (Eds), *op. cit.*
WHITBREAD, A. (1980) 'Female teachers are women first: Sexual harassment at work', in SPENDER, D. and SARAH, E. (Eds), *op. cit.*
WHITTING, D. (1981) 'Sex-role typing in Ladybird books', *Forum*, 23, 3, pp. 84–5.
WILLIS, P. (1981) 'Patriarchy, racialism and labour power', in DALE, R., ESLAND, G., FERGUSSON, R. and MACDONALD, M. (Eds), *op. cit.*
WILSON, D. (1978) 'Sexual codes and conduct: A study of teenage girls', in SMART, C. and SMART, B. (Eds), *op. cit.*
WOLPE, A.-M. (1974) 'The official ideology of education for girls', in FLUDE, M. and AHIER, J. (Eds), *op. cit.*
——————(1977) *Some Processes in Sexist Education*, London, Women's Research and Resources Centre Publications Collective.
——————(1978) 'Education and the sexual division of labour', in KUHN, A. and WOLPE, A.-M. (Eds), *op. cit.*
——————(1978) 'Girls and economic survival', *British Journal of Educational Studies*, 26, 2, pp. 150–62.
WOMENS STUDIES GROUP, Centre for Contemporary Cultural Studies, Birmingham (1978) *Women Take Issue*, London, Hutchinson.
WYNN, B. (1976) 'Domestic subjects and the sexual division of labour', in *Schooling and Society*, Milton Keynes, The Open University Press, Units 14–15, E202.

Journals

EOC News, Equal Opportunities Commission, Overseas House, Quay Street, Manchester M3 3HN (bi-monthly tabloid; free).
Feminist Review, 65 Manor Road, London N16 5EH (three times per year).
m/f, 22 Chepstow Crescent. London W11.
Spare Rib, 27 Clerkenwell Close, London EC1 OAT (monthly).
Womens Studies International Quarterly, Editor: Dale Spender, Institute of Education, University of London, 20 Bedford Way, London WC1H OAC; Publisher: Pergamon Press, Headington Hill Hall, Oxford, OX3 OBW, (formerly quarterly; bi-monthly from 1982 retitled Women's Studies International Forum).
Womens Studies Newsletter, Worker' Educational Association, 9 Upper Berkeley Street, London W1H 8BY (quarterly).

Groups

CASSOE (Campaign Against Sexism and Sexual Oppression in Education), C/o Liz Wynton, 17 Lymington Road, London NW6.
CISSY (Campaign to Impede Sex Stereotyping in the Young), 177 Gleneldon Road, London SW16.
GAMMA (Girls and MatheMatics Association), c/o Department of Teaching Studies,

School of Education, The Polytechnic of North London, Prince of Wales Road, London NW5 3LP.

GIST (Girls Into Science and Technology project), c/o Barbara Smail, 9a Didsbury Park, Manchester 20.

WOMEN AND EDUCATION (Group and Newsletter), c/o 14 St. Brendans Road, Manchester 20.

Resource Centres and Libraries

Equal Opportunities Commission Information Centre, Overseas House, Quay Street, Manchester, M3 3HN (open Monday to Friday, 9.00 to 5.00; list of publications and visual aids available).

The Fawcett Library, City of London Polytechnic, Calcutta House, Old Castle Street, London E1 (Tel: 01-283 1030 X570) (open Monday 1.00 to 8.30, Tuesday to Friday 10.00 to 5.00 in term time).

Women's Research and Resources Centre, 190 Upper Street, London N1 (Tel: 01-359 5773) (open Tuesday to Saturday, 11.00 to 5.30).

Bibliofem, A catalogue on microfiche, produced monthly, by the Equal Opportunities Commission and the Fawcett Library (available on subscription to any library or institution and for reference at either place).

12. Gender, Class and Education: A Teaching Bibliography of Australian and New Zealand Studies

Terry Evans, Gippsland Institute of Advanced Education

During the search for literature from Australia and New Zealand to compile the following bibliography two points became clear. First, Australia and New Zealand have developed quite different approaches to the study and publication of material on gender. In New Zealand much of the material has remained outside formal academic journals and has been disseminated typically through conference papers or local women's studies groups.[1] This has the advantage, as Bunce has claimed,[2] of research findings being located in the hands of people who are endeavouring to bring about a more just and equal New Zealand society. However, it also has the disadvantage of leaving much worthwhile material relatively inaccessible to international readers, scholars and feminists. Bates has lamented the fact that, due to its grassroots location, such research has not contributed to the mainstream of theoretical and critical development.[3] In Australia the academic journals, especially those of sociological or educational emphases, have contained substantial material on gender.[4] In fact, Musgrave has claimed that 'many of the scarce resources of sociological research' have been used to study gender within Australian society.[5] In another, earlier, context Musgrave referred to the changes which have taken place within the schooling of the sexes in Australia.[6] It is a matter of conjecture whether these two observations by Musgrave are related but one cannot fail to recognize a coincidence between research activity and changes of liberalizing nature in terms of gender occurring within schools and society at large. The second point of note is that women are by far the largest contributors to the field. One might expect that this is the case throughout the world, for historical, political and structural reasons. However, within the social sciences in general, and the sociology of education in particular, one might have anticipated that male researchers would also find the topic of gender (arguably the most crucial social division) as fascinating and important as any other. A sociological account of the sociology of education would need to consider the effect of patriarchy upon the sub-discipline's development.

The literature selected for inclusion in this bibliography represents a comprehensive list of that which has been published in Australia or New Zealand from 1973 onwards. As one may have concluded from the previous comments, gender was taken as the crucial topic for inclusion and material on class and education was selected for its pertinence to this topic. Conversely, the material on gender was expected to be related to education. The decisions about what material should be included or excluded were occasionally difficult; it is to be hoped that nothing substantial was excluded.[7] Some articles have been included which represent work from outside a sociological theoretical tradition because it was believed that the research evidence and discussion contained therein were pertinent to the sociology of education. Similarly, some texts have been included which contain comment on matters appertaining to gender, class and education in Australia or New Zealand even though this was not their central theme. Accessibility of material to an international audience was considered as a criterion for inclusion in the bibliography, hence the references included are generally those which a diligent student, researcher or scholar should be able to obtain. Some material from New Zealand may be amongst the most difficult to find, due to the tendency for local dissemination of material on the topic, however such material has been included because of its pertinence to the area.

A list has been appended to the end of the bibliography which encompasses special issues of journals; names and addresses of regular journals which occasionally contain material of an academic quality on the topic of this bibliography; and names and addresses of organizations and centres whose main focus falls within the topic.

Notes

1 See, for example, DAVEY, J.A. (1977) *One in Five: Women and School Committees*, Wellington, Society for Research on Women in New Zealand.
2 BUNCE, J. (1979) 'Far from the ivory tower: A review of research on women and education in New Zealand', a paper presented at the first National Conference of the New Zealand Association for Research in Education, Victoria University of Wellington, 7–10 December 1979.
3 BATES, R.J. (1980) 'Problems and prospects for a sociology of New Zealand education', *Australian and New Zealand Journal of Sociology*, 16, 2, p. 6.
4 It should be made clear that the major sociological journal is in fact a publication of the Sociological Association of Australia and New Zealand and, hence, not purely an Australian journal. However, in two symposia on 'Inequalities: Class and gender' published by the Association in 1979 only two out of 24 titles were contributed by authors with New Zealand institutional allegiances.
5 MUSGRAVE, P.W. (1980) 'The sociology of the Australian curriculum: A case study in the diffusion of theory', *Australian and New Zealand Journal of Sociology*, 16, 2, p. 18.
6 MUSGRAVE, P.W. (1979) *Society and the Curriculum in Australia*, Sydney, George Allen and Unwin, pp. 114–16.
7 I am grateful to Professor B. CALVERT of the Department of Education, University of Otago and to Dr S.N. SAMPSON, of the Faculty of Education Monash University for their advice on the compilation of this bibliography.

Bibliography

Books and Reports

BEARLIN, M.L. and SHELLEY, N.J. (1981) *Women in Education in the Australian Capital Territory*, Canberra, Australian College of Education, Australian Capital Territory Chapter.
BRANSON, J.E. and MILLER, D.B. (1979) *Class, Sex and Education in Capitalist Society: Culture, Ideology and the Reproduction of Inequality in Australia*, Melbourne, Sorrett.
BROWNE, J. *et al.* (1978) *Changes, Chances, Choices: A Report on the United Women's Convention*, Christchurch, United Women's Convention.
BUNKLE, P., LEVINE, S. and WAINWRIGHT, C. (1976) *Learning about Sexism in New Zealand*, Wellington, Learmonth.
BURNS, A. and GOODNOW, J. (1979) *Children and Families in Australia*, Sydney, George Allen and Unwin.
COMMITTEE ON THE STATUS OF WOMEN ACADEMICS (1977) *Project Reports. Survey on*

Women in Autralian Universities. Report on Characteristics of Academic Job Applicants, Melbourne, Federation of Australian University Staff Associations.

CONNELL, R.W., ASHENDEN, D.J., KESSER, S. and DOWSETT, G.W. (1982) *Making the Difference: Schools. Families and Social Division*, Sydney, George Allen and Unwin.

CONNELL, W.F., STROOBANT, R.E., SINCLAIR, K.E., CONNELL, R.W. and ROGERS, K.W. (1975) *12 to 20, Studies of City Youth*, Sydney, Hicks Smith.

DANIELS, K., MURNANE, M. and PICOT, A. (1977) *Women in Australia, Volume One: Tasmania, Western Australia and South Australia*, Canberra, Australian Government Publishing Service.

——————————————————————— (1977) *Women in Australia, Volume Two: Queensland, Victoria, Australian Capital Territory and New South Wales*, Canberra, Australian Government Publishing Service.

DAVIES, A., ENCEL, S. and BERRY, M. (Eds) (1977) *Australian Society: A Sociological Introduction*, third edition, Melbourne, Longman Cheshire.

DAWSON, M. (Ed.) (1974) *Families: Australian Studies of Changing Relationships within the Family and between the Family and Society*, Sydney, Searchlight, ANZAAS, John Wiley and Sons.

DEPARTMENT OF EDUCATION (1976) *Education and Equality of the Sexes: A Report on the National Conference in International Women's Year 1975*, Wellington, Department of Education.

DIXSON, M. (1976) *The Real Matilda: Women and Identity in Australia 1788–1975*, Ringwood, Penguin.

D'URSO, S. and SMITH, R.A. (Eds) (1978) *Changes, Issues and Prospects in Australian Education*, St. Lucia, University of Queensland Press.

EDGAR, D.E. (Ed.) (1975) *The Sociology of Australian Education*, Sydney, McGraw-Hill.

ENCEL, S., McKENZIE, N. and TEBBUTT, M. (1974) *Women and Society: An Australian Study*, Melbourne, Cheshire.

FENWICK, P. (1980) *Teacher Career and Promotion Study*, Wellington, Department of Education.

FITZGERALD, R.T. (1976) *Poverty and Education in Australia: Fifth Main Report of the Commission into Poverty in Australia*, Canberra, Australian Government Publishing Service.

FOSTER, L.E. (1981) *Australian Education: A Sociological Perspective*, Sydney, Prentice–Hall.

GRIEVE, N. and GRIMSHAW, P. (1981) *Australian Women: Feminist Perspectives*, Melbourne, Oxford University Press.

HARPER, J. and RICHARDS, L. (1979) *Mothers and Working Mothers*, Ringwood, Penguin.

HUGHES, B. and BUNKLE, P. (1981) *Women in New Zealand Society*, Sydney, George Allen and Unwin.

HUNT, F.J. (Ed.) (1978) *Socialization in Australia*, second edition, Melbourne, Australian International Press.

KARMEL, P. *et al.* (1973) *Schools in Australia: Report of the Interim Committee for the Australian Schools Commission*, Canberra, Australian Government Publishing Service.

KINGSTON, B. (1975) *My Wife, My Daughter and Poor Mary Ann: Women and Work in Australia*, Melbourne, Thomas Nelson.

MARTIN, J. (1978) *The Migrant Presence*, Sydney, George Allen and Unwin.

MERCER, J. (Ed.) (1975) *The Other Half: Women in Australian Society*, Ringwood, Penguin.

OECD (1974) *The Role of Women in the Economy: Background Information, Australia*, Canberra, Department of Labour.

RAMSAY, P. (Ed.) (1975) *The Family and The School in New Zealand Society*, Melbourne, Pitman.

REED, J. and OAKES, K. (1977) *Women in Australian Society*, Canberra, Australian Government Publishing Service.

REPORT TO THE PREMIER OF VICTORIA (1977) *Victorian Committee on Equal Opportunity in Schools*, Melbourne, Government Printer.

RITCHIE, J. (Ed.) (1975) *Psychology of Women: Research Record I, Psychology Research Series No. 5*, Hamilton, University of Waikato.

————— (Ed.) (1978) *Psychology of Women: Research Record II, Psychology Research Series No. 8*, Hamilton, University of Waikato.

ROBINSON, G. and O'ROURKE, B. (Eds) (1980) *Schools in New Zealand Society*, Auckland, Longman-Paul.

RYAN, E. and CONLON, A. (1975) *Gentle Invaders: Australian Women at Work 1788–1974*, Melbourne, Thomas Nelson.

SCHOOLS COMMISSION (1975) *Girls, School and Society*, Canberra, Australian Government Publishing Service.

————— (1978) *Report of the Triennium 1979–1981*, Canberra, Australian Government Publishing Service.

SEYMOUR, R. (Ed.) (1978a) *Research Papers 1978: Women's Studies*, Hamilton, New Zealand Women's Studies Association.

————— (Ed.) (1978b) *Women's Studies in New Zealand 1974–1977: A Pilot Bibliography Directory*, Hamilton, Department of Sociology, University of Waikato.

————— (Ed.) (1979) *Women's Studies in New Zealand 1978: A Bibliography–Directory*, Hamilton, Department of Sociology, University of Waikato.

SUMMERS, A. (1975) *Damned Whores and God's Police: The Colonization of Women in Australia*, Ringwood, Penguin.

TORSH, D., DRYER, R. and KAY, M. (1974) *A Bibliography of Social Change and the Education of Women*, Canberra, Schools Commission, Australian Government Publishing Service.

WHEELWRIGHT, E.L. and BUCKLEY, K. (Eds) (1975) *Essays in the Political Economy of Australian Capitalism, Volume One*, Sydney, Australian and New Zealand Book Company.

————— (Eds) (1978) *Essays in the Political Economy of Australian Capitalism, Volume Two*, Sydney, Australian and New Zealand Book Company.

————— (Eds) (1978) *Essays in the Political Economy of Australian Capitalism, Volume Three*, Sydney, Australian and New Zealand Book Company.

WILD, R.A. (1978) *Social Stratification in Australia*, Sydney, George Allen and Unwin.

Articles and Chapters

ABBEY, B. and ASHENDEN, D. (1978a) 'Explaining inequality', *Australian and New Zealand Journal of Sociology*, 14, 1.

————— (1978b) 'Unequal explanations: A rejoinder to Toomey and Edgar', *Australian and New Zealand Journal of Sociology*, 14, 2.

ALAI, B. and O'BRIEN, G. (1978) 'Sex role differentiation in a sample of Waikato University students', in RITCHIE, J. (Ed.) *Psychology of Women, Research Record II, Psychological Research Series No. 8*, Hamilton, University of Waikato.

ALLBURY, R.M., CHAPLES, E.A. and STUBBS, K. (1977) 'Sexism among a group of Sydney tertiary students', *Australian and New Zealand Journal of Sociology*, 13, 2.

ASHENDEN, D. (1979) 'Australian education: Problems of a Marxist practice', *Arena*, 54.

BERNARD, M.E. (1977) 'The effects of sex and sex role characteristics on teacher and student evaluations of each other. Research report', *Australian Journal of Education*, 21, 3.

BESSANT, B. (1976) 'Domestic science schools and woman's place', *Australian Journal of Education*, 20, 1.

BLOCH, C. (1975) 'Schools Commission looks at sexism', *Quest*, 17.

BOTTOMLEY, G. (1974a) 'Kinship and cultural change: Some observations of Greeks in

Sydney', in DAWSON, M. (Ed.) (1974) *Families: Australian Studies of Changing Relationships within the Family and between the Family and Society*, Sydney, Searchlight, ANZAAS, John Wiley.

——————(1974b) 'Some Greek sex-roles: Ideals, expectations and action in Australia and Greece', *Australian and New Zealand Journal of Sociology*, 10, 1.

BOTTOMLEY, M. and SAMPSON, S. (1977) 'The case of the female principal: Sex-role attitudes and perceptions of sex differences in ability', *Australian and New Zealand Journal of Sociology*, 13, 2.

BRYSON, L. (1974) 'Men's work and women's work: Occupation and family orientation', *Search*, 5, 7.

CASS, B. (1976) 'Women at University: Part One, family and class background', *Refractory Girl*, 10.

——————(1977) 'Family', in DAVIES, A., ENCEL, S. and BERRY, M. (Eds) (1977) *Australian Society: A Sociological Introduction*, third edition, Melbourne, Longman Cheshire.

—————— (1978) 'Women's place in the class structure', in WHEELWRIGHT, E.L. and BUCKLEY, K. (Eds) (1978) *Essays in the Political Economy of Australian Capitalism, Volume Three*, Sydney, Australian and New Zealand Book Company.

CONNELL, R.W. (1974) 'The causes of educational inequality: Further observations', *Australian and New Zealand Journal of Sociology*, 10, 3.

DONALDSON, M. (1978) 'Marx, women and bourgeois right: Feminism and class reconsidered', *Australian and New Zealand Journal of Sociology*, 14, 2.

EARLEY, P.D. (1981) 'Girls need jobs too you know! — Unemployment, sex roles and female identity', *Australian Journal of Social Issues*, 16, 3.

EDGAR, D.E. (1974) 'Adolescent competence and sexual disadvantage', *La Trobe University (Melbourne) Sociology Papers*, 10.

——————(1978) 'Reply to Abbey and Ashenden's "Explaining inequality"', *Australian and New Zealand Journal of Sociology*, 14, 1.

EDGAR, P.M. (1975) 'Sex type socialization and family comedy programmes', in EDGAR, D.E. (Ed.) (1975) *The Sociology of Australian Education*, Sydney, McGraw-Hill.

ELLEY, W.R. and IRVING, J.C. (1976) 'Revised socio-economic index for New Zealand', *New Zealand Journal of Educational Studies*, 11, 1. (See also IRVING, J.C. and ELLEY, W.R. (1977).)

ELLIOTT, L. (1975) 'Inequalities in the Australian education system, Part Two: Women in the professions', in MERCER, J. (Ed.) (1975) *The Other Half: Women in Australian Society*, Ringwood, Penguin.

FAUST, B. (1974) 'Feminism: Then and now', *Australian Quarterly*, 46, 1.

FRASER, B.J. (1980) 'Grade level and sex differences in attitude to several school subjects', *Australian Journal of Education*, 24, 1.

GALE, F. (1980) 'Academic staffing: The search for excellence', *Vestes*, 23, 1.

HAMILTON, A. (1975) 'Aboriginal women: The means of production', in MERCER, J. (Ed.) (1975) *The Other Half: Women in Australian Society*, Ringwood, Penguin.

HEALY, P. and RYAN, P. (1975) 'Sex stereotyping in children's books', in MERCER, J. (Ed.) (1975) *The Other Half: Women in Australian Society*, Ringwood, Penguin.

HERBISON, J.M. (1976) 'Girls, school and society: A report by a study group (review)', *Journal of Educational Administration*, 14, 2.

HUMPHREYS, D. (1975) 'School and the oppression of women', in MERCER, J. (Ed.) (1975) *The Other Half: Women in Australian Society*, Ringwood, Penguin.

HUNTER, T. (1975) 'Married women in academia — a personal view', *Vestes*, 18, 1.

IRVING, J.C. and ELLEY, W.B. (1977) 'A socio-economic index for the female labour force in New Zealand', *New Zealand Journal of Educational Studies*, 12, 2.

JEPSON, D. (1976) 'Women's education and feminism', *Arena*, 44–45.

JONES, J.M. and LOVEJOY, F.H. (1980) 'The perceived role of Australian female academics (research report)', *Australian and New Zealand Journal of Sociology*, 16, 2.

KELDERMAN, S., POTTS, W., WADE, L. and GUDSELL, K. (1978) 'Social change and sexist attitudes in high school students', in RITCHIE, J. (Ed.) (1978) *Psychology of Women:*

Research Record II, Psychological Research Series No. 8, Hamilton, University of Waikato.

KNIGHT, T. (1974) 'Powerlessness and the student role: Structural determinants of school status', *Australian and New Zealand Journal of Sociology*, 10, 2.

KOLLER, K., WADE, R. and GOSDEN, S. (1980) 'Youth unemployment: The special case of young women', *Australian Journal of Social Issues*, 15, 1.

LEDER, G.C. and WHITE, R.T. (1980) 'Three aspects of occupational aspirations of boys and girls', *Australian and New Zealand Journal of Sociology*, 16, 2.

LEVINE, S. (1974) 'Liberating research: The study of women', *Political Science*, 26, 1.

LITTLER, A. (1981) 'Transition education girls project', *Educational Magazine*, 38, 4.

LODGE, J. (1976) 'New Zealand women academics: Some observations on their status, aspirations and professional advancement', *Political Science*, 28, 1.

MACASKILL, S. (1976) 'Children's perceptions of sex roles', in BUNKLE, P., LEVINE, S. and WAINWRIGHT, C. (Eds) (1976) *Learning about Sexism in New Zealand*, Wellington, Learmonth.

MCCALLUM, D. (1980) 'Naturalizing educational inequality: An overview of the Australian intellectual field, 1935–1945', *Australian and New Zealand Journal of Sociology*, 16, 2.

MCDONALD, E.M.A. (1976) 'Girls, school and society: A report by a study group (review)', *South Pacific Journal of Teacher Education*, 4, 3.

MCDONALD, G. (1980) 'Education and the movement towards equality', in HUGHES, B. and BUNKLE, P. (Eds) (1980) *Women in New Zealand*, Sydney, George Allen and Unwin.

MARJORIBANKS, K. (1977) 'Educational deprivation thesis: A further analysis', *Australian and New Zealand Journal of Sociology*, 13, 1.

OVER, R. (1981) 'Women academics in Australian universities', *Australian Journal of Education*, 25, 2.

PHILLIPS, S. (1979) 'Sexual prejudice in Sydney middle school children (research report)', *Australian and New Zealand Journal of Sociology*, 15, 2.

POOLE, M.E. (1977) 'Social class — sex contrasts in patterns of cognitive style', *Australian Journal of Education*, 21, 3.

POWER, M. (1974) 'The wages of sex', *Australian Quarterly*, 46, 1.

RITCHIE, J., VILLIGER, J. and DUIGAN, P. (1977) 'Sex role differentiation in children: A preliminary investigation', *Australian and New Zealand Journal of Sociology*, 13, 2.

ROPER, T. (1975) 'Inequalitites in the Australian education system, Part One: An overview', in MERCER, J. (Ed.) (1975) *The Other Half: Women in Australian Society*, Ringwood, Penguin.

ROWLAND, R. (1980) 'Attitudes to sex roles: A discussion of Australian data and of methodology (research report)', *Australian and New Zealand Journal of Sociology*, 16, 3.

ROWLANDS, R.G. (1976) 'Are girls a disadvantaged group?', *Australian Journal of Education*, 20, 1.

SAMPSON, S.N. (1975) '*The Australian Women's Weekly* and the aspirations of girls', in EDGAR, D.E. (Ed.) (1975) *The Sociology of Australian Education*, Sydney, McGraw-Hill.

————(1976) 'Egalitarian ideology and the education of girls', *Australian Journal of Education*, 20, 1.

————(1977) 'Changes in Australian society and the education of teachers', *South Pacific Journal of Teacher Education*, 5, 3.

————(1978) 'Socialization into sex-roles', in HUNT, F.J. (Ed.) (1978) *Socialization in Australia*, second edition, Melbourne, Australian International Press.

SAMPSON, S.N. and CONNORS, L. (1977) 'Girls, school and society (review)', *Education News*, 16, 1.

SCUTT, J. (1979) 'The economics of sex: Women in service', *Australian Quarterly*, 46, 1.

SHARP, R. (1976) 'Girls school and society — a review', *Refractory Girl*, 11.

SINCLAIR, K.E., CROUCH, B. and MILLER, J. (1977) 'Occupational choices of Sydney teenagers: Relationships with sex and social class, grade level and parent expectations', *Australian Journal of Education*, 21, 1.

SMITH, A.B. (1980) 'The family, schools and sex roles', in ROBINSON, G. and O'ROURKE, B. (Eds) (1980) *Schools in New Zealand Society*, Auckland, Longman-Paul.

STEVEN, R. (1978) 'Towards a class analysis of New Zealand', *Australian and New Zealand Journal of Sociology*, 14, 2.

SYKES, B. (1975) 'Black women in Australia', in MERCER, J. (Ed.) (1975) *The Other Half: Women in Australian Society*, Ringwood, Penguin.

TOOMEY, D. (1974a) 'What causes educational disadvantage?', *Australian and New Zealand Journal of Sociology*, 10, 1.

_____(1974b) 'The school status theory of educational disadvantage — a rejoinder to Tony Knight', *Australian and New Zealand Journal of Sociology*, 10, 3.

_____ (1976) 'Educational disadvantage and meritocratic schooling', *Australian and New Zealand Journal of Sociology*, 12, 3.

_____ (1978) 'Two problems of educational inequality. A reply to Abbey and Ashenden', *Australian and New Zealand Journal of Sociology*, 14, 2.

WALES, D. (1978) 'Coeducational and single sex schools: Effects on pupils' attitudes', in RITCHIE, J. (Ed.) (1978) *Psychology of Women: Research Record II*, *Psychological Research Series No. 8*, Hamilton, University of Waikato.

WAUGH, P. (1976) 'Girls, school and society (review)', *Education* (New South Wales), 57, 9.

WENTWORTH, R.D. (1979) 'A comparison of the career aspirations of men and women trainee teachers', *South Pacific Journal of Teacher Education*, 7, 3/4.

WIDDUP, D. (1981) 'Women and maths. A wasting of talent', *Education News*, 17, 6.

WINKLER, A. (1976) 'Sex and student role stereotypes in Australian university students', *Australian Journal of Education*, 20, 3.

YOUNG, C. (1978) 'Adolescents' attitudes towards women in New Zealand', in RITCHIE, J. (Ed.) (1978) *Psychology of Women: Research Record II*, *Psychological Research Series No. 8*, Hamilton, University of Waikato.

ZAINU'UDDIN, A. (1973) 'Admission of women to the University of Melbourne', *Melbourne Studies in Education 1973*, Melbourne, Melbourne University Press.

Journals, Special Issues and Addresses

Australian Left Review, Box 247, South PO, Sydney, New South Wales. 2000, Australia.

Australian and New Zealand Journal of Sociology (1979) 15, 1. (Symposium: Inequalities: class and gender — Part One).

Australian and New Zealand Journal of Sociology (1979) 15, 2. (Symposium: Inequalities: class and gender — Part Two).

Australian and New Zealand Journal of Sociology (1980) 16, 2. (Symposium: Sociology of education).

Education News (1975) 15, 4 and 5. (Special issue: Women and education), Commonwealth of Australia, Department of Education.

Hecate (a women's interdisciplinary journal), PO Box 99, St Lucia, Brisbane, Queensland, 4067, Australia.

Refractory Girl, Women's Studies Group, 25 Alberta Street, Sydney, New South Wales, 2000, Australia.

RYAN, P. (Ed.) (1975) *A Guide to Women's Studies in Australia*, Carlton, Australian Union of Students. (Address: Australian Union of Students, 97 Drummond Street, Carlton, Victoria, 3053, Australia.)

School, Home and Work Project (an ongoing major project studying class, and gender and schooling in Sydney and Adelaide), for information: C/- Sociology, Macquarie University, North Ryde, New South Wales, 2113, Australia.

Society for Research on Women in New Zealand, PO Box 13–078, Johnsonville, Wellington, New Zealand.

Women's Studies Association, University of Waikato, Hamilton, New Zealand.

13. Gender, Class and Education: A Teaching Bibliography of American Studies

Emily J. Moskowitz, University of Rochester

Jessie Bernard refers to a world that is viewed through a 'prism of sex'. The research and study that goes on in universities is the study of men and men's institutions. Psychology, anthropology, sociology, literature, etc. all study and interpret a male world for men. Women are irrelevant and unimportant. The study of the world of women is not merely uninteresting to these researchers; they never even acknowledge that is exists. Knowledge is male knowledge. Culture is male culture. Women are barely seen as human; how could they be considered important enough to study? The reality of women's lives has been demeaned, if not totally denied. Men have owned women's reality and appropriated their knowledge. As Dorothy Smith has pointed out, women have never controlled the knowledge-making machinery. They have not been considered equals in the 'discourse' of intellectuals.

Feminist research is the attempt not only to alter the 'prism', but also to fill in the holes of the existing research, and to carve new roads where none have existed before. We must develop, as Adrienne Rich has called it, a 'Re-Vision'. This bibliography is part of that work of Re-Vision.

The bibliography has developed out of my own research and teaching in the area of women. The interest and study in this field has grown enormously over the past 15 years. Women's studies programs abound at American and Canadian universities. These programs vary, but almost all of them are interdisciplinary in approach, combining courses in literature, language, sociology, anthropology, education, economics, etc. — a characteristic reflected in this bibliography. The schools run the gamut from offering minors and electives in women's studies, to offering AA, BA, MA or PhD degrees in the area. The involvement and commitment of any school to a women's studies program is dependent upon the dynamic within that institution and not necessarily as an aspect of any external pressure from the national government. While Affirmative Action may be an impetus for the hiring of more women faculty, there is no concomitant pressure to establish women's studies programs or to fund research on women. The increase in research on and by women is much more a product of women's desire to control their own knowledge. (A list of women's studies programs is compiled annually by the Women's Studies Newsletter; Box 334, Old Westbury, New York 11568, USA and the National Women's Studies Association, 4102 Foreign Languages Building, University of Maryland, College Park, Maryland 20742, USA.)

As extensive as this bibliography appears to be, inevitably there are publications that have not been included. The prolific amount of research renders any published bibliography somewhat obsolete, yet this will begin to provide access even to those areas which are not given thorough coverage.

Bibliography

Women's Studies and Sex Roles

ARDENER, S. (Ed.) (1978) *Defining Female*, Somerset NJ, Halstead Press.

As, B. (n.d.) 'On female culture: An attempt to formulate a theory of women's solidarity and action', *Acta Sociologica*, 28, pp. 142–61.

ASTIN, H.S. (1975) *Sex Roles: A Research Bibliography*, Rockville, Md., National Institute.

BARDWICK, J.M. (1971) *Psychology of Women: A Study of Biocultultural Conflicts*, New York, Harper and Row.

BEECHEY, V. (1979) 'On patriarchy', *Feminist Review*, 3, pp. 66–82.

BELOTTI, E.G. (1978) *What Are Little Girls Made Of?*, New York, Schocken.

BERG, B.J. (1978) *The Remembered Gate, Origins of American Feminism: The Woman and the City*, 1800–1860, New York, Oxford.

BERKOWITZ, T., MANGI, J. and WILLIAMSON, J. (Eds) (1974) *Who's Who and Where in Women's Studies*, Old Westbury, The Feminist Press.

BERNARD, J. (1972) *The Sex Game*, Atheneum, New York.

BEZDEK, W. and STRODTBECK, F. (1970) 'Sex-role identity and pragmatic action', *American Sociological Review*, 35, pp. 491–502.

BLUMHAGEN, K. O'CONNOR and JOHNSON, W.D. (1978) *Women's Studies: An Interdisciplinary Collection*, Westport, Conn., Greenwood Press.

BROWNMILLER, S. (1977) *Against Our Will: Men, Women and Rape*, Penguin.

CANTOR, J.R. (1976) 'What is funny to whom: The role of gender', *Journal of Communication*, 26, pp. 164–72.

CARDEN, M.L. (1974) *The New Feminist Movement*, New York, Russell Sage.

——————— (1976) *Feminism in the Mid-1970's*, A Report to the Ford Foundation, New York.

CASSELL, J. (1977) *A Group Called Women: Sisterhood and Symbolism in the Feminist Movement*, New York, McKay.

CHAFETZ, J.S. (1974) *Masculine/Feminine or Human?*, Itasca, Ill., F.E. Peacock Publisher.

CHAPPELL, C.B. (1978) 'Status attainment process of women in Middletown in 1978', paper presented at American Sociological Association.

CLIFTON, A.K., MCGRATH, D. and WICK, B. (1976) 'Stereotypes of women: A single category?', *Sex Roles*, 2, pp. 135–48.

COOK, B.W. (Ed.) (1978) *Crystal Eastman on Women and Revolution*, New York, Oxford University Press.

COTT, N. (1977) *The Bonds of Womanhood*, New Haven, Yale University Press.

COWAN, M. and STEWART, B. (1977) 'A methodological study of sex stereotypes', *Sex Roles*, 3, pp. 205–16.

DALY, M. (1978) *Gyn/Ecology: The Metaethics of Radical Feminism*, Beacon Press, Boston.

DAVID, D. and BRANNON, R. (Eds) (1976) *The Forty-Nine Percent Majority: The Male Sex Role*, Reading, Mass., Addison-Wesley Publishing Co.

DAVIS, A.B. (1974) *Bibliography on Women*, New York, Science History Publications.

DAVIS, E.G. (1971) *The First Sex*, Baltimore, Md., Penguin Books.

DECKARD, B. (1979) *The Women's Movement*, second edition, New York, Harper and Row.

DINNERSTEIN, D. (1976) *The Mermaid and the Minotaur*, New York, Harper and Row.

DOYLE, N. (1974) *Woman's Changing Place: A Look at Sexism*, New York, Public Affairs Committee, No. 509.

DREIFUS, C. (1973) *Women's Fate: Raps from a Feminist Consciousness-Raising Group*, Bantam, New York.

DWORKIN, A. (1976) *Our Blood*, New York, Perigee Book.

FARRELL, W. (1975) *The Liberated Man*, New York, Bantam.

FASTEAU, M.F. (1975) *The Male Machine*, New York, Dell Publishing Co.

FAVA, S. (1978) 'Women's place', paper presented at American Sociological Association, San Francisco.

FELDMAN, S. (1974) *Escape from the Doll's House*, New York, McGraw-Hill.
—————— (1974) *The Rights of Women*, Rochelle Park, NJ, Hayden.
FELSHIN, J. (1974) *The American Woman in Sport*, Reading, Mass., Addison-Wesley Publishing Co.
FERGUSON, K.E. (1980) *Self, Society and Womanhood*, Westport, Conn., Greenwood Press.
FERRISS, A.L. (1971) *Indicators of Trends in the Status of American Women*, New York, Russell Sage Foundation.
FIRESTONE, S. (1970) *The Dialectic of Sex: The Case for Feminist Revolution*, New York, William Morrow.
FISHER, A.E. (1978) *Women's Worlds. NIMH-Supported Research on Women*, Rockville, Md., National Institute of Mental Health.
FORISHA, B.L. (1978) *Sex Roles and Personal Awareness*, NJ, General Learning Press.
FREEMAN, J. (1975) *The Politics of Women's Liberation*, New York, David McKay.
—————— (Ed.) (1979) *Women: A Feminist Perspective*, second edition, Palo Alto, Calif., Mayfield Publishing Company.
FRIEDAN, B. (1963) *The Feminine Mystique*, New York, Dell.
FRIEDAN, B. (1981) *The Second Stage*, New York, Summit Books.
FRIEDMAN, L.J. (1977) *Sex Role Stereotyping in the Mass Media: An Annotated Bibliography*, New York, Garland Publishing.
FLEXNER, E. (1971) *Women's Rights — Unfinished Business*, Public Affairs Pamphlet No. 468, New York, Public Affairs.
GARSKOF, M.H. (Ed.) (1971) *Roles Women Play: Readings towards Women's Liberation*, Wadsworth, Calif., pp. 68–83.
GIELE, J. (1979) *Women and the Future*, New York, Free Press.
GOLDBERG, S. (1973) *The Inevitability of Patriarchy*, New York, William Morrow and Co.
GORDON, L. (1976) 'Are the interests of men and women identical?', *Signs*, *1*, pp. 1011–18.
GORDON, L., BAXANDALL, R. and REVERBY, S. (1976) 'Boston working women protest, 1869', *Signs*, pp. 803–8.
GREER, G. (1971) *The Female Eunuch*, New York, McGraw-Hill.
—————— (1978) 'Flying pigs and double standards', *The Times Literary Supplement*, 26 July, p. 784.
GUNDRY, P. (1977) *Woman Be Free*, Grand Rapids, Mich., Zondervan Publishing House.
HAMMOND, D. and JABLOW, A. (1976) *Women in Cultures of the World*, Menlo Park, Calif., Cummings Publishing Co.
HART, M.M. (1971) 'Women sit in the back of the bus', *Psychology Today*, 5, pp. 64–6.
HASSELBART, S. (1978) 'Some underemphasized issues about men, women, and work', paper presented at American Sociological Association.
HERSCHBERGER, R. (1970) *Adam's Rib*, New York, Harper and Row.
HOCHSCHILD, A.R. (1973) 'A review of sex role research', *American Journal of Sociology*, 78, 4, pp. 11011–29.
HOGAN, C.L. (1977) 'From here to equality: Title IX', *Women Sports*, 4.
HOLE, J. and LEVINE, E. (1971) *The Rebirth of Feminism*, New York, Quadrangle Books.
HOWE, F. (1973) 'Sexism and the aspirations of women', *Phi Delta Kappan*, 55, 2, pp. 99–105.
—————— (1974) 'Report on the First Women's Studies Evaluation Conference', *Women's Studies Newsletter*, 3, March, pp. 8–10.
—————— (1977) *Seven Years Later: Women's Studies Programs in 1976*, Washington, National Advisory Council on Women's Education Programs.
HUNT, P. (1980) *Gender, Class and Consciousness*, NY, Holmest Meier.
JANEWAY, E. (1971) *Man's World, Woman's Place: A Study in Social Mythology*, New York, Delta.
—————— (1975) *Between Myth and Morning: Women Awakening*, New York, William Morrow.
JORDAN, J. (1969) *The Place of American Women*, Boston, Mass., The New England Press.
KARABELIAN, A.D. and SMITH, A.J. (1977) 'Sex role stereotyping in the United States: Is it

changing?', *Sex Roles*, 3, 2, pp. 193–8.

KELLEY, M. (Ed.) (1979) *Woman's Being*, Woman's Place, Boston, Mass., G.K. Hall and Co.

KOEDT, A., LEVINE, E. and RAPONE, A. (Eds) (1973) *Radical Feminism*, New York, Quadrangle Books.

KOMAROVSKY, M. (1953) *Woman in the Modern World*, Boston, Mass., Little, Brown.

KRADITOR, A. (Ed.) (1968) *Up from the Pedestal*, Chicago, Ill., Quadrangle.

KRICHMAR, A. (1977) *The Women's Movement in the Seventies*, Metuchen, NJ, The Scarecrow Press.

LAWS, J.L. (1979) *The Second X*, New York, Elsevier.

LAWS, J.L. and SCHWARTZ, P. (1977) *Sexual Scripts*, Illinois, Dryden Press.

LIPMEN-BLUMEN, J. (1978) 'Observations on the current status of the women's movement in the United States', paper presented at International Sociological Association, Uppsala.

——————— (1979) 'Emerging patterns of female leadership: Must the female leader go formal?', in HORNER, M. (Ed.), *Perspectives on the Patterns of an Era*, Cambridge, Mass., Harvard University Press.

LIPMEN-BLUMEN, J. and TICKAMEYER, A.R. (1975) 'Sex roles in transition: A ten year perspective', pp. 297–337 in INKELES, A. (Ed.), *Annual Review of Sociology, Vol. 1*, Palo Alto, Calif., Annual Reviews.

MCBEE, M.L. and BLAKE, K.H. (Eds) (1974) *The American Woman: Who Will She Be?*, Beverly Hills, Glencoe Press.

MCDOWELL, M.B. (1971) 'The new rhetoric of woman power', *Midwest Quarterly*, 12, pp. 187–98.

MCGUIGAN, D.G. (Ed.) (1973) *A Sampler of Women's Studies*, Ann Arbor, Mich., Center for Continuing Education of Women.

MARINI, M.M. (1978) 'Sex differences in the determination of adolescent aspirations: A review of research', *Sex Roles: A Journal of Research*, 4, 5, pp. 723–54.

MATTHIASSON, C.J. (Ed.) (1974) *Many Sisters: Women in Cross-Cultural Perspective*, New York, Free Press.

MERRIAM, E. (1964) *After Nora Slammed the Door*, New York, World Publishing Company.

MONEY, J. and EHRHARDT, A. (1972) *Man and Woman, Boy and Girl*, Baltimore, Md., Johns Hopkins University Press.

MORGAN, R. (Ed.) (1971) *Sisterhood is Powerful*, New York, Random House.

PETERS, B. and SAMUELS, V. (1976) *Dialogue on Diversity: A New Agenda for American Women*, New York, Institute on Pluralism and Group Identity.

PETRAS, J. (Ed.) (1975) *Sex: Male/Gender: Masculine*, Port Washington, NY, Alfred Publishing Co.

PLECK, J.H. (1976) 'The male sex role: Definitions, problems, and sources of change', *Journal of Social Issues*, 32, pp. 155–64.

PLECK, J.H. and SAWYER, J. (Eds) (1974) *Men and Masculinity*, Englewood Cliffs, NJ, Prentice-Hall.

REUTHER, R.R. (1975) *New Woman/New Earth: Sexist Ideologies and Human Liberation*, New York, The Seabury Press.

RICH, A. (1979) *On Lies, Secrets and Silence: Selected Prose*, New York, Norton and Co.

ROBERTS, J. (1976) *Beyond Intellectual Sexism: A New Woman, A New Reality*, New York, David McKay.

ROHR-LEAVITT, R. (Ed.) (1975) *Women Cross-Culturally: Change and Challenge*, The Hague, Mouton.

ROSEN, B. and JERDEE, T.H. (1974) 'Influence of sex-role stereotypes on personnel decisions, *Journal of Applied Psychology*, 59, pp. 9–14.

ROSS, S.D. (1973) *The Rights of Women*, New York, Avon.

——————— (Ed.) (1973) *The Feminist Papers*, New York, Bantam.

ROSZAK, B. and ROSZAK, T. (Eds) (1969) *Masculine/Feminine*, New York, Harper and Row.

RUTH, S. (1980) *Issues in Feminism: A First Course in Women's Studies*, Boston, Mass., Houghton Mifflin Co.

SABROSKEY, J.A. (1979) *From Rationality to Liberation: The Evolution of Feminist Ideology*, Westport, Conn., Greenwood Press.

SAHLI, N. (1978) 'Smashing: Women's relationships before the Fall', *Chrysalis*, 8, pp. 17–27.

SCHAEF, A. (1978) 'The female and male systems', paper presented at Women's Studies Conference, University of Maryland.

SHERMAN, J.A. and BECK, E.N. (Eds) (1979) *The Prism of Sex*, Madison, Wisc. University of Wisconsin Press.

SIGNS (1980) *Women and the American City*, Supplement, 5, 3.

SMITH, D. (1978) 'A peculiar eclipsing: women's exclusion from man's culture' *Women's Studies In Quarterly*, 1, 4, 281–96.

SNODGRASS, J. (1977) *For Men against Sexism*, New York, Times Change Press.

SNYDER, E.E. (Ed.) (1979) *The Study of Women: Enlarging Perspectives of Social Reality*, New York, Harper and Row.

SNYDER, E.E. and KIVLIN, J.E. (1977) 'Perceptions of the sex role among female athletes and nonatheletes', *Adolescence*, 12, 45, pp. 23–9.

STEPHENSON, M. (Ed.) (1973) *Women in Canada*, Toronto, New Press.

STEVENSON, C.L. (1975) 'Socialization participation in sport: A critical review of the research', *The Research Quarterly*, 46, 3, pp. 283–301.

STOLL, C.S. (1974) *Female and Male*, Dubuque, Iowa William C. Brown, Co.

STOLLER, R.J. (1968) *Sex and Gender: On the Development of Masculinity and Femininity*, New York, Science House.

STREATFIELD, (Ed.) (1976) *Women and the Future*, Binghamton, NY, Center for Integration Studies.

TANNER, L.B. (Ed.) (1970) *Voices from Women's Liberation*, New York, Signet.

TAVRIS, C. and OFFIR, C. (1977) *The Longest War*, New York, Harcourt, Brace Janovich.

TEITLEBAUM, M. (Ed.) (1976) *Sex Differences*, New York, Anchor Books.

TOBACH, E. and ROSOFF, B. (Eds) (1978) *Genes and Gender*, New York, Gardian Press.

TRESCOTT, J. (1979) 'Black feminist on the front line', *The Washington Post* (7 February).

TURK, M. (1971) *The Buried Life: A Nun's Journey*, New York, World.

VETTERLING-BRAGGIN, M., ELLISTON, F. and ENGLISH, J. (Eds) (1977) *Feminism and Philosophy*, New Jersey, Littlefield, Adams and Co.

WALUM, L.R. and MILDERN, N.D. (1974) 'Female roles and protest activity: The meat boycott of 1973', paper presented to the American Sociological Association Annual Meeting, New York.

WEITZ, S. (1977) *Sex Roles*, New York, Oxford University Press.

WEITZMAN, L.J. (1979) *Sex Role Socialization: A Focus on Women*, Palo Alto, Calif., Mayfield.

WEST, U. (1975) *Women in a Changing World*, New York, McGraw-Hill.

———— (1975) 'Friends and females', *Viva*, 2, 37–8, pp. 106–8.

WILMORE, J.H. (1974) 'They told you, you couldn't compete with men and you, like a fool, believed them. Here's hope', *Womensports*, (June) pp. 40–3.

WOMEN'S ACTION ALLIANCE (1976) *Women's Agenda*, 1, 1.

WOUDENBERG, R.A. (1977) 'The relationship of sexual attitudes, attitudes about women, and racial attitudes in white males', *Sex Roles: A Journal of Research*, 3, 2, pp. 101–10.

YORBURG, B. (1974) *Sexual Identity*, New York, Wiley.

Family and Women's Work

ALTMAN, S.L. and GROSSMAN, F.K. (1977) 'Women's career plans and maternal employment', *Psychology of Women Quarterly*, 1, 4, pp. 365–76.

ANDRE, R. (1981) *Homemakers — The Forgotten Workers*, University of Chicago Press.

ARONOFF, J. and CRANO, W.D. (1975) 'A re-examination of the cross-cultural principles of task segregation and sex role differentiation in the family', *American Social Review*, 40, pp. 12–20.

BARRETT, C.J. (1977) 'Women in widowhood', *Signs; Journal of Women in Culture and Society*, 2, 4, pp. 856–68.

BEARD, M. (1971) *Woman as Force in History*, New York, Collier.

BECKMAN, L.J. (1978) 'The relative rewards and costs of parenthood and employment for employed women', *Psychology of Women Quarterly*, 2, 3, pp. 215–34.

BERK, S.F. (1980) *Women and Household Labor*, Beverly Hills, Sage Publications.

BERNARD, J. (1972) *The Future of Marriage*, New York, Bantam Books.

——————— (1974) *The Future of Motherhood*, New York, Penquin Books.

———————(1975) 'Adolescence and socialization for motherhood', in DRAGASTIN, S. and ELDER, G. (Eds) *Adolescence in the Life Cycle, Psychological Change and Social Context*, Washington, DC, Hemisphere Publishing Co.

——————— (1975) *Women, Wives, Mothers: Values and Options*, Chicago, Aldine.

———————(1976) 'Where are we now? Some thoughts on the current scene', *Psychology of Women Quarterly*, 1, 1, pp. 21–37.

——————— (1980) 'Crisis, revolution, and the politics of the family', *Transaction-Society*.

——————— (1981) 'The good-provider role, its rise and fall', *The American Psychologist*, 36.

BIELBY, D. (1978) 'Maternal employment and socioeconomic status as factors in daughters' career salience: Some substantive refinements', *Sex Roles: A Journal of Research*, 4, 2, pp. 249–66.

BLANKENSHIP, J. (Ed.) (1976) *Scenes from Life: Views of Family, Marriage and Intimacy*, Boston, Mass., Little, Brown and Co.

BOULDING, E. (1976) 'Familial constraints on women's work roles', *Signs*, 1, pp. 95–118.

BREHM, H.P. and LOPATA, H.Z. (1982) *Widowhood*, New York, Praeger.

CHAPMAN, J.R. and GATES, M. (1977) *Women into Wives*, Beverly Hills, Sage Publications.

——————————————— (Eds) (1978) *The Victimization of Women*, Beverly Hills, Sage Publications.

CHESLER, P. (1975) 'Marriage and psychotherapy', in RADICAL THERAPIST COLLECTIVE (Eds), *The Radical Therapist*, New York, Ballantyne, pp. 197–80.

CHODOROW, N. (1978) *The Reproduction of Mothering: Psychoanalysis and the Sociology of Gender*, Berkeley, Calif. University of California Press.

COOMBS, L. (1977) 'Preferences for sex of children among US couples', *Perspectives*, 9, pp. 259–65.

COWAN, R.S. (1974) 'A case study of technological and social change: The washing machine and the working wife', in HARTMAN, M. and BANNER, L.W. (Eds) *Clio's Consciousness Raised*, New York, Harper Torchbooks, pp. 245–53.

———————(1976) 'The "Industrial Revolution" in the home: Household technology and social change in the twentieth century', *Technology and Culture*, 17, pp. 1–25.

———————(1976) 'Two washes in the morning and a bridge party at night: The American housewife between the wars', *Women's Studies*, 3, pp. 147–72.

——————— (1977) 'Women and technology in American life', in PICKETT, W.B. (Ed.) *Technology at the Turning Point*, San Francisco, San Francisco Press, pp. 23–33.

CRONKITE, C. (1977) 'The determinants of spouses' normative preferences for family roles', *Journal of Marriage and Family*, 39, pp. 575–85.

DEFRAIN, J.D. (1977) 'Sexism in parenting manuals', *The Family Coordinator*, 26, pp. 245–51.

DERR, C.B. (Ed.) (1980) *Work, Family, and the Career: New Frontiers in Theory and Research*, New York, Praeger.

DOBROFSKY, L.R. (1978) 'The wife: From military dependent to feminist?', *International Journal of Women's Studies*, 1, 3, pp. 248–58.

———————(1977) 'Women's power and authority in the context of war', *Sex Roles*, 3, pp. 141–57.

_____ and BATTERSON, C.T. (1977) 'The military wife and feminism', *Signs*, 2, pp. 675–84.

DOUVAN, E. (1978) 'Family roles in a twenty year perspective', paper presented at Radcliffe Centennial Conference.

DUBLIN, T. (1975) 'Women, work, and the family: Female operatives in the Lowell Mills, 1830–1860', *Feminist Studies*, 3, pp. 30–9.

_____ (1979) *Women at Work*, New York, Columbia University Press.

EHRLICH, C. (1971) 'The male sociologist's burden: The place of women in marriage and family texts', *Journal of Marriage and the Family*, 33, pp. 421–30.

EISENSTEIN, Z.R. (Ed.) (1979) *Capitalist Patriarchy and the Case for Socialist Feminism*, New York, Monthly Review Press.

FARMER, H.S. and BOHN, M.J. (1970) 'Home career conflict reduction and the level of career interest in women', *Journal of Counseling Psychology*, 17, pp. 228–32.

FEINSTEIN, K.W. (Ed.) (1979) *Working Women and Families*, Beverly Hills, Sage Publications.

FERREE, M.M. (1975) 'Working class jobs: Housework and paid work as sources of satisfaction', *Social Problems*, 23, pp. 431–41.

_____ (1976) 'The confused American housewife', *Psychology Today*, 10 (September), pp. 76–80.

FOGARTY, M.P., RAPOPORT, R. and RAPOPORT, R.N. (1980) *Sex, Career and Family*, Beverly Hills, Sage Publications.

FRITCHEY, C. (1976) 'The women's caucus', *The Washington Post* (24 April).

_____ (1977) 'The true champions of family life', *The Washington Post* (3 December).

GABRIEL, A. (1980) *Parenthood by Choice: Transition to Parenthood*, doctoral dissertation, University of Rochester.

GALBRAITH, J.K. (1973) 'Economics of the American housewife', *Atlantic Monthly*, 232 (August), pp. 78–83.

GETZ, J.G. and KLEIN, H.K. (1980) 'The frosting of the American woman: Hairdressing and the phenomenology of beauty', draft of paper presented at Society for Study of Social Problems, New York.

GIRALDO, Z.I. (1980) *Public Policy and the Family: Wives and Mothers in the Labor Force*, Lexington, Mass., Lexington Press.

GLADIEUX, J.D. (1978) 'Pregnancy — the transition to parenthood: Satisfaction with the pregnancy experience as a function of sex role conceptions, marital relationship, and social network', in MILLER, B. and NEWMAN, L.F. (Eds) *The First Child and Family Formation*, Chapel Hill, Carolina Population Center.

GLASTONBURY, M. (1979) 'The best kept secret — how working class women live and what they know', *Women's Studies International Quarterly*, 2, 2, pp. 171–83.

GLAZER, N. (Ed.) (1975) *Old Family/New Family*, New York, D. Van Nostrand.

GLAZER-MALBIN, N. (1976) 'The captive couple: The burden of gender roles in marriage', in ZIMMERMAN, D.H. and WIEDER, D.L. (Eds), *Social Problems in Contemporary Society*, New York, Praeger.

GUTTMAN, D. (1973) 'Men, women, and the parental imperative', *Commentary*, 56, pp. 59–63.

HACKER, H. (1971) 'The feminine protest of the working wife', *The Indian Journal of Social Work*, 31 (January), pp. 401–6.

HARTMANN, H. (1981) 'The family as the locus of gender, class and political struggle: The example of housework', *Signs*, 6, 3, pp. 366–95.

HAWKINS, M.H. (n.d.) '19th century household patents by women', in LEGHORN, L. and WARRIOR, B. (Eds) *Houseworker's Handbook*, Cambridge, Mass., Woman's Center.

HAWRYLYSHYN, O. (1979) *The Economic Value of Household Services*, New York, Praeger.

HOFFMAN, L.W. (1977) 'Changes in family roles, socialization and sex differences', *American Psychologist*, 32, pp. 644–57.

HOGELAND, R.W. (Ed.) (1973) *Women and Womanhood in America*, Lexington, Mass., D.C.

Heath and Co.

HOWE, L.K. (Ed.) (1972) *The Future of the Family*, New York, Simon and Schuster.

JOHNSON, C.L. and JOHNSON, F.A. (1977) 'Attitudes toward parenting in dual-career families', *American Journal of Psychiatry*, 134, 4, pp. 391–5.

KELLERMAN, J. and KATZ, E.R. (1978) 'Attitudes toward the division of child-rearing responsibility', *Sex Roles: A Journal of Research*, 4, 4, pp. 505–12.

KURIAN, G. and GHOSH, R. (Eds) (1981) *Women in the Family and the Economy: An International Comparative Survey*, Wesport, Conn., Greenwood Press.

LAMB, M.E. (1977) 'The development of parent preferences in the first two years of life', *Sex Roles*, 3, pp. 495–7.

LAWS, J.L. (1971) 'A feminist review of marital adjustment literature: The rape of the locke', *Journal of Marriage and the Family*, 33, pp. 483–516.

LEIBOWITZ, L. (1978) *Females, Males, Families: A Biosocial Approach*, North Scituate, Mass., Duxbury Press.

LEIFER, M. (1982) *Psychological Effects of Motherhood: A Study of First Pregnancy*, New York, Praeger.

LEWIS, D.K. (1975) 'The black family: Socialization and sex roles', *Phylon*, 36, pp. 221–37.

LOPATA, H.Z. (1971) *Occupation Housewife*, New York, Oxford Press.

_____ (1973) *Widowhood in An American City*, Cambridge, Mass., Schenkman Publishing Co.

MALOS, E. (1980) *The Politics of Housework*, London, Allison and Busby.

MANDELBAUM, D.R. (1981) *Work, Marriage, and Motherhood: The Career Persistence of Female Physicians*, New York, Praeger.

MARSHALL, H. and KNAFL, K. (1973) 'Professionalizing motherhood: La Leche League and Breast feeding', presented at the American Sociological Association, New York, 26–30 August.

MATTHEWS, S. (1979) *The Social World of Old Women: Management of Self Identity*, Beverly Hills, Sage Publications.

MOERS, E. (1973) 'Money, the job, and little women', *Commentary* (January), pp. 57–65.

NATIONAL COMMISSION FOR MANPOWER POLICY (1978) *Women's Changing Roles at Home and on the Job*, Washington, DC, Special Report No. 26, National Commission for Manpower Policy (September).

OPPENHEIMER, V.K. (1970) *The Female Labor Force in the United States*, Berkeley, University of California Press.

_____ (1977) 'The sociology of women's economic role in the family', *American Sociological Review*, 42, pp. 387–406.

_____ (n.d.) 'Rising educational attainment, declining fertility and the inadequacies of the female labor market', in WESTOFF, C. and PARKE, R. (Eds) *Demographic and Social Aspects of Population Growth*, Washington, DC, Government Printing Office, 305–29.

ORTH, P. (1972) *An Enviable Position: The American Mistress from Slightly Kept to Practically Married*, New York, David McKay.

PIOTRKOWSKI, C.S. (1979) *Work and the Family System: A Naturalistic Study of Working-Class and Lower-Middle-Class Families*, New York, Free Press.

POLATNICK, M. (1975) 'Why women don't rear children: A power analysis', *Berkeley Journal of Sociology*, 18, pp. 45–86.

POLOMA, M.M. and GARLAND, T. (1971) 'On the social construction of reality: Reported husband-wife differences', *Sociological Focus*, 5, pp. 40–54.

RAPOPORT, R. and RAPOPORT, R.N. (Eds) (1978) *Working Couples*, New York, Harper and Row.

RHEINGOLD, H.L. and COOK, K. (1975) 'The content of boys' and girls' rooms as an index of parents' behavior', *Child Development*, 46, pp. 459–63.

RICH, A. (1976) *Of Woman Born*, New York, Norton.

ROSEN, B., JERDEE, T.H. and PRESTWICK, T.L. (1975) 'Dual-career marital adjustment: Potential effects of discriminatory managerial attitudes', *Journal of Marriage and*

Family, 37, pp. 565–72.

ROSSI, A. (1968) 'Transition to parenthood', *Journal of Marriage and Family*, 30, pp. 26–39.

———(1977) 'A biosocial perspective on parenting', *Daedalus*, 106 (Spring), pp. 1–31.

ROTHBLATT, D.N., GARR, D.J. and SPRAGUE, J. (1979) *Women and the Suburban Environment*, New York, Praeger.

RUBIN, J.Z., PROVENZANO, F.J. and LURRA, Z. (1974) 'The eye of the beholder: Parents' views on sex of newborns', *American Journal of Orthopsychiatry*, 44, pp. 512–19.

RUBIN, L. (1976) *Worlds of Pain*, New York, Basic Books.

——— (1979) *Women of a Certain Age*, New York, Basic Books.

RYAN, M. (1982) *The Empire of Mothers: American Writings on Women and the Family, 1830–1860*, New York, Haworth.

SACKS, K. (1979) *Sisters and Wives: The Past and Future of Sexual Equality*, Westport, Conn., Greenwood Press.

SAEGERT, S. and WINKEL, G. (1978) 'The home: A critical problem for changing sex-roles', paper presented at American Sociological Association.

SAFILIOS-ROTHSCHILD, C. (1969) 'Family sociology or wives' family sociology?', *Journal of Marriage and the Family*, 31, pp. 290–301.

——————————— (1970) 'The study of family power structure: A review 1960–1969', *Journal of Marriage and the Family*, 32, pp. 70–90.

SAWHILL, I.V. (Ed.) (1978) *Women's Changing Roles at Home and on the Job*, Washington, DC, National Commission for Manpower Policy.

SCANZONI, J. and SZINOVACZ, M. (1980) *Family Decision-Making: A Developmental Sex Role Model*, Beverly Hills, Sage Publications.

SCANZONI, L. and SCANZONI, J. (1976) *Men, Women and Change: A Sociology of Marriage and Family*, New York, McGraw-Hill.

SENECA, G. (1980) 'The social meaning of maternity: Where do we go from here', unpublished paper, Geneseo, NY, Department of Sociology, State University of New York at Geneseo.

SILVERMAN, P.R. (Ed.) (1975) *Helping Each Other in Widowhood*, New York, Health Science Publishing Company.

SMITH, D. (1975) 'Women, the family, and corporate capitalism', *Berkeley Journal of Sociology*, 20, pp. 55–91.

——————— (1980) 'Women, class and family', paper prepared for SSHRC workshop on Women and the Canadian Labor Force, University of British Columbia.

STANLEY, J.P. (1972) 'Paradigmatic woman: The prostitute', paper presented at South Atlantic Modern Language Association.

STANTON, A.M. (1980) *When Mothers Go to Jail* Lexington, Mass., Lexington Press.

STEINMANN, A. and RAPPAPORT, A. (1970) 'Self achieving vs. family orientation of "professional-liberated" women' (perceptions of female sex roles among members of association of women psychologists), paper presented at the 78th Annual Convention of the American Psychological Association, Miami Beach, Florida, 3–7 September.

STOLLER, R.J. (1967) 'Effects of parents' attitudes on core gender identity', *International Journal of Psychiatry*, 4, p. 57.

SWERDLOW, A., BRIDENTHAL, R., KELLY, J. and VINE, P. (1981) *Household and Kin: Families in Flux*, New York, Feminist Press/McGraw-Hill.

TALLMAN, I. (1969) 'Working-class wives in suburbia, fulfilment or crisis?', *Journal of Marriage and the Family*, 31, pp. 61–72.

VANEK, J. (1974) 'Time spent in housework', *Scientific American*, 231, 14, pp. 116–20.

WAITE, L.D., and SPITZE, G.D. (1978) 'Female work orientation and marital events: The transition to marriage and motherhood', paper presented at American Sociological Association, San Francisco.

WALKER, K.E. and WOODS, M.E. (1976) *Time Use: A Measure of Household Production of Family Goods and Services*, Washington, DC, American Home Economics Association Center for the Family.

WALLACE, J. (1977) 'The honeymoon is over, and the houseworker gets hired', *Moving*

Mountains, A Feminist Quarterly, 2 (Winter), pp. 4–5.

WALSHOK, M.L. (1977) 'Occupational values and family roles: A descriptive study of women working in blue-collar and service occupations', paper presented at a seminar at the National Institute of Mental Health, February.

WALUM, L.R. and FRANKLIN, C. Jr. (1972) 'Structural components of wives' working', report prepared for Center for Human Resources, Columbus, Ohio, Ohio State University.

WARRIOR, B. and LEGHORN, L. (1975) *Houseworker's Handbook*, Cambridge, Mass., Leghorn and Warrior Woman's Center.

WEITZMAN, L. (1974) 'Legal regulation of marriage: Tradition and change', *California Law Review*, 62, pp. 1169–288.

WERTZ, R.W. and WERTZ, D.C. (1977) *Lying-In: A History of Childbirth in America*, New York, Free Press.

WHITEHURST, R.N. (1974) 'Sex role equality and changing meanings in cohabitation', presented to the North Central Sociological Association Meetings, Windsor, Canada (May).

WILLIAMSON, N. (1976) *Sons or Daughters*, Beverly Hills, Sage Publications.

ZARETSKY, E. (1973) *Capitalism, the Family and Personal Life*, New York, Harper and Row.

ZIHLMAN, A.L. (1978) 'Motherhood in transition: From ape to human', in MILLER and NEWMAN (Eds), *The First Child and Family Formation*, Chapel Hill, NC, Carolina Population Center, pp. 35–50.

—————— and TURNER, N. (1976) 'Women in evolution: Part I: Innovation and selection in human origins', *Signs*, 1, pp. 585–608.

Education

ABRAMSON, J. (1975) *The Invisible Woman: Discrimination in the Academic Profession*, New York, Jossey-Bass.

AHLUM, C. and FRALLEY, J. (1976) *High School Feminist Studies*, Old Westbury, NY, The Feminist Press.

AMSLER, D., et al. (1976) *Undoing Sex Stereotypes: Research and Resources for Educators*, New York, McGraw-Hill.

ANDERSON, S. (Ed.) (1972) *Sex Differences and Discrimination in Education*, Ohio, Charles A. Jones Publishing Co.

ASTIN, H. (Ed.) (1976) *Some Action of Her Own, The Adult Woman and Higher Education*, Lexington, Mass., Lexington Books.

ASTIN, H.S. and HARWAY, M. (1977) *Sex Discrimination in Career Counseling and Education*, New York, Praeger.

ASTIN, H.S. and HIRSCH, W.Z. (Eds) (1978) *The Higher Education of Women: Essays in Honor of Rosemary Parks*, New York, Praeger.

BEM, D.L. and BEM, S.L. (1973) 'On liberating the female student', *The School Psychology Digest*, 2 (Summer), pp. 10–17.

BERNARD, J. (1970) *Academic Women*, New York, Meridian.

BIEMER, L. (1973) 'Female studies: K-8 suggestions', *Social Science Record*, 10, 3, pp. 8–13.

—————— (1975) 'Female studies: The elective approach', *Social Science Record*, 12, 3, pp. 7–11.

BIKLEN, S.K., et al. (Eds) (1980) *Women and Educational Leadership*, Lexington, Mass., Lexington Press.

BOSWELL, S.L. (1979) 'Study on women's career choice and academic achievement', *Association for Women in Mathematics Newsletter*, 9, pp. 14–15.

BROWN, P. and DAVIES, H. (1975) 'Sexism in education: A review of the ERIC data base', *Journal of Teacher Education*, 26, 4, pp. 356–9.

BUDD, M.W. and LEE, M. (1974) *A Guide for Teaching about Women in History*, San Diego, San Diego City Schools.

BUREAU OF GENERAL EDUCATION CURRICULUM DEVELOPMENT (1978) *Balancing the Picture: Integrating Women into American History*, Albany, NY, State Education Department.

BURSTYN, J.N. and CORRIGAN, R.R. (1975) 'Images of women in textbooks', *Teachers College Record*, 76, pp. 431–40.

CARLSON, D. (1973) *Girls Are Equal Too*, New York, Atheneum.

CAUCUS FOR WOMEN IN STATISTICS (1979) 'Factors related to young women's math achievement', *Association for Women in Mathematics Newsletter*, 9, pp. 3–4.

CEBIK, L.B. (1975) 'Women's studies and home economics', *Journal of Home Economics*, 67 (January), pp. 27–30.

CLEMENT, J.P. (1975) *Sex Bias in School Leadership*, Evanston, Ill., Integrated Education Associates.

COHEN, M. (Ed.) (1975) *Growing Free; Ways to Help Children Overcome Sex-Role Stereotypes*, Washington, Association for Childhood Education International.

COLLINS, J.A. (1975) 'Reflective examination of the feminine role: Teaching strategies', *High School Journal*, 58 (March), pp. 259–73.

COUNCIL ON INTERRACIAL BOOKS (1977) *Stereotypes, Distortions and Omissions in US History Textbooks*, New York.

CUSICK, J. (Comp.) (1976) *A Resource List for Non-Sexist Education*, Washington, DC, The Resource Center on Sex-Roles in Education, National Foundation for the Improvement of Education.

DEPARTMENT OF HEALTH, EDUCATION AND WELFARE (1977) *Salaries, Tenure and Fringe Benefits of Full-Time Instructional Faculty in Institutions of Higher Education*, Washington, DC, Government Printing Office.

DWECK, C.S. and REPPUCCI, N.D. (1973) 'Learned helplessness and reinforcement responsibility in children', *Journal of Personality and Social Psychology*, 25, 1, pp. 109–16.

DWECK, C.S. and BUSH, E.S. (1976) 'Sex differences in learned helplessness: I: Differential debilitation with peer and adult evaluators', *Developmental Psychology*, 12, 2, pp. 147–56.

DWECK, C.S., DAVIDSON, W., NELSON, S. and ENNA, B. (1978) 'Sex differences in learned helplessness: II: The contingencies of evaluative feedback in the classroom and III: An experimental analysis', *Developmental Psychology*, 14, pp. 268–76.

EDUCATION COMMITTEE OF PENNSYLVANIANS FOR WOMEN'S RIGHTS (1974) *Self-Study Guide to Sexism in Schools*, Harrisburg, Pennsylvania Department of Education.

EDUCATIONAL CHALLENGES, INC. (1974) *Today's Changing Roles: An Approach to Non-Sexist Teaching*, Washington, Resource Center on Sex-Roles in Education, NFIE.

EMMA WILLARD TASK FORCE (1972) *Sexism in Education*, Minneapolis.

FALLON, C. (1980) 'Women's studies in the social studies curricula of secondary schools', unpublished doctoral dissertation, University of Rochester.

FARQUHAR, N. and MOHLMAN, C. (1973) 'Life competence: A non-sexist introduction to practical arts', *Social Education*, 37, 6, pp. 516–19.

FEDERBUSH, M. (1973) *Let Them Aspire* (third edition with addenda), Pittsburgh, Penn., Know Inc.

FENNEMA, E. and SHERMAN, J. (1977) 'Sex related differences in mathematics achievement: Spatial visualization and affective factors', *American Educational Research Journal*, 14, pp. 51–71.

FIELDS, R.M. (n.d.) *Public Education: Training for Sexism*, Philadelphia, Penn., Know Inc.

FISHELL, A. (1977) *National Politics and Sex Discrimination in Education*, Lexington, Mass., Lexington Books.

FISHELL, A. and POTTKER, J. (1971) *Sex Bias in Schools: The Research Evidence*, New York, Fairleigh Dickinson University Press.

FITZGERALD, F. (1980) *America Revised*, New York, Vintage Books.

Fox, L.H. (1974) *Facilitating the Development of Mathematical Talent in Young Women*, unpublished PhD dissertation, Baltimore, Johns Hopkins University.

_____ (1977) 'The effects of sex role socialization on mathematics participation and achievement', *Women and Mathematics: Research Perspectives for Change*, Washington, DC, National Institute of Education, Papers in Education and Work, No. 7.

Frashe, R. and Walker, A. (1972) 'Sex roles is early reading textbooks', *The Reading Teacher*, 25 (May), pp. 741–9.

Frazier, N. and Sadker, M. (1973) *Sexism in School and Society*, New York, Harper and Row.

Froschl, M. and Williamson, J. (1977) *Feminist Resources for Schools and Colleges*, Old Westbury, NY, The Feminist Press.

Gardner, J. (1971) 'Sexist counseling must stop', *Personnel and Guidance Journal*, 49 (May), pp. 705–14.

Gerson, B. (1973) 'The theory and practice of consciousness-raising groups with elementary school girls', *School Psychology Digest*, 2, 3, pp. 38–46.

Gersoni-Stavn, D. (1974) *Sexism and Youth*, New York, Bowker.

Gordon, N.M., Morton, T.E. and Braden, I.C. (1974) 'Faculty salaries: Is there discrimination by sex, race and discipline?', *American Economic Review*, 64, pp. 419–27.

Gough, P.B. and Snell, A.C. (1975) 'Middle-graders focus on sexism', *Childhood Education*, 51 (January), pp. 128–31.

Graebner, D.B. (1972) 'A decade of sexism in readers', *The Reading Teacher*, 26 (October).

Graham, P.A. (1978) 'Expansion and exclusion: A history of women in American higher education', *Signs*, 3, 4, pp. 759–73.

Grambs, J.D. (1972) 'Sex-stereotypes in instructional materials, literature and language: A survey of research', *Women's Studies Abstracts*, 1, 1–4, pp. 91–4.

_____ (1976) *Teaching about Women in the Social Studies*, Bulletin No. 48, Arlington, Va., National Council for the Social Studies.

Gross, N. and Trask, A. (1976) *The Sex Factor and the Management of Schools*, New York, John Wiley and Sons.

Gruberg, M. (1973) 'Women's studies in America', *International Review of Education*, 19, 1, pp. 127–33.

Guttenberg, M. and Bray, H. (1976) *Undoing Sex Stereotypes: Research and Resources for Educators*, New York, McGraw-Hill.

Hahn, C.L. (1975) 'Strategies for teaching about women in social studies', *Social Science Record*, 12, 3, pp. 1–2.

_____ (1975) 'The role of a professional organization in promoting social justice for women', *Social Science Record*, 12, 3, p. 37.

Harris, A.S. (1970) 'The second sex in academe', *American Association of University Professors Bulletin*, 56, pp. 283–95.

Harrison, B.G. (1974) *Unlearning the Lie: Sexism in School*, New York, William Morrow and Co.

Harway, M. and Astin, H.S. (1977) *Sex Discrimination in Career Counseling and Education*, New York, Praeger.

Hawke, S. (1975) 'Women's studies in the junior high school', *Profiles of Promise*, No. 42. Boulder, Col., ERIC Clearinghouse for Social Studies.

Helgeson, C. (1976) 'The business of texts: Male chauvinism in college handbooks and rhetorics', *College English*, 38, 4, pp. 396–406.

Hoffman, N. (1981) *Woman's 'True' Profession: Voices from the History of Teaching*, New York, Feminist Press-McGraw-Hill.

Howard, S. (1975) *Liberating Our Children, Ourselves*, Washington, DC, American Association of University Women.

Howe, F. (Ed.) (1975) *Women and the Power to Change*, New York, McGraw-Hill.

_____ (1977) *Seven Years Later: Women's Studies Programs in 1976*, Report of the

National Advisory Council on Women's Educational Programs.

_____ (1979) 'Introduction: The first decade of women's studies', *Harvard Educational Review*, 49, 4, pp. 413–21.

JACKLIN, C., HEUPERS, M., MISCHELL, H. and JACOBS, C. (1972) 'As the twig is bent: Sex role stereotyping in early readers', unpublished paper, Department of Psychology, Stanford University.

JACKSON, P. and LAHADERNE, H. (1971) 'Inequalities of teacher-pupil contacts', in SILBERMAN, M. (Ed.), *The Experience of Schooling*, New York, Holt, Rinehart and Winston, pp. 123–34.

JONES, J.M. and LOVEJOY, F.H. (1980) 'Women's college and women achievers revisited', *Signs*, 5, 3, pp. 504–18.

KAUFMAN, D.R. (1978) 'Associational ties in academe: Some male and female differences', *Sex Roles: A Journal of Research*, 4, 1, pp. 9–21.

KASCHAK, E. (1978) 'Sex bias in student evaluations of college professors', *Psychology of Women Quarterly*, 2, 3, pp. 233–43.

KATZ, D. (1973) 'Faculty salaries, promotions and productivity at a large university', *American Economic Review*, 63, pp. 469–77.

KERSEY, S.N. (1981) *Classics in the Education of Girls and Women*, New Jersey, The Scarecrow Press.

KEY, M.R. (1971) 'The role of male and female in children's books — Dispelling all doubt', *Wilson Lib. Bulletin*, 46 (October), pp. 167–76.

KILSON, M. (1976) 'The status of women in higher education', *Signs*, 1, 4, pp. 935–42.

KINGSLEY, J.L., BROWN, F.L. and SEIBERT, M.E. (1977) 'Social acceptance of female athletes by college women', *The Research Quarterly*, 48, 4, pp. 727–33.

KNOB, H. and KELLY, F. (1972) 'A look at women in education: Issues and answers for HEW', unpublished report of the Commissioner's Task Force on the Impact of Office of Education Programs on Women, Washington, DC, (November).

LAGEMANN, E.C. (1978) 'Educational biography: An approach to the history of women's education', paper presented at Berkshire Conference.

LANTZ, A.E., WHITTINGTON, M.C., FOX, M.C., ELLIOTT, L. and SACKETT, K. (1980) *Re-Entry Programs for Female Scientists*, New York, Praeger.

LEE, P. and GROPPER, N. (1974) 'Sex-role culture and educational practice', *Harvard Educational Review*, 44, pp. 369–410.

LESERMAN, J. (1981) *Men and Women in Medical School: How They Change and How They Compare*, New York, Praeger.

LEVER, J. (1976) 'Sex differences in the games children play', *Social Problems*, 23, pp. 478–87.

_____ (1978) 'Sex differences in the complexity of children's play and games', *American Sociological Review*, 43, pp. 471–83.

LEVY, B., *et al.* (1973) *Sex Role Stereotyping in the Schools*, Washington, DC, National Education Association.

LIEBERMAN, M. (Ed.) (1973) 'Education and the feminist movement', *Phi Delta Kappan*, 55 (October), pp. 93–137.

LOTT, B. (1979) 'Sex-role ideology and children's drawings: Does the Jack of O'Lantern smile or scare', *Sex Roles*, 5, pp. 93–8.

LYNN, N.B. (1974) *Research Guide in Women's Studies*, Morristown, NJ, General Learning Press.

LYON, C.D. and SAARIO, T.N. (1973) 'Women in public education: Sexual discrimination in promotions', *Phi Delta Kapan*, 55, 2, pp. 120–3.

MACDONALD, J. and MACDONALD, S.C. (1981) 'Gender, values and curriculum', *Journal of Curriculum Theorizing*, 3, 1, pp. 299–305.

McGHEE, P. and GRODZITSKY, P. (1973) 'Sex-role identification and humor among pre-school children', *Journal of Psychology*, 84, pp. 189–93.

'McGraw-Hill Guidelines for Equal Treatment of the Sexes' (1975) *School Library Journal*, 21, 5, pp. 23–7.

MACKE, A., RICHARDSON, L. and COOK, J. (1980) *Sex Typed Teaching Styles of University Professors and Student Reactions*, Final Report, Washington, DC, National Institute of Education (Grant #NIE-G-78-0144).

McLURE, G.T. and McLURE, J.W. (1977) *Women's Studies*, Washington, National Education Association.

MARTIN, J.R. (1981) 'Sophie and Emile: A case study of sex bias in the history of educational thought', *Harvard Educational Review*, 51, 3, pp. 357–73.

MILLER, J.L. (1980) 'Women: The evolving educational consciousness', *Journal of Curriculum Theorizing*, 2, 1.

_____ (1981) 'The sound of silence breaking: Feminist pedagogy and curriculum theory', *Journal of Curriculum Theorizing*, 4, 1.

MOSKOWITZ, E.J. (1982) *Why Did the Little Girls Grow Crooked?: Images of Females in Elementary School Readers*, unpublished doctoral dissertation, University of Rochester.

MULLEN, J.S. (1972) 'Freshman textbooks', *College English*, 34, 1, pp. 79–93.

NASAW, D. (1979) *Schooled to Order*, New York, Oxford University Press.

NATIONAL EDUCATION ASSOCIATION (1977) *Status of the American School Teacher*, Washington, DC, National Education Association.

NEMEROWICZ, G.M. (1979) *Children's Perceptions of Gender and Work Roles*, New York, Praeger.

NILSEN, A.P. (1971) 'Women in children's literature', *College English*, 32, 8, pp. 918–26.

O'DONNELL, R.W. (1973) 'Sex bias in primary social studies textbooks', *Educational Leadership*, 31 (November), pp. 137–41.

OLIVER, L. (1974) 'Women in aprons: The female stereotype in children's readers', *Elementary School Journal*, 74, pp. 253–9.

ORTIZ, F.I. (1981) *Career Patterns in Education: Women, Men, and Minorities in Public School Administration*, New York, Praeger.

PARKER, F. and PARKER, B.J. (Eds) (1979) *Women's Education, A World View: Annotated Bibliography of Doctoral Dissertations*, Westport, Conn., Greenwood Press.

PEARSON, E.O. and TRECKER, J.L. (1973) 'Teaching the role of women in American history', *NSSE Yearbook*, 43, pp. 278–97.

PERUN, P.J. (Ed.) (1982) *The Undergraduate Woman: Issues in Educational Equity*, Lexington, Mass., Lexington Books.

PINAR, W. (1981) 'Gender, sexuality, and curriculum studies: The beginning of the debate', *McGill Journal of Education*, 16, 3.

_____ (1982) 'Curriculum as gender text: Notes on reproduction, resistance, and male-male relations', *Journal of Curriculum Theorizing*, 4, 2.

PIVNICK, P.T. (1974) *Sex-Role Socialization: Observations in a First-Grade Classroom*, unpublished doctoral dissertation, University of Rochester.

REINIGER, M.E.R. (1982) *Traces of Misogyny in Women's Schooling: Autobiographical Search for Gyn/ecology*, unpublished doctoral dissertation, University of Rochester.

RICHARDSON, L.W., COOK, J.A. and MACKE, A.S. (1980) 'Classroom authority management of male and female professors', unpublished paper presented at the Americal Sociological Association Meetings, New York.

ROBERTS, D.F. and ROBERTS, G. (1973) 'Techniques for confronting sex-role stereotypes', *School Psychology Digest*, 2, 3, pp. 47–54.

ROBERTS, E.J. (Ed.) (1980) *Childhood Sexual Learning: The Unwritten Curriculum*, Cambridge, Mass., Ballinger.

ROSE, C. (Ed.) (1975) *Meeting Women's New Educational Needs*, San Francisco, Jossey-Bass.

ROSSI, A. and CALDERWOOD, A. (Eds) (1973) *Academic Women on the Move*, New York, Russell Sage.

ROTHSCHILD, N. (1973) *Sexism in Schools: A Handbook for Action*, available from author, 14 Hickory St., Mahtomedi, Minnesota.

ROWLEY-ROTUNNO, V. and DOBKIN, W.S. (1974) 'Curriculum considerations and learning strategies in the teaching of women's studies', *High School Journal*, 57, (February), pp. 182–9.

SAARIO, T., JACKLIN, C. and TITTLE, C. (1973) 'Sex role stereotyping in the public schools', *Harvard Educational Review*, 43, pp. 386–416.

SADKER, D., SADKER, M. and SIMON, S. (1973) 'Clarifying sexist values', *Social Education*, 37, 8, pp. 756–60.

SADKER, D. and SADKER, M. (1974) 'Sexism in schools: An issue for the 70's', *Education Digest*, 39 (April), pp. 58–61.

SADKER, P. and SADKER, D.M. (1980) 'Sexism in teacher education texts', *Harvard Educational Review*, 50, pp. 36–46.

——————————— (1982) *Sex Equity Handbook for Schools*, New York, Longman Press.

SAFFIOTI, H.I.B. (1978) *Woman in Class Society*, New York, Monthly Review Press.

SEEMAN, J. (1974) 'The hidden curriculum: Gender stereotyping in sixth grade mathematics books: 1963–1974', unpublished paper, Columbus, Ohio, Ohio State University.

SEXTON, P.C. (1976) *Women in Education*, Bloomington, Ind., Phi Delta Kappan Educational Committee.

SHAPIRO, N. (1976) 'The Shapiro Report: An analysis of salaries of men and women faculty at Ohio State University', Columbus, Ohio, Ohio State University.

SMITH, D.E. (1975) 'An analysis of ideological structures and how women are excluded: Considerations for academic women', paper at Women's Studies Conference, University of Alberta.

SOLMON, L.C., KENT, L., OCHSNER, N.L. and HURWICZ, M.-L. (1981) *Underemployed Ph.D.'s*, Lexington, Mass., Lexington Books.

SOLMON, L.C. and GORDON, J.J. (1981) *The Characteristics and Needs of Adults in Postsecondary Education*, Lexington, Mass., Lexington Books.

SPEARS, B. (1978) 'Prologue: The myth', in OGLESBY, C.A. *Women and Sport: From Myth to Reality*, Philadelphia, Lea and Febiger, pp. 3–15.

SPEIZER, J.J. (1981) 'Role models, mentors, sponsors: The elusive concepts', *Signs*, 6, 4, pp. 692–713.

SPRUNG, B. (Ed.) (1978) *Perspectives On Non-Sexist Early Childhood Education*, New York, Teachers College Press.

STACEY, J., BEREAUD, S. and DANIELS, J. (Eds) (1974) *And Jill Came Tumbling After: Sexism in American Education*, New York, Dell Publishing.

STERN, M. (Ed.) (n.d.) *Changing Sexist Practices in the Classroom*, Washington, Women's Rights Committee of the American Federation of Teachers.

STROBER, M.H. and TYACK, D. (1980) 'Why do women teach and men manage? A report on research on schools', *Signs*, 5, 3, pp. 494–504.

TAUBMAN, P. (1982) 'Gender and curriculum: Discourse and the politics of sexuality', *Journal of Curriculum Theorizing*, 4, 1.

THEODORE, A. (Ed.) (1971) *The Professional Woman*, Cambridge, Mass., Schenkman Publishing.

TIBBETTS, S.L. (1979) 'Research in sexism: Some studies on children's reading material revisited', *Educational Research Quarterly*, 4, 4. (Winter)

TITTLE, C.K. and DEKKER, E.R. (1980) *Returning Women Students in Higher Education*, New York, Praeger.

TRECKER, J.L. (1971) 'Women in U.S. history high school textbooks', *Social Education* (March), pp. 249–260; 338.

——————————— (1973) 'Sex stereotyping in the secondary school curriculum', *Phi Delta Kappan*, 55, 2, pp. 110–12.

VARTULA, S. (Ed.) (1982) *The Ph. D. Experience: A Woman's Point of View*, New York, Praeger.

VECSEY, G. (1975) 'Lesson for a day: Consciousness-raising', *Times School Weekly*, New York, 17 March.

VINCENT, M.F. (1976) 'Comparison of self-concepts of college women: Athletes and physical education majors', *The Research Quarterly*, 47, 2, pp. 218–25.

WALLENSTEIN, S. (1979) 'Notes toward a feminist curriculum theory', *Journal of Curricu-*

lum Theorizing, 1, 1.

WEITZMAN, L.J. (1972) 'Sex-role socialization in picture books for preschool children', *American Journal of Sociology*, 77, 6, pp. 1125–50.

WOLFSON, S. (1970) 'She was Stan's girl', *This Magazine Is about Schools*, 4, 3, pp. 145–52.

'Women and the Educational Enterprise' and 'Exploding the Myth of Sexism in Secondary School Administration' (1980) *National Association of Secondary School Principals Newsletter*, 27, 6, (Feb.) pp. 19–20.

WOMEN ON WORDS AND IMAGES (1975) *Dick and Jane as Victims: Sex Stereotyping in Children's Readers*, Princeton, NJ, N.O.W.

'Women's Studies Stamp out Sexist Stereotypes' (1974) *Nation's Schools*, 93 (April), pp. 29–30.

'Women's Studies: Up and away from Stereotypes' (1970) *Nation's Schools*, 86 (November), pp. 42 ff.

YANNETTI, R. (1975) 'Lesson plan: How to help students learn about the origins of sex-roles in society', *Social Science Record*, 12, 3, pp. 27–9.

ZARET, E. (1975) 'Women/schooling and society', *Schools in Search of Meaning*, MAC-DONALD, J. and ZARET, E. (Eds) Washington, Association for Supervision and Curriculum.

Sociology: Law, Politics, Employment, Society

ABRAMSON, J. (1979) *Old Boys-New Women*, New York, Praeger.

ACKER, J. (1973) 'Women and social stratification: A case of intellectual sexism', *American Journal of Sociology*, 78, pp. 936–45.

AGASSI, J.B. (1979) *The Attitudes of Women to Their Work*, Lexington, Mass., Lexington Books.

ALMQUIST, E.M. (1977) 'Women in the labor force', *Signs*, 2, 4, pp. 843–55.

AMUDSEN, K. (1977) *A New Look At the Silenced Majority: Women and American Democracy*, Englewood Cliffs, NJ, Prentice-Hall.

ANGRIST, S.S. and ALMQUIST, E.M. (1975) *Careers and Contingencies*, New York, Dunellen.

BABCOCK, B.A., FREEMAN, A.E., NORTON, E.H. and ROSS, S.C. (1975) *Sex Discrimination and the Law: Causes and Remedies*, Boston, Little, Brown.

BAKER, E.F. (1964) *Technology and Woman's Work*, New York, Columbia University Press.

BAXANDALL, G. and REVERBY (Eds) (1976) *America's Working Women*, New York, Vintage.

BEER, W. (1982) *Househusbands: Men and Housework in American Families*, New York, Praeger.

BEHR, M. and LAZAR, W. (1981) *Women Working Home*, New Jersey, WWH Press.

BENSTON, M. (1969) 'The political economy of women's liberation', *Monthly Review XX*, 20, pp. 13–27.

BERNARD, J. (1971) *Women and the Public Interest*, Chicago, Aldine.

——————— (1973) *My Four Revolutions*, New York, Knopf.

——————— (1976) 'Change and stability in sex-role norms', *Journal of Social Issues*, 32, 3, pp. 207–24.

———————(1976) 'Where are we now? Some thoughts on the current scene', *Psychology of Women Quarterly*, 1, 1, pp. 21–37.

——————— (1978) 'Models for the relationship between the world of women and the world of men', in KRIESBERG, L. (Ed.), *Research in Social Movements, Conflicts and Change*, Greenwich, Conn., Jal, pp. 291–340.

——————— (1981) *The Female World*, New York, The Free Press.

BLACK, N. and COTTRELL, A.B. (1981) *Women and World Change: Equity Issues in Development*, San Francisco, Sage Publications.

BLAKE, J. 'The changing status of women in developed countries', *Scientific American*, 231 (September), pp. 36–147.

BLAU, F.D., (1976) 'Economists' approaches to sex segregation in the labor market: An appraisal', *Signs*, 1, pp. 181–99.

BLAXALL, M. and REAGAN, B. (1976) *Women and the Workplace: The Implications of Occupational Segregation*, Chicago, University of Chicago Press.

BLUMBERG, R.L. (1976) 'Women and world development: Veil of invisibility, world of work', *International Journal of Intercultural Relations*.

——————— (1978) *Stratification: Socioeconomic and sexual inequality*, Dubuque, Iowa, William C. Brown.

——————— (1980) *Females, Farming and Food: Rural Development and Women's Participation in Agricultural Systems*, Washington, DC, Office of Women in Development, FAO.

BOOTH, A. (1972) 'Sex and social participation', *American Sociological Review*, 37, pp. 123–92.

BOSERUP, E. (1970) *Woman's Role in Economic Development*, New York, St Martin's Press.

BOWKER, L.H. (1978) *Women, Crime and the Criminal Justice System*, Lexington, Mass., Lexington Books.

BROWN, B.A., FREEDMAN, A.E., KATZ, H.N. and PRICE, A.M. (1977) *Women's Rights and the Law*, New York, Praeger.

BUNCH, C. and MYRON, N. (Eds) (1974) *Class and Feminism*, Baltimore, Diana Press.

BURKHART, K.W. (1976) *Women in Prison*, New York, Popular Library.

CAHN, A.F. (Ed.) (1978) *Women in the United States Labor Force*, New York, Praeger.

CANTOR, M. and LAURIE, B. (1977) *Class, Sex and the Woman Worker*, Westport, Conn., Greenwood Press.

CHAFE, W.H. (1972) *The American Woman, Her Changing Social, Economic and Political Roles 1920–1970*, New York, Oxford University Press.

——————— (1977) *Women and Equality: Changing Patterns in American Culture*, New York, Oxford University Press.

CHAPMAN, J.R., (Ed.) (1976) *Economic Independence for women*, Beverly Hills, Sage Publications.

——————— (1980) *Economic Realities and the Female Offender*, Beverly Hills, Sage Publications.

CHISHOLM, S. (1970) 'Racism and anti-feminism', *The Black Scholar*, 43, pp. 40–5.

CLARDY, M.L. and ALESSI, F.V. (1975) 'Helping the American woman to step outside her stereotypical political role', *Social Science Record*. 12, 3, pp. 3–6.

COOK, B.W. (1976) 'The personal is the political: Women, alternative lifestyles and political activism', paper presented at Berkshire Conference, Bryn Mawr, Penn.

CONSTANTINI, E. and CRAIK, K.H. (1972) 'Women as politicians: The social background, personality and political careers of female party leaders', *Journal of Social Issues*, 28, pp. 217–36.

DANIELS, A.K. (1979) 'Development of feminist networks in the professions', *Annals of the New York Academy of Sciences*.

DAVIS, A. (1982) *Women, Race and Class*, New York, Random House.

DeCROW, K. (1974) *Sexist Justice*, New York, Vintage Books.

DOUVAN, E. (1976) 'The role of models in women's professional development', *Psychology of Women Quarterly*, 1, 1, pp. 5–20.

DYE, N.S. (1975) 'Creating a feminist alliance: Sisterhood and class conflict in the New York Women's Trade Union League, 1903–1914', *Feminist Studies*, 2, pp. 24–38.

EAGLETON INSTITUTE OF POLITICS (1974) Conference on American Women and Politics, Rutgers, report in *Carnegie Quarterly*, 22 (Summer).

EICHLER, M. (1979) 'The origin of sex inequality: A comparison and critique of different theories and their implications for social policy', *Women's Studies International Quarterly*, 2, 3, pp. 329–46.

——————— (1980) *The Double Standard: A Feminist Critique of the Social Sciences*, New York, St Martin's Press.

ENGLAND, P. (1979) 'Women and occupational prestige: A case of vacuous sex equality',

Signs, 5, 2, pp. 522–66.

EPSTEIN, C.F. (1970) *Women's Place: Options and Limits on a Professional Career*, Berkeley, Calif., University of California Press.

——————— (1974) 'Changing sex-roles: A review of sociological research development and needs', *Current Sociology* (Summer), pp. 245–77.

——————— (1981) *Women in Law*, New York, Basic Books.

EPSTEIN, L.K. (Ed.) (1975) *Women in the Professions*, Lexington, Mass., Lexington Books.

FABE, M. and WIKLER, N. (1979) *Up against the Clock. Career Women Speak on the Choice to Have Children*, New York, Random House.

FAHEY, M. (n.d.) 'Block by block: Women in community organizing', *Women*, 6, pp. 24–9.

FARLEY, L. (1978) *Sexual Shakedown: The Sexual Harassment of Women on the Job*, New York, McGraw Hill.

FEINMAN, C. (1980) *Women in the Criminal Justice System*, New York, Praeger.

FENNELL, M.L., BARCHAS, P.R., COHEN, E.G., McMAHON, A.M. and HILDEBRANDE, P. (1978) 'An alternative perspective on sex differences in organizational settings: The process of legitimation', *Sex Roles: A Journal of Research*, 4, 4, pp. 589–604.

FIDELL, L.S. and DeLAMATER (Eds) (1971) *Women in the Professions: What's All the Fuss About?*, San Francisco, Sage Publications.

FONER, P.S. (1979) *Women and the American Labor Movement, from Colonial Times to the Eve of World War I*, New York, Free Press.

FONOW, M.M. (1972) *Women in Steel: A Case Study of the Participation of Women in a Trade Union*, unpublished PhD dissertation, Columbus, Ohio, Department of Sociology, Ohio State University.

FOX, G.L. (1977) '"Nice girl": Social control of women through a value construct', *Signs: A Journal of Women in Culture and Society*, 2, 4, pp. 803–17.

FRAMSWA, H. (1974) 'Working women in fact and fiction', *Journal of Communication*, 24, pp. 104–9.

FRANK, F.D. and DRUCKER, J. (1977) 'The influence of evaluatee's sex on evaluations of a response on a managerial selection instrument', *Sex Roles: A Journal of Research*, 3, 1, pp. 59–64.

FREEMAN, J. (1975) *The Politics of Women's Liberation: A Case Study of an Emerging Social Movement and It's Relation to the Policy Process*, New York, David McKay Company.

FULENWIDER, C.K. (1979) *Feminism in American Politics*, New York, Praeger.

GIALLOMBARDO, R. (1974) *The Social World of Imprisoned Girls. A Comparative Study of Institutions for Juvenile Delinquents*, New York, Wiley.

GITHENS, M. and PRESTAGE, J.L. (1972) *A Portrait of Marginality. The Political Behavior of the American Woman*, New York, David McKay.

GLAZER, N. (1980) 'Overworking the working woman: The double day in a mass-magazine', *Women's Studies International Quarterly*, 3, pp. 79–93.

GLAZER, N. and WAEHRER, H.Y. (Eds) *Women in a Man-Made World*, Chicago, Rand McNally Publishers.

GLENNON, L.M. (1979) *Women and Dualism*, Philadelphia, Longmans, Green.

GOFFMAN, E. (1977) 'The arrangement between the sexes', *Theory and Society*, 4, pp. 301–31.

——————— (1979) *Gender Advertisements*, New York, Harper and Row.

GORNICK, V. and MORAN, B.K. (Eds) (1971) *Woman in Sexist Society: Studies in Power and Powerlessness*, New York, New American Library.

GOULD, M. (1980) 'The new sociology', *Signs*, 5, 3, pp. 459–68.

GUETTEL, C. (1974) *Marxism and Feminism*, Toronto, Canadian Women's Educational Press.

GUTEK, B.A. (Ed.) (1979) *Enhancing Women's Career Development*, San Francisco, Jossey-Bass.

HART, M.M. (1972) 'On being female in sport', in HART, M.M. (Ed.), *Sport in the Socio-Cultural Process*, Dubuque, Iowa, Wm. Brown Co., pp. 291–302.

HELLER, T. (1981) *Women and Men As Leaders. Contemporary Images*, New York, Praeger.

HELSEN, R. (1972) 'The changing image of the career woman', *Journal of Social Issues*, 28, pp. 33–46.

HENNIG, M. and JARDIN, A. (1977) *The Managerial Woman*, New York, Anchor/Doubleday.

HEPPERLE, W. and CRITES, L. (Eds) (1978) *Women in the Courts*, Williamsburg, Va., National Center for State Courts.

HERNTON, C.C. (1965) *Sex and Racism in America. An Analysis of the Influence of Sex on the Race Problem*, New York, Doubleday.

HESSELBART, S. (1977) 'Sex role and occupational stereotypes: Three studies of impression formation', *Sex Roles: A Journal of Research*, 3, 5, pp. 409–22.

HOCHSCHILD, A. (1973) *The Unexpected Community*, Englewood Cliffs, NJ, Prentice-Hall.

HOLTER, H. (1970) *Sex Roles and Social Structure*, Oslo: Universitetforlaget.

_____ (1978) 'Typology of women's relations and associations with each other: Five categories', paper presented at International Sociological Association, Uppsala.

HOWE, L.K. (1977) *Pink Collar Workers: Inside the World of Women's Work*, New York, Avon.

HUBER, J. (Ed.) (1973) *Changing Women in a Changing Society*, Chicago, Ill., University of Chicago Press.

_____ (1976) 'Toward a socio-technological theory of the women's movement', *Social Problems*.

JAIN, H.C. and SLOANE, P.J. (1981) *Equal Employment Issues: Race and Sex Discrimination in the United States, Canada and Britain*, New York, Praeger.

JAQUETTE, J.S. (Ed.) (1974) *Women in Politics*, New York, Wiley Interscience.

JENNINGS, K. and NORMAN, T. (1968) 'Men and women in party elites: Social roles and political resources', *Midwest Journal of Political Science*, 12, pp. 469–92.

KANOWITZ, L. (1969) *Women and the Law: The Unfinished Revolution*, Albuquerque, New Mexico, University of New Mexico Press.

KANTER, R.M. (1977) *Men and Women of the Corporation*, New York, Basic Books.

_____ (1978) 'Work in a new America', *Daedalus: Journal of the American Academy of Arts and Science*, 107, pp. 47–8.

KAY, H.H. (1974) *Text, Cases and Materials on Sex-Based Discrimination in Family Law*, St Paul, Minn., West Publishing Co.

KELLER, S. (Ed.) (1981) *Building for Women*, Lexington, Mass., Lexington Books.

KELLY, R.M. and BOUTILIER (1970) *The Making of Political Women*, Chicago Nelson-Hall.

KIRKPATRICK, J.J. (1974) *Political Woman*, New York, Basic Books.

KRAMER, J.H. and KEMPINEN, C. (1978) 'Erosion of chivalry? Changes in the handling of male and female defendants from 1970 to 1975', paper presented at Society for Study of Social Problems.

KUPINSKY, S. (1982) *Working Women*, New York, Praeger.

LARWOOD, L. and WOOD, M.M. (1977) *Women in Management*, Lexington, Mass., Lexington Books.

LARWOOD, L. and BLACKMORE, J. (1978) 'Sex discrimination in managerial selection: Testing prediction of the vertical dyad linkage model', *Sex Roles: A Journal of Research*, 4, 3, pp. 359–68.

LeGRANDE, L.H. (1978) 'Women in labor organizations: The ranks are increasing', *Monthly Labor Review*, US Department of Labor, Bureau of Labor Statistics, 10, pp. 8–14.

LEVEZEY, B. and ANDERSON, J. (1974) 'Trials of a woman lawyer', *Women's Rights Law Reporter*, 2, 6, p. 38.

LEWIS, M. and WEINTRAUB, M. (1979) 'Origins of early sex-role development', *Sex Roles*, 5, 2.

LIPMEN-BLUMEN, J. (1976) 'Toward a homosocial theory of sex roles: An explanation of the sex segregation of social institutions, *Signs: Journal of Women in Culture and Society*, 2, 3, part 2, pp. 15–31.

LIPMEN-BLUMEN, J. and BERNARD, J. (Eds) (1979) *Sex Roles and Social Policy*, Beverly Hills, Calif., Sage Publications.

LLOYD, C.B. (Ed.) *Sex, Discrimination and the Division of Labor*, New York, Columbia University Press.

LLOYD, C.B. and NIEMI, B.T. (1979) *The Economics of Sex Differentials*, New York, Columbia University Press.

LOWE, M. (1978) 'Sociobiology and sex differences', *Signs*, 4, pp. 118–25.

LYLE, H.R. and ROSS, J. (1973) *Women in Industry. Employment Patterns of Women in Corporate America*, Lexington, Mass., Lexington Books.

MCCOURT, K. (1977) *Working-Class Women and Grass-Roots Politics*, Bloomington, Ind., Indiana University Press.

MCGUIGAN, D.G. (Ed.) (1974) *New Research on Women at the University of Michigan*, Ann Arbor, Mich., University of Michigan.

MACKINNON, C.A. (1979) *Sexual Harassment of Working Women*, New Haven, Conn., Yale University Press.

MCNALLY, F. (1979) *Women for Hire: A Study of the Female Office Worker*, New York, St Martin's Press.

MCTAGGERT-ALMQUIST, E. (1979) *Minorities, Gender, and Work*, Lexington, Mass., Lexington Books.

MANDLE, J. (1979) *Women and Social Change*, Princeton, NJ, Princeton Book Co.

MARCH, A. (1978) 'Female invisibility in androcentric sociological theory', paper presented at American Sociological Association.

MEDNICK, M.T.S., TANGRI, S.S. and HOFFMAN, L.W. (Eds) (1975) *Women and Achievement: Social and Motivational Analyses*, New York, Wiley.

MILLER, A.G. (1981) *In the Eye of the Beholder. Contemporary Issues in Stereotyping*, New York, Praeger.

MILLET, K. (1970) *Sexual Politics*, New York, Doubleday and Co.

MILLMAN, M. (1973) 'Autobiography and social mobility, life accounts of working class daughters', paper presented at Society for Study of Social Problems, San Francisco.

MISCHEL, J. (1974) 'Sex bias in the evaluation of professional articles', *Journal of Educational Psychology*, 66 pp. 157–66.

MOORE, J.W. (1961) 'Patterns of women's participation in voluntary associations', *American Journal of Sociology*, 46, pp. 592–8.

NADELSON, T. and EISENBERG, L. (1977) 'The successful professional women: On being married to one', *American Journal of Psychiatry*, 134, 10, pp. 1071–76.

NAGEL, S.S. and WELTZMAN, L.J. (1962) 'Women as litigants', *The Hastings Law Journal*, 23, pp. 171–98.

NATIONAL COMMISSION ON WORKING WOMEN CENTER FOR WOMEN AND WORK. *National Survey of Working Women: Perceptions, Problems and Prospects* Washington, DC, National Manpower Institute (June).

NELSON, C. and OLESEN, V. (1977) 'Veil of illusion: A critique of the concept of equality in Western thought', Catalyst, *10–11*, pp. 8–36.

NICHOLAS, S.C., PRICE, A. and RUBIN, R. (1981) *Rights and Wrongs: Women's Struggle for Legal Equality*, New York, Feminist Press.

NIELSEN, J. (1978) *Sex in Society*, Calif. Wadsworth.

———•——— (1979) 'From corrective to creative progress in sex strategies', *International Journal of Women's Studies*, 2, 4, pp. 324–39.

NORLAND, S. and SHOVER, N. (1977) 'Gender roles and female criminality: Some critical comments', *Criminology*, 15, pp. 67–87.

OPPENHEIMER, K. (1973) 'Demographic influence on female employment and the status of women', *American Journal of Sociology*, 78, pp. 184–99.

PALLEY, M.L. and PRESTON, M.B. (Eds) *Race, Sex, and Policy Problems*, Lexington, Mass., Lexington Books.

PECK, T. (1978) 'When women evaluate women, nothing successds like success: The differential effects of status upon evaluation of male and female professional ability', *Sex Roles: A Journal of Research*, 4, 2, pp. 205–14.

PEZZULLO, T.R. and BRITTINGHAM, B.E. (Eds) (1979) *Salary Equity. Detecting Sex Bias in*

Salaries among College and University Professors, Lexington, Mass., Lexington Books.

QUINN, J.B. (1978) 'Managerial men and women are found remarkably alike', *The Washington Post*, 17 July.

RAPHAEL, N. (1975) *Being Female: Reproduction, Power and Change*, Chicago, Aldine Publishing Co.

RECKLESS, W. and KAY, B. (1967) *The Female Offender*, report to the President's Commission on Law Enforcement and the Administration of Justice. Washington, DC, US Government Printing Office.

RICHARDSON, L.W. (1981) *The Dynamics of Sex and Gender*, second edition, Boston, Houghton Mifflin Co.

ROBINSON, L.S. (1978) *Sex, Class, and Culture*, Bloomington, Ind., Indiana University Press.

ROBY, P. and KERR, V. (1972) 'The politics of prostitution', *The Nation*, 10 April, pp. 463–6.

ROMER, N. (1981) *The Sex-Role Cycle: Socialization from Infancy to Old Age*, New York, Feminist Press.

ROSS, M.W., ROGERS, L.J. and McCULLOCH, H. (1978) 'Stigma, sex, and society: A new look at gender differentiation and sexual variation', *Journal of Homosexuality*, 3, 4, pp. 315–30.

ROTHBLATT, D.N., GARR, D.J. and SPRAGUE, J. (1979) *The Suburban Environment and Women*, New York, Praeger.

SAFILIOS-ROTHSCHILD, C. (Ed.) (1972) *Toward a Sociology of Women*, Lexington, Mass., Xerox Publishing Co.

SAFRON, C. (1976) 'What men do to women on the job: A shocking look at sexual harassment', *Redbook* (November).

SANDAY, P.R. (1973) 'Toward a theory of the status of women', *American Anthropologist*, 75, pp. 1682–700.

SCANZONI, J. (1978) *Sex Roles, Women's Work, and Marital Conflict*, Lexington, Mass., Lexington Books.

SCHEPPELE, K.L. (1977) 'Feminism as a response to sociological ambivalence', paper presented at Sociologists for Women in Society.

SCHOENBERG, S.P. and DABROWSKI, I. (1978) 'Factors which enhance the participation of women in urban neighborhood social life', paper presented at American Sociological Association.

SCOTT, A.F. (1970) *The Southern Lady from Pedestal to Politics 1830–1930*, Chicago, University of Chicago Press.

SEIDENBERG, R. (1973) *Corporate Wives, Corporate Casualties?*, Garden City, NY, Anchor.

SEIFER, N. (1973) *Absent from the Majority, Working Class Women in America*, New York, National Project on Ethnic Research.

————(1975) 'The working family in crisis: Who is listening?', New York, Institute on Pluralism and Group Identity.

———— (1976) 'The key to our future: Coalition building', in *Women's Agenda*, 1 February, pp. 12–13.

———— (Ed.) (1976) 'Forty-two years a maid', *Nobody Speaks for Me, Self-Portraits of American Working Class Women*, New York, Simon and Schuster, pp. 136–77.

———— (1976) 'Where feminism and ethnicity intersect: The impact of parallel movements', New York, Institute on Pluralism and Group Identity, Working Paper No. 16 (February).

————(n.d.) 'Equal rights and working class women', New York, Institute of Human Relations (draft).

SIMON, R. (1975) *The Contemporary Woman and Crime*, NIMH, Washington, DC, Government Printing Office.

———— (1976) 'American women and crime', *Annals American Academy Political and Social Science*, 423, January, pp. 31–46.

SMITH, D. (1974) 'Women's perspective as a radical critique of sociology', *Sociological*

Inquiry, 44, 1, pp. 7–13.

SMITH, R.E. (1979) *The Subtle Revolution*, Washington, DC, The Urban Institute.

——— (1979) *Women in the Labor Force in 1990*, Washington, DC, The Urban Institute.

SNYDER, E.E. and SPREITZER, E. (1978) 'Socialization comparisons of adolescent female athletes and musicians', *The Research Quarterly*, 49, 3, pp. 342–50.

SNYDER, E. (Ed.) (1979) *The Study of Women: Enlarging Perspectives of Social Reality*, New York, Harper and Row, pp. 228–61.

SOKOLOFF, N.J. (1980) *Between Money and Love. The Dialectics of Women's Home and Market Work*, New York, Praeger.

——— (1980) 'Theories of women's labor force status: A review and critique', paper presented at the National Women's Studies Association Meetings, Bloomington, Ind. (May).

SOTO, D.H. and COLE, C. (1975) 'Prejudice against women: A new Perspective', *Sex Roles: A Journal of Research*, 1, 4, pp. 385–94.

SPRADLEY, J.P. and MANN, B.J. (1975) *The Cocktail Waitress: Woman's Work in a Man's World*, New York, Wiley.

STAUDT, K. and JAQUETTE, J. (Eds) (1982) *Women and Development*, New York, Haworth.

STIMPSON, C., DIXLER, E., NELSON, M.J. and YATRAKIS, K.B. (Eds) (1981) *Women and the American City*, Chicago, University of Chicago Press.

STROMBERG, H. and HARKESS, S. (Eds) (1978) *Women Working: Theories and Facts in Perspective*, Palo Alto, Calif., Mayfield Publishing Company.

SZALAI, A. (1973) *The Use of Time: Daily Activities of Urban and Suburban Populations in Twelve Countries*, The Hague, Mouton.

——— (1975) 'Women's time. Women in the light of contemporary time-budget research', paper distributed as an official document at the United Nations International Women's Year Conference, Mexico City.

TERRY, R.M. (1978) 'Trends in female crime: A comparison of Adler, Simon, and Steffensmeier', paper presented at Society for Study of Social Problems, San Francisco.

TIFFANY, S. (Ed.) (1979) *Women and Society*, Montreal, Eden Press.

TOLCHIN, S.J. (1976) *Women in Congress 1917–1976*, Washington, DC, House of Representatives Report No. 94–1732, 25 June.

TRAHEY, H. (1978) *Women and Power*, New York, Rawson.

US BUREAU OF THE CENSUS, POPULATION DIVISION (1976) *A Statistical Portrait of Women in the United States*, Special Studies Series P-23, No. 58 (April).

US DEPARTMENT OF LABOR, WOMEN'S BUREAU. *The Earnings Gap between Women and Men*, Washington, DC, US Government Printing Office.

VINCENT, C. (1976) *Women in Prison*, New York, Popular Library.

VINYARD, J.E.M. (1974) 'Women and the city: Immigrants and native Americans in Detroit, 1880', paper presented at Berkshire Conferences.

WALLACE, P.A. and LAMOND, A.M. (Eds) (1977) *Women, Minorities, and Employment Discrimination*, Lexington, Mass., Lexington Books.

WALUM, L.R. (1970) 'The origins of the women's movement', lecture, Columbus, Ohio, Ohio State University.

——— (1974) 'The changing door ceremony: Some notes on the operation of sex-roles in everyday life', *Urban Life and Culture*, 2, pp. 506–15.

WARREN, M.B. (1975) 'The work role and problem coping: Sex differentials in the use of helping systems in urban communities', paper at American Sociological Association, San Francisco.

WEISSTEIN, N. and BOOTH, H. (n.d.) 'Will the women's movement survive?', *Sister*, 4, 12, pp. 1–6.

THE WELLESLEY EDITORIAL COMMITTEE (Ed.) (1978) *Women and National Development. The Complexities of Change*, Chicago, University of Chicago Press.

WOLMAN, C. and FRANK, H. (1975) 'The solo woman in a professional peer group', *American Journal of Orthopsychiatry*, 45, pp. 164–71.

WOMEN'S BUREAU (1975) *Handbook of Women Workers*, Washington, DC, Government Printing Office.

WOMEN'S EQUITY ACTION LEAGUE (WEAL) AND LEGAL DEFENSE FUND, 'What WEAL and WEAL FUND have done for women and girls in sports', Washington, DC.

ZUCKERMAN, E.L. (Ed.) *Women and Men, Roles, Attitudes, and Power Relations*, New York, The Radcliffe Club.

Contributors

Sandra Acker	Lecturer, School of Education, University of Bristol, Bristol, England.
Jean Anyon	Associate Professor, School of Education, Rutgers University, Newark, New Jersey, USA.
Michael Apple	Professor, Department of Curriculum and Teaching Studies, University of Wisconsin, Madison, USA.
Madeleine Arnot	Lecturer, Faculty of Educational Studies, The Open University, Milton Keynes, England.
Len Barton	Senior Lecturer, Education Department, Westhill College, Selly Oak, Birmingham, England.
Maggie Coats	Research Student, Department of Education, Loughborough University, Loughborough, England.
Lorraine Culley	Tutor, Department of Social Sciences and Public Administration, Leicester Polytechnic, Leicester, England
Miriam David	Lecturer, Department of Social Administration, University of Bristol, Bristol, England.
Lynn Davies	Lecturer, Faculty of Education, University of Birmingham, Birmingham, England.
Rosemary Deem	Lecturer, Faculty of Educational Studies, The Open University, Milton Keynes, England.
Sara Delamont	Senior Lecturer, Sociology Department, University College, Cardiff, Wales.
Jack Demaine	Lecturer, Department of Education, Loughborough University Loughborough, England.
Terry Evans	Lecturer, School of Social Sciences, Gippsland Institute of Advanced Education, Churchill, Victoria, Australia.
Emily Moskowitz	Doctoral Student, Graduate School of Education, University of Rochester, Rochester, USA.
Stephen Walker	Principal Lecturer, Education Department, Newman College, Bartley Green, Birmingham, England.

Author Index

Subject Index

abortion, 148
access
  to senior positions, 12–13
accommodation
  to ideologies, x, xi, 19–37, 161–72
adult education, 107–21
  see also popular education
Australia, 183–90

Bibliofem, 182
Britain, 8, 10, 41–52, 54, 62, 71, 74, 81,
  93–105, 107–21, 123–39, 141–59

Campaign against Sexism and Sexual
  Oppression
  in Education (CASSOE), 181
Campaign to Impede Sex Stereotyping in
  the Young
  (CISSY), 181
Canada, 191–213
capitalism, 42, 51, 161–72
careers
  in teaching, 123–39
  see also professionalism
class
  and education, *passim*
  and gender, *passim*
clubs
  and women's education, 107–21
co-education, x, 69–91, 131
comparative analysis, xi, 107–21
comprehensivation, 81–2
conformity, 101–3
conservatism, 141–59
  and co-education, 85–6
  and sex roles in schools, 93–9
'contestation'
  concept of, 16
'contradiction'
  concept of, 14–15
cultural production
  and women's groups, 113–14
curriculum, 8–12, 55–60, 63, 76–80, 94,

96–7, 114–17, 135, 141, 146, 149–54,
155–6

Department of Education and Science
  (DES)
  (UK), 111
discipline
  in schools, 96

education
  and class, *passim*
  and gender, *passim*
educational transmission
  and women's groups, 114–17
employers
  and sex-role stereotyping, 99–101
Equal Opportunities Commission (EOC),
  85, 146
Equal Opportunities Commission
  Information Centre, 182
equal opportunity
  in education, 141, 143–7
Equal Rights Amendment, 29, 32
Europe, 173–82
  see also Britain

family, 12–14, 123–39, 148, 154, 155–6,
  195–200
Fawcett Library, The, 182
feminism, *passim*
femininity, 19–37, 46, 48–9, 75
Flower Arranging Club, 109–10, 114–15,
  116, 117–19

gender
  and class, *passim*
  and curriculum differentiation, 8–12
  and education, *passim*
  and schooling, 2–14
Girls and Mathematics Association
  (GAMMA), 181–2
Girls Into Science and Technology Project
  (GIST), 182

233